Jacq

Paris Noir

The Secret History of a City

translated with an introduction and notes
by Christine Donougher

Dedalus

Dedalus would like to thank The Burgess Programme of the French Ministry of Foreign Affairs, The French Ministry of Culture in Paris and The Arts Council England in Cambridge for their assistance in producing this book.

LOTTERY FUNDED

Published in the UK by Dedalus Ltd, Langford Lodge,
St Judith's Lane, Sawtry, Cambs, PE28 5XE
email: info@dedalusbooks.com
www.dedalusbooks.com

ISBN 1 903517 48 6
ISBN 978 1 903517 48 2

Dedalus is distributed in the United States by SCB Distributors,
15608 South New Century Drive, Gardena, California 90248
email: info@scbdistributors.com   web site: www.scbdistributors.com

Dedalus is distributed in Australia & New Zealand by Peribo Pty Ltd,
58 Beaumont Road, Mount Kuring-gai N.S.W. 2080
email: peribo@bigpond.com

Dedalus is distributed in Canada by Disticor Direct-Book Division,
695 Westney Road South, Suite 14 Ajax, Ontario, LI6 6M9
web site: www.disticordirect.com

Publishing History
First published in France in 1954
First Dedalus edition in 2006

Rue des Maléfices copyright © Editions Phébus, Paris 1987
Translation, introduction and notes copyright © Christine Donougher 2006

The right of the estate of Jacques Yonnet to be indentified as the copyright holder and Christine Donougher to be identified as the translator of this work has been asserted by them in accordance with the Copyright, Designs and Patent Act, 1988.

Printed in Finland by WS Bookwell
Typeset by RefineCatch Limited, Bungay, Suffolk

A C.I.P. listing for this book is available on request.

THE TRANSLATOR

Christine Donougher's translation of *The Book of Nights* won the 1992 Scott Moncrieff Translation Prize.

Her translations from French for Dedalus are: 6 novels by Sylvie Germain, *The Book of Nights*, *Night of Amber*, *Days of Anger*, *The Book of Tobias*, *Invitation to a Journey* and *The Song of False Lovers*, *Enigma* by Rezvani, *The Experience of the Night* by Marcel Béalu, *Le Calvaire* by Octave Mirbeau, *Tales from the Saragossa Manuscript* by Jan Potocki, *The Land of Darkness* by Daniel Arsand and *Paris Noir* by Jacques Yonnet.

Her translation from Italian for Dedalus are *Senso (and other stories)* by Camillo Boito, *Sparrow and Temptation (and other stories)* by Giovanni Verga.

Christine Donougher is currently translating *Magnus* by Sylvie Germain for Dedalus.

ïi institut français

French Literature from Dedalus

French Language Literature in translation is an important part of Dedalus's list, with French being the language *par excellence* of literary fantasy.

The Land of Darkness – Daniel Arsand £8.99
Séraphita – Balzac £6.99
The Quest of the Absolute – Balzac £6.99
The Experience of the Night – Marcel Béalu £8.99
Episodes of Vathek – Beckford £6.99
The Devil in Love – Jacques Cazotte £5.99
Les Diaboliques – Barbey D'Aurevilly £7.99
Milagrosa – Mercedes Deambrosis £8.99
An Afternoon with Rock Hudson – Mercedes Deambrosis £6.99
The Man in Flames – Serge Filippini £10.99
Spirite (and Coffee Pot) – Théophile Gautier £6.99
Angels of Perversity – Rémy de Gourmont £6.99
The Book of Nights – Sylvie Germain £8.99
The Book of Tobias – Sylvie Germain £7.99
Night of Amber – Sylvie Germain £8.99
Days of Anger – Sylvie Germain £8.99
The Medusa Child – Sylvie Germain £8.99
The Weeping Woman – Sylvie Germain £6.99
Infinite Possibilities – Sylvie Germain £8.99
Invitation to a Journey – Sylvie Germain £7.99
The Song of False Lovers – Sylvie Germain £8.99
Parisian Sketches – J.K. Huysmans £6.99
Marthe – J.K. Huysmans £6.99
Là-Bas – J.K. Huysmans £8.99
En Route – J.K. Huysmans £7.99
The Cathedral – J.K. Huysmans £7.99
The Oblate of St Benedict – J.K. Huysmans £7.99
Lobster – Guillaume Lecasble £6.99

The Mystery of the Yellow Room – Gaston Leroux £7.99
The Perfume of the Lady in Black – Gaston Leroux £8.99
Monsieur de Phocas – Jean Lorrain £8.99
The Woman and the Puppet – Pierre l ouÿs £6.99
Portrait of an Englishman in his Chateau – Pieyre de
    Mandiargues £7.99
Abbé Jules – Octave Mirbeau £8.99
Le Calvaire – Octave Mirbeau £7.99
The Diary of a Chambermaid – Octave Mirbeau £7.99
Sébastien Roch – Octave Mirbeau £9.99
Torture Garden – Octave Mirbeau £7.99
Smarra & Trilby – Charles Nodier £6.99
Manon Lescaut – Abbé Prévost £7.99
Tales from the Saragossa Manuscript – Jan Potocki £5.99
Monsieur Venus – Rachilde £6.99
The Marquise de Sade – Rachilde £8.99
Enigma – Rezvani £8.99
Paris Noir – Jacques Yonnet £9.99
Micromegas – Voltaire £4.95

Anthologies featuring French Literature in translation:

The Dedalus Book of French Horror: the 19c – ed T. Hale
    £9.99
The Dedalus Book of Decadence – ed Brian Stableford
    £7.99
The Dedalus Book of Surrealism – ed Michael Richardson
    £9.99
Myth of the World: Surrealism 2 – ed Michael Richardson
    £9.99
The Dedalus Book of Medieval Literature – ed Brian
    Murdoch £9.99
The Dedalus Book of Sexual Ambiguity – ed Emma
    Wilson £8.99
The Decadent Cookbook – Medlar Lucan & Durian Gray
    £9.99
The Decadent Gardener – Medlar Lucan & Durian Gray
    £9.99

Contents

Translator's Introduction

First issued in 1954 under the publisher's choice of title *Enchantements sur Paris* (Paris Spellbound), reissued in accordance the author's wishes as *Rue des Maléfices* (Witchcraft Street), Jacques Yonnet's only published book fits into no single category. Personal diary, memoir of some of the darkest hours in a nation's history, guide to a city's lower depths, ethnographical study of an urban population that no longer exists or has been driven elsewhere, record of a number of paranormal incidents and experiences – *Paris Noir* is all of these.

Jacques Yonnet is twenty-four years old when war breaks out in 1939. Captured by the Germans in June 1940, as France's eastern defences crumble before the invasion, Yonnet escapes and returns to his native city, but not to where he is known, at home among old friends and family (of socialist inclinations). A hunted man, sought by the Nazis and by the collaborationist French police, he goes underground in the heart of Paris, in the 'villages' of the 5th arrondissement on the Left Bank – Maubert, Montagne, Mouffetard, Gobelins. Here he finds refuge, as though in another world, another dimension.

It is a world that would have been familiar to the great French poet of the 15th century, François Villon, a world peopled by beggars and rag-pickers, mercenary soldiers, petty criminals, police informers, penniless artists, whores, healers, drunks, exiles, exorcists, gypsies, wayward wives and defrocked priests. And the common ground on which they all meet are the numerous bars and drinking establishments that offer a curious combination of anonymity and community, an ideal environment for a young man who is to become active in the Resistance.

Because as the war progresses, Yonnet, for all his natural scepticism and non-conformist anarchist tendencies, gets involved in clandestine warfare and ends up running a mapping and radio transmission centre, liaising with London to ensure that Allied bombings on German targets in the Parisian region are carried out with the fewest possible civilian casualties. But far from being motivated by any notion of patriotism or ideology, it is a personal sympathy for the plight of a parachutist in hiding that draws him in. It is the individual story to which he responds.

And this curious world that he now inhabits throws up the most extraordinary individual stories, which for Yonnet constitute the real fabric of the city he loves: stories of love and hatred, friendship and betrayal, obsession and jealousy, persecution and revenge – but always with a curious edge to them, a suggestion that things could not have happened otherwise, at that time, in that place.

What emerges from Yonnet's stories is a sense that it is the city itself that creates its own history. It is not an inanimate construct. It exists on a level that transcends the physical evidence of the here and now. And events are in some mysterious way determined by their location, even as the location is defined by the events that have occurred there.

Whilst these are conclusions that Yonnet himself has reached, through reflection and observation and extensive reading of historical documents and literature on Paris, some of the low-life characters with whom he becomes acquainted – the cool killer Keep-on-Dancin', for instance, or the Gypsy who exacts a terrible revenge for being insulted – turn out to be extraordinary repositories of this kind of wisdom about the nature of the city, and willing to share their arcane knowledge with him.

Tantalizingly, not all of their confidences does he pass on, having been sworn to secrecy. For such knowledge is not to be trifled with. It can be a matter of life and death, as we see in the story of the shipwreckage doll or the room where nothing but the truth can be spoken. Not that Yonnet makes any attempt to argue a case. That is not his style. He presents himself simply as a witness, although Yonnet himself is the protagonist of one of the most thrilling, chilling stories of all.

A born raconteur, he records with consummate narrative skill, an eye for the compelling detail and a finely attuned ear for the raw energy and economical humour of a Parisian argot redolent of its period, what he has seen and heard and experienced. In doing so, he brings to life a cast of unforgettable characters – from Mina the Cat, Cyril the Watchmaker and Poloche the Shrimp-Fisher to Pepe the Pansy, Dolly-the-Slow-Burner and the Old Man Who Appears After Midnight, to name only a few – and with all the accomplishment of a verbal sorcerer conjures up a Paris that has long since disappeared along with the population that once used to inhabit it.

In translating Yonnet's book I have tried to capture the flavour of the argot – which sounds dated to contemporary French ears – without resorting to a vocabulary too suggestive of a non-Parisian environment – American or Cockney, for instance. I have also appended a few explanatory notes on some of the references in Yonnet's text that would not necessarily be understood by English readers today.

Christine Donougher

Chapter I

An age-old city is like a pond. With its colours and reflections. Its chills and murk. Its ferment, its sorcery, its hidden life.

A city is like a woman, with a woman's desires and dislikes. Her abandon and restraint. Her reserve – above all, her reserve.

To get to the heart of a city, to learn its most subtle secrets, takes infinite tenderness, and patience sometimes to the point of despair. It calls for an artlessly delicate touch, a more or less unconditional love. Over centuries.

Time works for those who place themselves beyond time.

You're no true Parisian, you do not know your city, if you haven't experienced its ghosts. To become imbued with shades of grey, to blend into the drab obscurity of blind spots, to join the clammy crowd that emerges, or seeps, at certain times of day from the metros, railway stations, cinemas or churches, to feel a silent and distant brotherhood with the lonely wanderer, the dreamer in his shy solitude, the crank, the beggar, even the drunk – all this entails a long and difficult apprenticeship, a knowledge of people and places that only years of patient observation can confer.

It is in tumultous times that the true temperament of a city – and even more so, of the coagulated mass of sixty villages or so that make up Paris – reveals itself. For thirteen years I've been compiling all kinds of notes, especially historical, for such is my profession. From them I have extracted what relates to a series of events I witnessed, or of which I was the very unlikely protagonist. A kind of diffidence, of indescribable fear prevented me from bringing this work to fruition before now.

Maybe it is due to particular circumstances that the bizarre events that are the subject of this work struck me as fantastic – but fantastic on a human scale.

I discovered in every fortuitous circumstance, weird occurrence and freak of coincidence a logic so rigorous that in my constant concern for truthfulness I felt compelled to introduce myself into the narrative much more than was perhaps strictly necessary. But it was essential to capture the period, and this period I lived through, more intensely than many others. I was steeped in it to the core. All the same, it would never have occurred to me to relate a personal story had I not been aware how intimately related it is to that, infinitely more complex and worthy of interest, of the City itself.

There are no fictional characters here, nor any anecdotes arising solely from the imagination of the narrator – who could just as well be any one else.

So what should be seen in this book then is not the most disquieting but disquieted of testimonies.

1941

Beyond the island and the two branches of the river, the city changes. In the square, on the site of the old morgue, stones dating from different periods that cannot abide each other have been cemented on top of one another. There's a muted hatred between them. It grieves me as much as it does them. It's inconceivable that no one gave any thought to this.

The Seine is sulking. Showing the same moodiness as before, when I came to pay my respects after a rather longer trip than I would have liked. This river is no easy mistress.

It will be a hard winter. There are already seagulls at La Tournelle, and it's only September.

In June 1940, at Boult-sur-Suippe, I was wounded and taken prisoner. I found out that the Germans had identified me as a radical journalist. I escaped at the first opportunity.

I have a little money. Enough to survive two weeks, perhaps three. But all I have in terms of identity papers is the service record of Sergeant Ybarne, a priest with no family, who died in my camp – and a demobilization document I concocted for myself.

I don't know whether it will be possible one day to regain

14

my own family name. I have constantly to beware of patrols and raids, especially those carried out by French policemen.

I don't yet know where to sleep. I'm not without trust-worthy friends: a good dozen. I've lurked beneath their windows and always thought better of calling on them.

I wandered through the Ghetto, behind the Hotel de Ville. I know its every paving stone, every brick of every house. I came away disappointed, almost angry. There's an atmosphere of despair, acceptance, resignation. I wanted to breath a more vigorous air. It was towards Maubert, with its secret smile, that an overriding instinct guided my steps. I'm drawn to Rue des Grands-Degrés. I've just got this feeling I'm sure to shake hands with a friend there.

The Watchmaker of Backward-Running Time

This little green clapboard shed is the 'shop' (not quite three square metres in size) of Cyril the master watchmaker. Born in Kiev, God knows when.

Old Georgette the washerwoman, one of the doyennes of La Maube, who remembers the Château-Rouge and Père Lunette and the opening of Rue Lagrange, told me in 1938, 'That guy's incredible. I'm getting on for seventy and I've known him for ever. Watchmender with second-hand watches to flog. Never any trouble. Every now and then he changes his name. Says he's entitled to. That's the fourteenth woman he's on to now. He's buried more than half the rest. And his face still looks the same as ever. I can't figure it out.'

It was certainly curious. More immediate concerns pre-vented me from paying much attention to 'the case' of Cyril. And then, some time later, I meet him in a bar and tell him the story (that I'd just pieced together) of the building his shack leans up against.

A colonel in the days of the Empire (when all colonels were courageous) lost a leg at Austerlizt. This led to his retirement. The officer sought permission from the Emperor to return to Paris with his horse, with whom he had developed a close friendship. The Emperor was in a good mood that day. Permission was granted.

Colonel and horse bought the house, and had an extra storey built on to it. It has a big courtyard paved with sandstone. A huge watering trough was installed in it at great expense. For His Nibs the Horse was in the habit of taking baths and could only drink from running water. The colonel's assets and pension were insufficient to pay for the three or four fellows who shuttled back and forth with their buckets, between the Seine and the sybaritic nag's intermittently flowing stream. Colonel and mount expired simultaneously, locked in each other's embrace.

Cyril found this highly amusing. We drank a lot and became bosom pals.

Cyril has found me a refuge. He took me to Rue Maître-Albert. A street that dog-legs down to the river. Pignol's – a low dive – is a tiny place, crammed with people. Snacks are served behind closed shutters.

Hourly patrols come storming up the street. Their boots can be heard a long way off. It sounds as though the asphalt answers 'turd' to every resounding step. As soon as they turn the corner, we dim the light and keep our traps shut. They feel a sense of desecration. They penetrate the hostile darkness with a tremendous fear in their guts, like a man who'd force himself on a woman who resists.

A power failure. Apparently this is now a frequent occurrence. The proprietress, Pignolette, the only person Cyril introduced me to, lights some candles. I then observe the watchmaker's face (in normal light he looks forty years old at most).

Countless, extraordinarily fine, parallel wrinkles leave no area of his skin unmarked. He looks mummified. I recall Georgette's words. Cyril has already got me to recount my adventures. Now it's his turn.

Having joined the Foreign Legion under an assumed name at the outbreak of hostilities, luckily he put up a good fight.

Military Cross and distinguished service medal. Didn't get caught. They let him keep the name he'd adopted: so he's issuing his own bill of health. But since Cyril, as I well recall, once described to me, in great detail, the fighting he was involved in on the French Front in the 1914–1918 war, as well as the famous Kiev massacres, when the Shirkers were tied to the rails and slow-moving locomotives sliced off their heads, this story bothers me slightly. This matter of time. And of being in so many different places.

People considered 'reputable' because of their three-piece suits are gathered here together with genuine tramps, shovelling down the same grub. I noticed the bespectacled fellow on the end of the bench, his crew-cut hair, his very dark-ringed protruding eyes. Cyril whispers, 'Apparently he's a poet. His name's Robert Desnos.'

I asked for the key to my room.

Exhaustion has made me hypersensitive. A rheumy lorry passes by, a very long way off. I hear it, I sense it descending Rue Monge. It's going to drive round the square, turn into the boulevard on the left. I can 'see' it. I'm sure of it. It sends a shudder through cubic kilometres of buildings. This evening the neighbourhood's nerves are on edge.

Ici tous les plafonds ont eu la scarlatine
Ça pèle à plâtre que veux-tu – ô Lamartine . . .
[Here all the ceilings have had scarlet fever
As you'd expect the plaster's peeling – O Lamartine . . .]

That dark, circular, ringed stain above the bedside table is where the petrol lamp used to hang, stinking and leaking like nobody's business. A nasty fly-specked light bulb dangles over my head, swinging fractionally. It makes the shadows move. The lorry draws closer, and the disturbed shadows cannot quite settle back into place: then the room itself shares in the general unease.

Mobilization had caught me by surprise on my return from a trip to Eastern Europe. In my bohemian two-roomed apartment, I'd accumulated documents and books about the history of Paris. I'd not had time to read them.

I slipped into my place during the day. The Germans have put a seal on my front door: that's to say, two strips of what looks like brown wrapping paper stamped with the eagle and swastika. They think they can impress the world by such pathetic means. For me, it was child's play to get inside, gather together a bundle of linen, documents and books, put everything back in order and leave without being seen.

So I retrieved, among others, *Paris Anecdote* by Privat d'Anglemont, the 1853 edition; a huge and a very old collection of *Arrests Mémorables du Parlement de Paris*; and two precious notebooks that will enable me to collate records of events, places and dates. Besides, the Nationale has once again opened its doors to me. Also, the Arsenal, St Geneviève, and the Archives. I've managed to reconstruct a medieval legend, which relates to the very place where Cyril has been working for so many years. Here it is.

In 1465 the Ruelle d'Amboise, which led from the river to Place Maubert, originated in the teeming industriousness of Port-aux-Bûches. The sluggish Bièvre formed a kind of delta at that point, before mingling its muddy tannin-polluted waters with those of the Seine. Unsquared logs were left to pile up in the stagnant mud that made them imperishable. A brooding unease overhung Paris. Charles the Bold's forces were sweeping down from the north. Along the Loire, the Bretons, won over to the Burgundian cause, were pressing hard on the Duke of Maine's people. Francis of Brittany and the Duke of Berry had also joined forces against the crowned king, Louis XI. In the City itself, the Burgundians were plotting. The overextended police forces were unreliable. So there was a relaxation of the vigilant watch kept on the serfs, semi-slaves, vagabonds, pedlars and hawkers congregated below the walls of the town.

On the very site of Cyril's shack, a watchmaker who had arrived from the Orient, a convert to Christianity who displayed 'great piety', set up business. He made, sold and repaired time-pieces, which were extremely valuable and rare in those days.

His clients were inevitably members of the nobility or wealthy merchants. Tristan the Hermit, who lived in a house very close by, appreciated the watchmaker's skill and had taken him under his patronage.

The watchmaking trade was thriving. The Oriental had repudiated his barbarous name and called himself Oswald Biber. (Which means 'beaver' as does the old French word 'Bièvre'.) The wily fellow lived frugally, and yet he was known to have become very wealthy. Meanwhile, some Gypsies who had been driven out of the City established their encampment in the vicinity of Port-aux-Bûches. They read the future in tracings made in the sand with the end of a stick, in the palms of women and the eyes of children.

Some prelates got upset and condemned this as magic. But there wasn't enough wood in the entire port to burn all those who rightly or wrongly would have been accused of witchcraft. The Gypsies – at that time they were called 'Egyptians' – were on good neighbourly terms with the watchmaker. Perhaps it was because of this that a rumour developed and gained currency, according to which the pious Biber was in reality in possession of forbidden secrets. With the passage of time it had to be acknowledged that such was the case.

Some of his clients – the oldest and wealthiest – seemed less and less affected by the burden of their years. They were rejuvenated, and old men beheld with astonishment those whom they believed to be their contemporaries become once again men in their prime.

It was discovered that Biber had in great secrecy made watches for them that were little concerned with telling the time: they ran backwards. The fate of the person whose name was engraved on the watchwork arbors became linked to that of the object. His life went into reverse, returning through the term of existence he'd already lived. He grew younger.

A brotherhood established itself among the beneficiaries of this marvellous secret. Many years passed.

And then one day Oswald Biber received a visit from his assembled clients. They entreated him, 'Could you not make the mechanisms that rule our lives just mark time now, without regressing any further?'

'Alas! That's impossible. But consider yourselves lucky. You'd have been long dead if I hadn't done this for you.'

'But we don't want to get any younger! We dread adolescence, oblivious youth, the dark night of early childhood, and the inescapable doom of returning to limbo. We can't bear the haunting prospect of that inexorable date, the preordained date of our demise.'

'There's nothing to be done about it, nothing more I can do for you.'

'But we've known you for so many years now, and why do you still look the same as ever? You seem to be ageless.'

'Because the master I had in Venice in times long gone by, who did not to my great regret instil all of his knowledge in me, made for me this watch here.

'The hands run alternatively clockwise and anticlockwise. I age and rejuvenesce every other day.'

Unconvinced, these aspirants to eternal life of the flesh went away and conferred. It was decided they would return to Biber the sorcerer after nightfall and compel him by whatever means necessary to do as they wanted.

They invaded his house but he wasn't there. Every one of them had come, too, with the secret intention of stealing the watchmaker's watch, the only one of its kind offering such comfort.

They fought savagely among themselves, and in their struggle the object that controlled all the others was shattered.

Their watches stopped immediately, and immediately these fine fellows died. Their corpses were discovered and solemnly execrated. They were piled up in a charnel house in a place where 'the soil was so putrefying that a body decayed in nine days.'

At the time I almost regretted having mentioned this to Cyril. I'd already noticed his subtle turn of thought, appreciated the soundness of some of his advice. The unanimous opinion of folk in the neighbourhood could be summed up in these words: Cyril knows things that others don't. But I wasn't aware that he was the holder of a secret – his own – and that to be reminded of it was so painful to him.

All I said was, 'Are you at all familiar with a legend about time running backwards. . . Oswald Biber . . .'

He paled, began to tremble. In a broken voice, staring at me with a kind of terror, he said as if to himself, 'So you too are in the know? It's much more serious than I thought.'

For a moment there was infinite distress in his eyes, rising from the most distant past.

And then he recovered, and we spoke of other things.

Chapter II

Occupied Paris is on its guard. Inviolate deep down to its core, the City has grown tense, surly and scornful. It has reinforced its interior borders, as the bulkheads of an endangered ship are closed. You no longer see between the villages of Paris that self-confident and good-natured human traffic that existed just a few months ago. I sense a resurgence and reassertion, growing stronger every day, of the age-old differences that set apart Maubert and La Montagne, Mouffetard and Les Gobelins. To say nothing of crossing the bridges: left bank and right bank are not two different worlds any more, but two different planets. Often I feel the need to get snugly settled in a corner seat, quiet and alone, with the complicit smile of some boundary-mark, some stone, on the other side of the window, addressed to me alone. With the pleasure of seeing, on this stretch of wall, the poster that flutters in the drama of early morning calling for my attention. It knows that I'm responding.

I make this neighbourhood my own. But bowing to social conventions is now a thing of the past. I literally turn my back on one fellow, said to be likeable and of irreproachable behaviour, who offers me his plump paw. But I've no objection to being surrounded, like some precious stone embedded in rock, by a bunch of sweet-natured winos. There's Gérard the painter, who has a trichological obsession. On the first of every month he gets his hair dressed like that of a musketeer. By the second week he looks like a Russian peasant. There's Séverin the anarchist, who deserted for the sake of a girl. And there's Théophile Trigou. In order to attend mass at St Séverin every morning without being seen, this Breton resorts to the same cunning as the rest of us do in pretending to be unaware of his harmless subterfuge. Théophile is a first-rate Latinist, to which we owe some terrific evenings now and again. The four of us form 'the Smart Gang'. That's the name Pignolette gave us. She's fond of us and so she looks after us.

Yesterday we descended on the Vieux-Chêne, run by the Captain. A genuine ex-merchant marine officer.

Sunset's the best time to take a stroll down Mouffetard, the ancient Via Mons Cetardus. The buildings along it are only two or three stories high. Many are crowned with conical dovecotes. Nowhere in Paris is the connection, the obscure kinship, between houses very close to each other more perceptible to the pedestrian than in this street.

Close in age, not location. If one of them should show signs of decrepitude, if its face should sag, or it should lose a tooth, as it were, a bit of cornicing, within hours its sibling a hundred metres away, but designed according to the same plans and built by the same men, will also feel it's on its last legs.

The houses vibrate in sympathy like the chords of a *viola d'amore*. Like cheddite charges giving each other the signal to explode simultaneously.

The Man Who Repented of Betraying a Secret

The Vieux-Chêne was the scene of bloody brawls between arch thugs. By turns a place of refuge, conspiracy, crime, it was frequently closed down by the police.

I was planning on a session of sweet silent thought, with a pipe to smoke and memories ready to be summoned.

It was not to be. Silence, like madness, is only comparative. We felt embarrassed, almost intimidated, my companions and I, by the absence of the usual screen that guaranteed our isolation: that cacophony of belching, gurgling, stomach-rumbling, incoherent ranting, singing, belly-aching, swearing, drunken snoring – all this was missing.

The local dossers and tramps were there as usual. But silent, anxious, watchful – fearfully so, it seemed – as they gazed at a spare lean man dressed in black, and disgustingly dirty.

Leaning forward with his elbows on the table, huge-eyed with pouches that sagged down his face, he sat staring at a newly lighted candle standing some distance in front of him.

The Captain signalled to us – shh – and went creeping out to bolt the door.

The minutes seeped away like wine from a barrel.

The dossers' eyes went from the candle to the man, from the man to the candle. This carried on for a while, a very long while. When the candle had burned two-thirds of the way down, the flame lengthened, sputtered, turned blue and flickered drunkenly, like the delinquent dawn of a bad day. Then I knew who the man was. I'd encountered him before.

Just after the last war, I spent some of my childhood (the summer months, for several years in a row) at E, a small town in the Eure-et-Loir. I had some playmates, who were entranced by all the things the 'big boys' got up to, that's to say, boys three or four years their senior. These 'big boys' affected to despise us. They never joined in our games, but they were happy to capture the admiring attention of an easily impressed gaggle of kids. The most conceited, big-mouthed show-off, and sometimes the meanest of these older boys, was called Honoré.

We hated him as much as we loved his father: Master Thibaudat, as he was known. This good-hearted fellow – I can still see his blue peaked cap, his Viking moustache, and the reflection on his face of his smithy's furnace – repaired agricultural machinery. He was also captain of the town's fire brigade. This was no small distinction. Every Sunday morning he'd gather together his helmeted and plumed subordinates for fire drill. He'd get them lined up in rows outside the town hall, and direct operations in his manly voice with a thick Beauce accent.

'*Pompe à cul! Déboïautéi!*

'*Mettez-vous en rangs su l'trottouèr comm' dimanche dargniéi!*

'*Hé là-bas: gare les fumelles . . . on va fout'un coup d'pompe . . .*'

[Drop the hose reel! Let it run!

Line up on the pavement like last Sunday!

Hey, watch out there, lasses . . . we're going to give it burst . . .]

What a laugh!

The rest, I found out later.

For there was something else: Master Thibaudat was '*marcou*'. In other words, he'd inherited from his ancestors the secret, passed down from father to son, of mastering fire.

Thibaudat had the ability to extinguish a blazing hayrick, to isolate a burning barn, the strategic genius to contain a forest fire. But more importantly, he was a healer. Mild burns disappeared at once; the rest never withstood him more than a few hours. In very serious cases, he would be sent to the hospital. There he would pass his hands over the agonized patient who would be screaming and in danger of suffocating. At the same time he would recite in an undertone set phrases known only to himself. The pain would cease immediately. And flesh and skin would regenerate with a speed that astounded numerous doctors. From Maintenon to Chartres, and even as far afield as Mans, Thibaudat is still remembered by many people.

The day came when Master Thibaudat sensed that his powers were failing. He feared that he no longer had the vital energy he needed to be able to do his job. His only son, Honoré, was a now grown man: for his eighteenth birthday he'd been given a new bicycle and a pair of long trousers. His third pair.

Under solemn oath to hold his tongue, Honoré was initiated into the family secret and in turn became '*marcou*'.

Honoré got more and more above himself. He'd stuck with the same bunch of friends because, being better dressed than they were, and with plenty of money in his pocket, he more easily cut a dash at the country dances, especially at a time when the day-labourers, not satisfied with the sluts they were fobbed off with in the bordellos – 'Good enough for peasants! Incapable of screwing without the rest of the gang in tow, and drunk as skunks!' – were happily treating themselves to young housemaids, getting them pregnant or giving them a dose of the clap, without a by-your-leave or thank-you and no time to call mother.

Honoré at least had some style and manners. And the means to compensate his partners for the loss of half-a-day's pay. And to find modest sheets to lie between, under a feather counterpane that with two kicks and a pelvic thrust was soon sent flying in the direction of the ceramic-edged chamber-pot with the blue enamel lid.

'Now, what was it your father told you, Honoré? What do you have to say to draw the heat? Is it a prayer or a spell? Go on, tell me, Honoré . . .'

Forgetting his oath, Honoré spilled the beans on several occasions. He'd already exercised the power passed on to him, on some not very serious injuries. The patients had been cured: less rapidly, however, than if they'd been treated by the father. But allowances had to be made. Honoré would eventually get the hang of it.

The hat shop in Rambouillet had prospered. In the workshop, twenty women in front of twenty sewing machines turned out twenty snoods of woven straw, dreadful things for imprisoning chignons. Two girls from the area round E found themselves working side by side. One of them boasted of her experience – and enjoyment – of the seductive charms of the handsome Honoré. Her neighbour, stung to jealousy, claimed to be equally knowledgeable on this subject. There was no way they could start tearing each other's hair out. But the girls were obdurate. At a loss for insults, vying to have the last word, they hurled at each other those phrases that were not to be uttered, the phrases unwisely divulged by Honoré. And once let loose, those words were soon all over town.

The child that had fallen on to the fire in the hearth was brought before Honoré, who with the laying-on of his hands began to murmur. A quarter of an hour later the child was dead.

Then the rumours gained substance. And people grabbed their pitchforks, their flails and some their guns. The '*marcou*' had become '*malahou*', in other words, forsworn, a traitor to his word, a traitor to everyone.

It required the energetic protection of the police to allow Honoré to get on his bike and reach the very distant station of Gazeran, where the Paris train stopped.

Old Thibaudat died shortly afterwards – broken-hearted, so they say. Banished from that region for ever, Honoré got on the wrong side of the law. He spent his military service doing time with one of the Africa Disciplinary Battalions.

The extinguished wick was still smoking, through distraction – amazement, perhaps.

The dossers began to talk among themselves, suspecting one another of being the one that had blown out the candle without anyone noticing. The man in black seemed at once crushed and relieved. I don't know why I was so cruel.

'Honoré Thibaudat?'

His lined face became even more gaunt. The same terrified bewilderment, the same overwhelming distress I'd witnessed in Cyril. But this lasted much longer. With great difficulty he formed the words, 'What . . . what do want?'

'Nothing. Are you the son of the fireman at E? We used to know each other.'

'So . . . so what? What do you want of me?'

'Nothing, I tell you, nothing at all. Let me buy you a drink.'

'He only drinks lemonade,' said our host.

Honoré seemed unable to breathe. 'Yes . . . yes . . . with lots of ice,' he said.

In three large glassfuls, three single draughts, he'd emptied his bottle of lemonade. He looked at me. This time with the eyes of a beaten dog.

'So . . . you know the story?'

We still had twenty minutes before the curfew. Honoré and I walked back up La Mouffe side by side. He pointed to a basement window. 'I sleep there, in the cellar. It's cooler. Since back then, especially since Africa, I have this burning sensation. Here.' He ran a trembling hand over his larynx. 'Nothing I can do to relieve it. Tried everything, including injections. Afterwards, it comes back, worse than ever. Sometimes I can even extinguish live embers. But that takes it out of me. I'm already an old man.'

It was true. At forty years of age, he looked seventy.

He yelled, he bellowed, 'What must I do? What must I do?'

And I left him there in the dark, sobbing in repentance for the secret he'd betrayed.

It's really very, very cold. People are hungry. Rations are inadequate. Nothing to line your stomach. The tramps, who for years have been part of the landscape, are dying like flies. Only the strongest survive. For those that deign to stir themselves there's no lack of work – luckily. They have only to be on the street by five in the morning (any earlier is prohibited) and start going through the dustbins. Never has the price of paper, fabric and scrap metal been so high. And it's still soaring. The master rag-pickers – wholesale rag-traders – are beginning to build up real fortunes. The tramps couldn't care less. They'll earn just enough to stuff their faces with no matter what, no matter how, no matter where – and to fill their stomachs with enough plonk to keep them in a drunken stupor till the next time they waken. That's all they ask.

The Shipwreckage Doll

Yesterday Old Hubert was found dead, frozen stiff, behind the bar. The rats had started in on the exposed softer parts: the neck, the cheeks and the fat of his palms. We'd seen it coming for a long time. No one was surprised. You can still make out on the front of his shop: Coffee – Wines – Liqueurs – Hotel with Every Comfort. Every comfort? What a joke!

Rue de Bièvre, number 1A, right by the river. Two and a half storeys – in other words, you'd have to be a dwarf or amputated at the knees to able to stand upright under the sloping roof. From the outside it looks at least as respectable as the other hovels in the street. But just go up to the first floor, and you know the score. The walls are caving in or bulging with damp. The landings are pitted with holes – pot-holes. The resident population is made up of (or breaks down into) five households, three unsanctioned by marriage, with a total of twenty-one children between the ages of two and ten, not to mention the babes-in-arms. All the fathers share a physical resemblance: they're midgets. Not one of them even as tall as one metre sixty. Nowhere near it. And there's another defining characteristic they have in common: they've done absolutely nothing for many, many years. Just a matter of bad luck! All of them skilled workers of one kind or another, but so highly skilled, and as ill luck would have it so inappropriately skilled, that any job that might be available never matches their skill. It's a near thing every time. Which means unemployment, welfare, child allowance, assistance for this, benefits for that, social, unsocial, antisocial . . .

A man can get by pretty well on this, and keep his whistle wet. But paying the rent, that's another story. Wait till the landlord starts moaning before you give him something to keep him off your back. It wasn't in old Hubert's nature to give anyone a hard time. He'd already been served notice to carry out urgent health and safety repairs to his building. And with what millions? Forget it! With the Huns here, and everyone hard up, this was no time to be hoping for so much as a brass farthing. So what? Evict them? Unthinkable! Old Hubert simply decided to ignore the existence of the hotel. He condemned his own bedroom on the first floor as unfit for habitation, and started living in the bar.

For the past three months he'd been dossing down behind the counter. During the day he served plonk, in the morning 'coffee' – a dark foul brew – accompanied with more or less adulterated spirits. This gave him enough to live on, until that winter dawn when, finding the door closed, the tramps discovered Hubert dead, in perishing cold weather, surrounded by empty wines bottles, tins of food and dirty dishes.

Not a pretty sight was the late Hubert, scowling and grimacing, with his spittle frozen, sprawled out on his pile of refuse. Alas, I've seen all too many corpses and could have spared myself this spectacle.

Théophile Trigou was there too. No more motivated by morbid curiosity than I was. He snatched Tutur's pipe from his mouth and threw La Voltige's cap on the ground. And because One-Eyed Ida, either drunk already or still drunk, was bawling her head off and making a nuisance of herself, he literally booted her out.

After that, he gave the three or four guys there a job to do – he knows how to take charge. They hadn't worked so hard for a long time. Bottles in one corner, rags in another. Rubbish, out into the gutter, then down the drain. A quick sweep, and a going over with the floor cloth as well.

He got the body laid out on a not too wobbly table covered with brand new pieces of sacking.

The end result was an almost shocking semblance of decency.

Théophile stood there motionless beside the dead man. I realized he was praying. La Voltige, the spurious tough guy, took a while to twig. He sniggered. Someone said, 'Don't be stupid!' He wiped the grin off his face and adopted a serious expression.

Everyone scarpered when the cops arrived.

Old Hubert must have had a premonition of his squalid demise. In October he said to me, 'Forty-two years I've had this place. I'd really like to go back home, but I ain't got the energy since my old girl died. And I can't sell it the way it is now. But anyway before I hang my hat up I'd be curious to know what's in that third cellar of mine.'

The third cellar has been walled up by order of the civil defence authorities after the floods of 1910. A double barrier of cemented bricks prevents the rising waters from invading the upper floors when flooding occurs. In the event of storms or blocked drains, the cellar acts as a regulatory overflow.

The weather was fine: no risk of drowning or any sudden emergency. There were five of us: Hubert, Gérard the painter, two regulars and myself. Old Marteau, the local builder, was upstairs with his gear, ready to repair the damage. We made a hole.

Our exploration took us sixty metres down a laboriously-faced vaulted corridor (it must have been an old thorough-fare). We were wading through a disgusting sludge. At the far end, an impassable barrier of iron bars. The corridor continued beyond it, plunging downwards. In short, it was a kind of drain-trap.

That's all. Nothing else. Disappointed, we retraced our steps. Old Hubert scanned the walls with his electric torch. Look! An opening. No, an alcove, with some wooden object that looks like a black statuette. I pick the thing up: it's easily removable. I stick it under my arm. I told Hubert, 'It's of no interest . . .' and kept this treasure for myself.

I gazed at it for hours on end, in private. So my deductions, my hunches were not mistaken: the Bièvre–Seine confluence was once the site where sorcerers and satanists must surely have gathered. And this kind of primitive magic, which the blacks of Central Africa practise today, was known here several centuries ago. The statuette had miraculously survived the onslaught of time: the well-known virtues of the waters of the Bièvre, so rich in tannin, had protected the wood from rotting, actually hardened, almost fossilized it. The object answered a purpose that was anything but aesthetic. Crudely carved, probably from heart of oak. The legs were slightly set apart, the arms detached from the body. No indication of gender. Four nails set in a triangle were planted in its chest. Two of them, corroded with rust, broke off at the wood's surface all on their own. There was a spike sunk in each eye. The skull, like a salt cellar, had twenty-four holes in which little tufts of brown hair had been planted, fixed in place with wax, of which there were still some vestiges. I've kept quiet about my find. I'm biding my time.

Chapter III

'Your Body's Tattooed'

The other day some of La Mouffe's most egregious specimens of humanity went over to La Maube and fetched up
at Pignol's. They were carrying baskets. I think they sold
Pignolette, on the semi-black market, the rabbits we've been
eating since. There was Fanfan-No-Kidding, Smoke-Sucker
and Butterfly. Butterfly is so called because the stem of his
nose runs into the abdomen of a blue bombyx that spreads its
delicately veined wings across his forehead.

During a period of his life when he wasn't making much
use of his, what Rabelais referred to as, 'quickening peg',
Smoke-Sucker thought it a good idea to have it decorated
with delicate spiral motifs. Something of a Don Juan by nature,
he said it was his practice to invite his partners to use this
instrument in a subtle manner reminiscent of Baudelairean
chibouk-smokers. Hence the nickname.

Fanfan-No-Kidding gets his moniker from the unruffled
nerve with which he describes Guyana, the penal colony he
'very nearly' went to. Condemned to five years' hard labour,
he had his sentence commuted to detention, which he served
on French soil. He retains a deep grudge against his overzeal-
ous defence lawyers. Fanfan is tattooed all over his lower body.
From his navel to his toes, from his coccyx to the soles of
his feet, is all flowers, weird plants, fantastic animals romping
among playing cards, dice boxes, cryptic devices.

We bolted the door to admire at closer quarters the hidden
splendours of our mates, who willingly displayed them.

Then, taking our cue from Théophile, ever ready to discuss
problems of 'the marginalized', we conferred. Interminably.

Fanfan told us of the grinding boredom in top-security
prisons, the stupefying effect of freezing-cold or stifling-hot

cells, the friendships forged amid disgusting overcrowding. And the pleasure derived from outwitting 'the screws', getting hold of ink and needles by the most incredible means. And the horrible relief, for someone who knows he's branded, of branding himself in a visible and indelible way to make him part of that vast and uncouth brotherhood of eternal reprobates.

Théophile seemed obsessed with the subject. He recalled the various images, figures and mottoes he had observed on the epidermis of his contemporaries. There was no stopping him as he launched into a very interesting and knowledgeable disquisition on the 'symbolism of tattoos'.

I caught myself declaring, with an authoritativeness that was totally unjustified, how dangerous it was for any man to subject his body to such an intervention. I think I even said: 'to such an experience'. I learned from my own lips that tattoos were not only, in my opinion, a mark of identification, more often than not lewd, but the sign of a kind of acceptance of defeat. Abandonment of the struggle against an unrelentingly hostile fate.

Fanfan agreed with me. He said, 'That's for sure. With your tattooed man, there's powers at work. Just look at what goes on at the Salève.'

'Tell me.'

'Oh! It's not that easy to explain. Better go and see for yourself.'

'Where?'

'Rue Zacharie, St-Séverin.'

'Come and show me.'

I was excited. The others objected. Not now. It was nice and comfortable here. Let's have another round. Why move to another bar?

No, no, right now. Théophile eyed me with anxiety. He gave the nod. We set off, Fanfan leading the way.

Rue Zacharie: they've renamed it after the cabaret singer Xavier Privas, but it's the old name that sticks in the mind. Nothing to do with the prophet. In the seventeenth century it was Rue Sac-à-Lie. While waiting for the quality of their merchandise to be certified at the Petit-Châtelet, the vinegar sellers kept stored in bonded warehouses the leather bottles containing the lees – the so-called mother of vinegar. For a while, under St Louis, it was called Rue des Trois-Chandeliers. And for just a few years, Rue de l'Homme-Qui-Chante. But I know an Englishman, Dr Garret, who possesses an extraordinary document: he showed it to me in Sydenham, in 1935. It's a map of the Sorbonne district, drawn up by the scholars resident at the Irish College. Rue Zacharie, between St Séverin and La Huchette – on the map, there's no question about it – appears under the name of Witchcraft Street.

'Rue des Maléfices. Why?'

This intrigues me, especially as I've never been able, since long before the war, to walk down that dark and narrow street on my own without a sense of painful disquiet. That feeling you get in the presence of a dear friend under the constraint of an unaccountable reserve.

I would compel this gloomy secretive street to lift a corner of its veil. I was already savouring my revenge.

Enemy Tattoos

An indentation on either side of Rue Zacharie creates a little square where trolleys loaded with all kinds of things stand idling. Outside the charcoal store, the dismantled hand-cart, collapsed wheel to wheel, handshafts together, cart-prop dangling, looks like the skeleton of some Apocalyptic wader bird mounted on an axle. From all round exudes the sound of droning voices, Arab, African, Greek or Armenian. This wooden balcony was once painted white. There's washing drying on it that will be stuck like eye patches over the sightless windows. A bunch of North Africans has clocked us. They want to know what these new faces are doing here. One of them steps towards us, a young guy. At the bidding of the Elders, he asks us what time it is. We shrug our shoulders without replying. As if it could be any ordinary time in such a street as this.

At the Salève, the stove is drawing badly. This and the stale tobacco, rough wine and a perpetual acrid pungency (disinfectant or vomit, or both) are almost intolerable. But there's that tingling you've only got to register once: within two seconds it gets you at the back of your throat, and then immediately diffuses like a drop of oil. A sudden and surprising sweetness. Breathe in through your mouth, out through your nose. That's it. You're hooked.

Someone here is smoking hashish.

The *patron* looks like a higher form of rodent. Almost fit for society. Around him stews sozzled flesh. Sozzled not only with adulterated wine. But hunger, tiredness. And boredom. Out of a dark corner, three pairs of brown eyes look daggers at us. There are some wide-awake people over there. The smell of hashish comes from that direction.

The rodent stares at Théophile and me. Fanfan delivers some spiel. As the patter goes on, the overfed rat-face grows wary. He signals to the pair of peepers furthest away: a tall guy comes over. A Frenchman, very dark, very bitter. Neither old nor bowed. But for ever down on his luck. You can tell straight away. Introductions: Edgar Jullien. Journalist and explorer. Théophile and I give our names. Or someone else's. You can never be too careful. A beardless and smaller-sized rat-face – a twelve-year-old version – passes for the only son of the rat-face behind the counter. 'Go and fetch Dimitri,' says the pater.

The kid opens the door, heads off to some other factory of despair.

It would take too long to tell the whole story.

Besides, I've no right to.

Only a few years ago Edgar Jullien – let's say that's his name – was a very well-known journalist. A specialist on Islamic issues. A member of the Society of French Explorers. He knows North Africa well, but more importantly has travelled all over the Near East where he managed to pass as a Muslim for months on end. It's easy to imagine him turbanned, shod in Turkish slippers, with a djellaba draped casually over his shoulders. He carried out some very dangerous assignments in his day. But he made the mistake of indulging from one day to the next in the most foolish, pointless and disarming of idle 'precautions'. It was in Syria that the dreaded fit of aberration overcame him. He made the acquaintance of some exiled Greek monks, who had converted to a satanic sect and wanted to initiate him in their rites. So far, the whole thing sounds like some ludicrous burlesque of neurotic mystics. But, prompted by inertia and perhaps some other concerns that he doesn't disclose, Edgar Jullien allowed his chest to be tattooed with the sect's tutelary emblem: a bat.

Ever since then his life has been an incredible series of terrible disasters.

Dimitri B was a great pianist, listened to with knuckles pressed to brow in all the concert halls of Europe. Son of a White Russian, he applied for French citizenship, and in order to obtain it had to do eighteen months' military service in the French army much later than the normal age. He chose Tunisia. He was already a heavy drinker. The rotgut, the raki, the malaria – his brain couldn't take it. Brought up by a fanatically orthodox family in the constant and strictest observance of his liturgical 'duties', he wouldn't rest until a huge intricate crucifix, like an icon, was tattooed on his pectorals. In contrast with the appallingly lucid Edgar Jullien, Dimitri now gives the impression of being a hopeless moron.

Dimitri prepares himself for what is about to happen with a litre of red. Edgar Jullien, with what I don't know. Or dare not contemplate.

In the middle of the back room, now emptied of its dozy occupants, a table has been cleared. On it has been placed a glass filled with water, on the surface of which rat-face junior has set to float a previously greased and magnetized sewing needle.

Naked to the waist, with their backs to opposite walls of the room, the two tattooed men confront each other – they don't so much abhor as ignore each other. They advance slowly towards the table that separates them. The improvised compass is thrown into confusion – it wavers, spins round, and the needle sinks. They did this four times.

'Apparently on some stormy evenings,' says the *patron*, 'the water's even bubbled a bit.'

I'd very much like to 'conclude' something from this experiment. Or that it should raise a question in my mind, and a commitment to get to the bottom of the matter, to investigate, to come up with an outline of the beginning of an answer, however ill-defined or trite it might be . . . But no. I'm here to see, hear, observe – to experience. Let others explain.

It's splendid how much at home we feel at Pignol's. A tacit complicity at every moment prevails among the regulars here. A process of self-selection operates: starving crooks, thirsty whores, witless grasses working for low-grade cops, middle-class types a bit too willing to conform (leaving aside the pound of blackmarket meat and the camembert without ration tickets) – all feel too ill at ease here. They've only got to stay away. Along with anyone else who doesn't meet the requirements of this establishment: first and foremost, to keep your trap shut. The war? Past history. The Krauts? Don't know any. Russia? Change at Réaumur. The police? There was a time when they were needed for directing the traffic. At Pignol's, silence constitutes the most important, most difficult and lengthiest induction ordeal.

After that, it's a matter of imponderables. It works according to the rule of three: the people who don't get along with the people that I get along with are people I can't get along with. Syllogisms, of course. Now clear out!

Oh, goodness gracious! Don't be shocked by my vocabulary. It's not an affectation. To use any other words would be to play false with these people for whom I've too great a regard. And to play false with you too, in so far as you'll assume I have 'all the time in the world', or else conclude the opposite. Understand?

So the most unlikely solidarity has grown up between characters who normally would heartily despise each other. My, what a crowd!

There's Pepe the Pansy. Beyond belief. A poof like you wouldn't have thought possible. He has the audacity to solicit at the entrance to the hotel opposite. On crutches, toothless, outrageously made up, he sometimes wears a filthy wig and a skirt, with his single trouser leg and his wooden leg with the naked end of his stump showing, extending below it. This human detritus claims to be an hermaphrodite. Before, he lived in a brothel in Le Havre, where he was called Miss Mexico. Now he fleeces the Jerries, especially the young SS who turn up one by one, not very proud of themselves – the street is out of bounds to them. He'd be thrown out anywhere else. Here he's tolerated. Why, I'll be wondering for the rest of my life. And to my own surprise that I don't instinctively recoil in disgust at his presence somewhat appals me.

There's Léopoldie the West Indian. A tart, a fine girl who's stopped turning tricks for the duration of the war. The green of the German uniform, she says, doesn't suit her complexion. So she sells flowers, mostly to us, whenever possible.

There's Bizinque. With a face that's all cheekbone. A conk like a carbuncle. For a mouth, an orifice like a hen's arsehole (an ostrich hen). And big, red-rimmed, flat eyes, reminiscent of a bream. He's a junk dealer, but makes real finds – he'd find you a gramophone in the desert. There's also Riton the Pimp, who's latched on to Catherine because of her small annuity. One day, when he was drunk and couldn't buy any more booze because he was skint, Riton gave Catherine's kids a terrible thrashing. And while the kids were bawling their heads off, the neighbours didn't hear Riton removing the door that opened on to the landing. He chopped it up as firewood and sold it straight away to Constant, the charcoal seller on Rue de Seine.

The rest of the gang aren't worth mentioning. But every one of them's got a story.

I catch myself writing 'not worth mentioning'. According to what criteria? No reason whatever to feel superior.

No, I know what it is. I'm nice to them, I seem harmless, and I've no desire to lecture them the way Théophile does. So they all want to tell me their story. They crave acceptance, an excuse for their often abominable behaviour, a hint of commiseration. Théophile listens to them. He's something of a saint. But I don't always have the patience. But here come the guys from the place opposite that my down-and-outs rub shoulders with. Géga, purveyor of all things. A wholesale ragman these days. A crooked smile, brimmed hat, pipe and patter. Sheer Balzac. Heart of gold. But he ought to shut up. There's Monsieur Moniaud, presently history teacher in a private school, ousted from the senior position he held in the Aliens Bureau at the Tour Pointue on account of his insufficiently pro-Nazi sentiments. There's Papa Bonnechose, qualified barrister and drunkard, dyspeptic and stunted, accompanied by two or three old wags and many a time by Henri Vergnolle, a tall guy with big fat lips, architect and socialist but out of the game for the time being, for the sole reason there's only one game in town, that of the Wehrheim.

Here, in a few words, you've said all you need to say. People stand by each other, but they don't talk. It's remarkable. I've investigated the extraordinary history of these walls. I think I'm the only person who knows that it's the stones, the stones alone that set the tone here.

The House That No Longer Exists

There's news regarding Rue de Bièvre. Henri Vergnolle has kept in touch with his old cronies. It was he who told us.

In Lugny (Saône-et-Loire), a twenty-seven-year-old vine-grower has just been told by lawyers that he's the sole heir of his uncle – Old Hubert – who basically left him a 'hotel located in Paris, close to the Boulevard St-Michel'. To take possession of it, some fairly considerable debts would have to be discharged. But according to the letter, of which I have a copy before my eyes, 'something could be worked out'.

There's open speculation (purely conjectural) on how things will develop. We're wondering whether the young man will try to sell his 'property' (!) or decide to apply from the Unoccupied Zone for authorization to come and run the place 'in person'.

Everyone's chortling in anticipation of the look on his face. I'm not at all happy about it. Vergnolle too is laughing derisively. I've taken a liking to him since this evening.

What's going on? Théophile Trigou has long puzzled and exasperated me. He earns his living, and not badly at that, offering his services as a Latinist, at La Source and D'Harcourt, to wealthy numbskulls studying for a degree, struggling with their textual analyses of Cicero, or with a tough translation. In response to a tactless question he once said to me, 'What do you expect? This lousy neighbourhood gave me the come-on. I couldn't resist.' So what? Me too. I'm now so jealous of 'my' buildings that, filled with a sort of elemental anxiety, I go off on my own and examine them one by one to try and determine which will be the first to dash my hopes. It's mostly Rue de Bièvre that I haunt, after midnight, between patrols, and I've got my eye in particular on Old Hubert's house, now completely taken over by tramps. I can't bear the idea that some outsider, some stranger, from far away, should have more rights to this crumbling edifice than I do. If that someone shows up, I want to be the first to meet him, fully prepared. Depending on what he looks like, it'll be up to me whether he's forever blacklisted, or immediately becomes one of the lads. Accepted straight off, if I so decide.

A little twinge woke me. I'd been forewarned: the intruder was due to arrive in these parts at about seven thirty. He would come over the Seine, cross 'my' frontier. I hastily dressed and raced over to Rue de Bièvre. I spotted him from a distance, pretending to be taking a casual stroll in the acid morning light. All those well-laid plans are scuppered: there are two of them, he and his wife. I wasn't expecting that.

They were each carrying a small suitcase: they must have walked from the station, and put their trunks in left luggage. Tramps laden with their bags emerged like moles out of dark warrens. The dancing light played over their etched faces, transformed the bearded men into prophets. Children began squealing. Vexed eiderdowns unwillingly put out to air at open windows wept feathers. The man, with a sheet of paper in his hand, located number 1A. He gave a start. His wife was surveying the embankment, the rooftops, looking down her nose at the tramps who passed close by, already reeling drunkenly. The couple walked up the street to Place Maubert, then retraced their steps. The man consulted Madame Cooked-Vegetables-to-Take-Away, who was sweeping sawdust out of her shop into the gutter. There was no denying the fact: this was the place. The man's distress, the woman's indifference – none of this could escape my attention. We agreed, Séverin and Théophile and I, to keep a close eye on developments, and apply ourselves to finding out, very soon, what measure of satisfaction or concern these two newcomers to our domain would bring us.

I happen to have gazed at length on two surrealist paintings: one depicts a sewing machine standing on a work table; the other, a bull charging into a grand piano.

Wrested from their familiar world, the Valentin couple suggested to me the same sense of dramatic absurdity.

Valentin isn't cut out for this sort of thing. He serves this unkempt, scruffy crowd with such bad grace that the tramps have soon written him off as 'a fat-head'. The clientele will probably desert him, go and tipple elsewhere? Not a bit of it. These people are like bedbugs: when they've made up their minds to infest a place, there and nowhere else, the owner of the premises has to capitulate willy-nilly and let them take over. This is what happens to Valentin. He eventually resigns himself to getting down here by four thirty to prepare the dreadful dishwater he serves.

Sullen-faced, he scarcely responds to his customers who, completely plastered from as early as eight to ten in the morning, tell him their tales of woe.

All the same, he had to behave more sociably when it became necessary to establish categories: those that work – the rag-pickers – to whom some credit could be allowed, or even a little money loaned, without too much risk; and those that not only don't do a stroke, but make it a point of honour.

Paulette dolls herself up in her room, comes down late and goes off to do her shopping after a vague good morning addressed to anyone in the room. A reproachful silence, a kind of irritated disapproval greets her every time: no one's entitled at a time like this, least of all round La Maubert, to go flaunting such casual displays of attractiveness and even elegance. Because she sure knows how to dress, that woman, she's bursting with youthful vitality, and when she walks up the street, without putting on any of that hip-swinging typical of tarts, eyes follow her, sidelong glances full of desire, jealousy and regret.

She and Valentin talk to each other very little, at work at least. After a lunch prepared with care but dispatched in ten minutes, Valentin puts on his raincoat and goes out for a walk. On his own, he strolls for an hour or two, sometimes three, along the banks of the Seine, which he follows up to Austerlitz and beyond. He doesn't drop in anywhere, or talk to anyone. A loner.

That's the moment we pick, the rest of the gang and I, to go and pay court, as they say – in other words, to try and win over Paulette – that's all. We now know that, behind that pretty face cast in shadow by her light chestnut hair, that slightly ill-defined countenance, that vexing little forehead, there lurks a dangerous feather-brain, fey and romantic. We've found out the key facts about her past life or as much of it as concerns us: studies too soon interrupted for her liking, married off – her parents wanted her 'comfortably settled' – to a boy she didn't love. Once upon a time, back home before the war, a Gypsy woman foretold a long journey ahead of her. Paulette declares with a false laugh that she doesn't know which she regrets most: the journey she hasn't made or the few coins the fanciful fortune-teller cost her.

Not another word about her married life, but it's easy to see that the time she spends with Valentin is kept to the minimum.

In a joint, now closed, near Place de la Contrescarpe, Fréhel sings for her friends. You have go down a long corridor and knock four times – three hard raps, and then a more tentative one – to get the heavy low door to open up.

She stands there, a big ravaged brute of a woman, in her

black costermonger's apron, clasping over her belly her two uselessly swollen hands. She sings '*Chanson Tendre*' and '*La Vielle Maison*' in a voice like a cheese-grater, its musicality now lost. Unobtrusive, ecstatic, La Lune accompanies her on the harmonica. La Lune the tramp, and doing so well, La Lune the weirdo, La Lune the extraordinary musician, of such feeling . . . There are those that take their time coming back from the pisser, having stepped out for a shoulder-heaving crying jag, their hooters and peepers buried in purple-checked snot-rags. Talk about tough guys.

Fréhel is shacked up with a girlfriend over by Montmartre. But for tonight we've found her a room nearby. We're keeping her over here. We take them all for a drink at the Vieux-Chêne, her, La Lune and the guy that has the room for her.

As coincidences go, this is some coincidence. Gathered round the stove at the Vieux-Chêne, having a chinwag, are all of La Mouffe's very finest. There's La Puce. Just out of jail. He'd nicked the priest's ceremonial vestments from the sacristy of St Médard. Retired officer Cyclops, one-eyed as his name suggests, listens to a wizened skeleton, a real swank, snuggly wrapped in a long cloak, holding forth. Next to the skeleton is seated a very old man with a goatee beard and glasses.

'Right back there is where the rostrum was,' explains the skeleton, rolling his rs. 'When I sang, I used to wear a scarf or a cap; sometimes a *bat' d'Af*' képi. It was Georges Darien, the guy that wrote *Contre Biribi*, who first brought him here. He used to turn up with guys I didn't know, sometimes with floozies. Just before the war, he treated me to dinner in Montparnasse. There were some incredible characters. And filthy dirty. It was a long time afterwards that someone showed me his memoirs. He wrote that he admired me, that I had a gift as a real "singer of the people". Well, after all, knowing what he came to be, that actually counts for something, especially now.'

The skeleton in question is called Montehus. He's talking about a fellow named Vladimir Illitch Lenin, who, in his day, also enjoyed some renown.

I got up to shake hands with the bearded Gypsy who was sitting in a corner, having a bite to eat in silence. Got to keep up your contacts.

This man intrigues me. He's tall, not old, shows no signs of being a wino, with distinguished angular features that confer a certain nobility on his dark face framed with a thick black shiny beard. His sunken eyes are very far-searching. A clear gaze. His long thin hands have preserved an astonishing delicacy for one of his profession – rag-picker, like the others. One detail: in his pierced left ear is a tiny gold ring. I saw one like it attached to the ear lobe of a Russian singer, a former Cossak.

I always have on me something to draw with. After offering him a drink, I wanted to knock off a quick portrait of the Gypsy in red chalk. Five minutes is a long time. He posed patiently.

As I was about to leave with the rest of the gang, the Gypsy comes up to me, almost formally – and gives me permission to keep for myself his likeness.

I made this tactless reply: 'But I'm not asking for any favours, I'd happily pay you for posing for me, or do you another portrait, if it were of any use to you.'

He insisted, almost angrily, 'I only get paid for the work I do. Here I drink. And I'm telling you, it's just as well for you that you have my permission.'

I had no alternative but to order another two glasses. La Lune was slumped on the table, snoring. The sound of the Gypsy's voice, his barely detectible accent, the metallic precision of his words are engraved on my memory.

I know that the Germans have begun to round up the Romanies, even those that are settled. I vowed that, if I came across the fellow again, I'd warn him of the danger – give him advice or help, if wanted. Today we ran into each other in the market on Rue des Carmes. I led Blackbeard off to Rue de Bièvre. On the way I told him about my fears for his safety. He stopped dead and looked me in the eye. 'Gypsy? Why that rather anything else? I didn't select the words used round here.

As for the Germans, if you knew how much grief I gave them, the cops and all the others.'

'You're no grass, though?'

At that, he laughed heartily and patted me on the shoulder.

'Anyway, the fact you wanted to help me out makes me happy,' he said.

At Paulette's, he called her '*Madame*' and not '*la patronne*', and ordered tea. No one had ever seen the like of it. He insisted on paying his round. Phenomenal. I don't know what prompted me to mention my trip to Prague. Not only did he know Prague, but also Hungary, Romania, Galati and the mouths of the Danube. With a real gift for words, he was able to describe the people to be found there, their customs, occupations, the colour of their clothes, the shape of their houses.

Contrary to her usual practice, Paulette didn't retreat behind her counter. She sat with us, put the shawl she was knitting down on the table and listened with pleasure to what Blackbeard was saying. Why did she have to go and tell her story of the Gypsy woman, the 'long journey', and the few coins?

The Gypsy gave that characteristic smile of his. It was as if this was just what he'd been waiting for.

'Let's see if she was telling the truth.' And at the same time he placed in front of the young woman a strange deck of cards, decorated with images unknown in these parts. 'Cut.'

Under Blackbeard's guidance Paulette had to lay the cards out in a circle, cover them, turn them over, repeat the process, build up little piles.

'That's it.'

The Gypsy seemed to be concentrating, and deliberately disposed not to speak frivolously – when Valentin came bursting in. The cards were still lying on the oilcloth-covered table.

In her sudden exasperation Paulette's face expressed disappointment, weariness and resentment of an unforgiving kind.

Valentin instantly realized what was going on. He turned pale. I'd never seen him like that before.

'Go on! Get out of here!'

The sturdy Gypsy gathered up his cards and without haste very calmly got to his feet.

'Excuse me! I know how to behave, and I'm not doing any harm!'

Valentin was foaming.

'Beat it! Scram!'

'All right, if that's the way you want it,' said the Gypsy sullenly.

Outside on the pavement he turned and gave his new enemy a smile that was just as strange but different. I tried to get Valentin to listen to reason.

'Look, about that guy, I'm the one that . . .'

'Fine, fine, let's change the subject.'

His hands, his neck, his jaws were trembling.

The Gypsy came by Pignol's very late. He was in no mood for talking. We could only extract these disturbing words from him:

'That friend of yours, he should never have done that. Never. If he only knew.'

Obviously Valentin's behaviour still rankles. It's really got to him.

Séverin and I left, feeling preoccupied, rather worried.

Well! He's got some nerve, that Gypsy. He showed up at Rue de Bièvre at dawn. He asked for a black coffee. Valentin threw him out straight away. The rag-pickers there at the time, who scarcely knew who Blackbeard was – the people of La Maube and La Mouffe are fraternal enemies – made it clear that one of these days there could be trouble. Valentin cut short his constitutional, on the Pont de la Tournelle. A few days ago he picked up a starving dog. A beauceron. Today the animal was tied up behind the counter, with a generous help-ing of mash. Paulette sewed in silence, sulking. She's plotting God knows what revenge. It's blatantly obviously. I daredn't say anything to her but the tritest things. Valentin, who wanted to ease the tension, shared some weak joke with me. He gave a forced laugh. His red wine's turning sour.

Little by little, the Gypsy has changed his stamping ground.

He's drawn closer to the embankment. According to his 'colleagues', he works immensely hard and 'salvages' an astonishing quantity of old papers, rags and metal. He drinks less than the others. No one knows where he dosses. Not far away, that's for sure; because every morning he comes up Rue de Bièvre, and to Valentin's exasperation stops in front of his window and stares at him with that famous smile at the corners of his mouth, ever more full of teasing menace.

This morning Blackbeard couldn't restrain himself any longer. He made so bold as to try and enter the café. Valentin, who'd just been waiting for an excuse, set his dog on him. With one bound, the beauceron – it's a ferocious beast – leapt over the counter. With its fangs bared, it looked as if it was going to attack Blackbeard. But it stopped dead. The smiling Gypsy held it in check. Two fingers of his right hand parted in a V and pointed at the hound halted it in its tracks. Then the Gypsy made some gravelly utterances. And the dog began to tremble. It backed off, showing its teeth, and once it thought it was beyond reach of some unspecified danger, known only to itself, it fled and ran to cower against its master's legs. The Gypsy didn't push things any further. He ambled off.

Now the dog trembles incessantly. It won't eat anything. It has to be dragged out. It keeps escaping and comes straight back. Its fur's falling out in handfuls. Valentin decided to wrap it up in a blanket and carry the whining creature in his arms to the vet near by. This specialist, Doctor N, a black man, is well known for his intuitive expertise, which never fails. He nodded at Valentin's story. He spoke of 'sorcery' with the air of a man who knows what he's talking about.

He gives the bald skeletal creature two injections a day. Without holding out much hope for it. He wants this to be known.

It's all over. The dog has been put down.

Throughout the dog's 'treatment', the Gypsy didn't reappear in Rue de Bièvre. The nights finally grew shorter, the weather milder, and Valentin more and more gloomy. He nursed a brooding anger. We were all dreading the day when . . .

And then it happened.

The Gypsy came in quietly while Valentin had his back turned, as he was arranging his bottles. I was in the back of the room, at the end of the counter.

Valentin fell into a frightful fit of fury. He shouted insults left hanging in the air. 'Son of a . . . Sodding . . .' He ended up brandishing a heavy stick.

Blackbeard – still with that exasperating smile – levelled both hands this time, his fingers set in two horizontal Vs. And again he spoke.

Yes, it was a force, a real force that emanated in successive waves from the hands of this demonic man and immobilized Valentin, now suddenly as limp as a rag.

Blackbeard put one hand behind him, opened the door and backed out, taking his time. His nasty smile deepened.

Overwhelmed with unconquerable lethargy, Valentin had to retire to bed. He wasn't seen again for several days. Blackbeard took advantage of his absence to come by in the afternoons and lay out his deck of cards in front of Paulette. We never found out whatever it was he told her – she wouldn't let anyone come near. 'It's my own business,' she said.

Valentin has returned to his counter. He's unrecognizable. Emaciated, pasty-faced, he stares dull-eyed at his clients. You often have to repeat your order. He's acquired nervous ticks. He scratches between his fingers. Paulette watches this without seeming to be very much affected by it.

Valentin is turning into a monkey. He starts scratching at his armpits, then his groin, then all over. This disgusts the clients, though they're far from fastidious and accustomed to some pretty insalubrious behaviour. It's only curiosity that brings people to see him. At the same time his mind wanders. He's incapable of finishing a sentence. Usually a man of so few words, he launches into bombastic speeches and after a few words, dries up.

His hands and his neck are nothing but open wounds, with

suppurating scabs here and there. We made him go to Hôtel-Dieu. He was sent straight off to St-Louis. No one's able to give a definite diagnosis of the type of leprosy that's eating away at his skin. The agony – it's like being flayed alive – is driving him berserk.

Paulette wasn't opening the bar now until the afternoon, and refused to serve clients she didn't like. Meanwhile, a ceiling in the hotel partly collapsed, and the fire brigade had to prop it up.

We only saw the Dutchman twice. He was solidly built, and looked young despite his grey hair. Pullover, loose garments of dark blue heavy woollen cloth. Sailor's cap. He claimed to be the owner of a barge moored not far from here, and we wondered how, with most of the canals blocked, he'd managed to get inside the city walls.

Whenever he was around, Paulette had eyes only for him. Apparently one day he invited her to visit his barge. Paulette turfed out the few regulars in the bar at the time, locked up and posted the key through the letterbox. They headed off together in the direction of the Seine. None of us has ever set eyes on them again.

So the hotel was left to itself, Paulette's room pillaged, the bar ransacked. At night the tramps, who'd forced their way in through the back door, would come down the corridor and invade the bar, where they slept all piled on top of each other.

There was another, much more serious cave-in. The city authorities got involved: immediate evacuation of the building was ordered. The police had to be called in to evict a whole gaggle of tramps, moaning and shouting, dragging their brats and bundles away with them. The doors and windows were bricked up.

Meanwhile, an architect came, assessed the damage and took samples of the building material. We hear that the walls of the house are infected with a real disease: a kind of 'mushroom' gets inside them, and eats away at them, right to heart. The stones crumble like blown plaster. And what's more, the 'disease' is apparently contagious, and a threat to other buildings.

The whole lot has to be demolished, and very soon.

Every morning the Gypsy passes by, and stops in front of the house, just for a little while.

It was a team of French workers that started the job. From the upper storey they set up a kind of shoot made of planks, and shored up the front walls. They began taking down the roof, or what was left of it. But all this is thirsty work, and every quarter of an hour these lads would go off for a drink, at this bar or that: the Vieux-Palais, Chez Dumont, Chez Bébert. The owners of these different establishments, the regulars too, didn't fail to tell the whole story of the Gypsy, the sick hairless dog, the now leprous and crazed Valentin, Paulette's elopement. A professional demolition worker doesn't much like stories that prey on his mind.

Work had scarcely begun on the second storey when these six fellows – including the foreman – also began to feel peculiar pricklings in their hands, armpits, groins.

They all, simultaneously, found actionable grounds for breaking the contract they had with the public works' contractor. And the site remained abandoned: no one wanted to take a pickaxe to those jinxed walls.

The spring rains turned the staircases into cascades, the ceilings into waterfalls. The house was in danger of collapsing into the street at any moment.

I don't know how the Germans got to hear about it, but it was a team of Poles, conscripted from the mines in the North, and brought on site by truck, with a couple of armed German soldiers on guard, who razed it to ground in two days.

The rubble was removed as it came down.

Today it's all tidied up, the ground properly levelled. The Gypsy comes by every morning at about eleven o'clock, loaded with bags. Deliberately, he settles himself on a crate in the middle of the plot, and sorts out the 'goods' he's collected, to be passed on to the master ragmen: scraps of wool, rags of other textiles, paper, metal, old bones, refuse of all sorts.

At last the smile that Blackbeard has is the one for happy days. He's on conquered soil.

Chapter IV

The Ancients understood the omnipotence
of the underside of things.

Pasteur

Followed step by step, relived hour by hour, the story of the house that no longer exists would not by itself give a total picture of that period. Since my escape I'd been unable to shake off an immense fatigue that from time to time suddenly and at totally unexpected interludes completely knackered me, so overwhelmed me I was afraid of collapsing on the spot.

I consulted Cyril.

'Sleep,' he prescribed. 'No other solution. Whenever you feel the urge, go and lie down, somewhere nice and warm, and take a nap. But mind you don't just fall asleep anywhere when you're in a weak state. If you've found a good spot where you feel relaxed, it's because you're protected there. Try and stick to it. That's very important.'

He's right. At his suggestion, I moved the position and orientation of the bed in my room five or six times. Now that it's at an angle by the window, I feel comfortable in it, quite safe. What Cyril said holds true to within a metre.

Cyril's not the only one who has contributed to completing my education. Several people have taught me that there exists, in the underlying order of things, a potential for humour that corresponds to paradoxical requirements. Laughter is proper to the man? Perhaps. But the incident that provokes us to laughter, the comical incident, belongs to all creation, from the amoeba to the crystal. In short, nothing should be taken too seriously.

On receiving his call-up papers for military service, a fellow by the name of Borjois noticed that his first name was Alfophonse. You read that correctly: efohpeeaitchohen. He started laughing, and showed it to his mates, who cracked up, as well they might, and Alfophonse thereupon embarked on a discreet but necessary investigation. He likes to report his findings in the argot he speaks better than anyone else. For Alfophonse is a purist: he's from Glacière, where traditions are not about to die out.

'You see, when my old lady pupped me, I had three older sisters. "A boy, at last!" says the old man.' (At this point, I'll pass over the physiological details that would lack colourfulness in correct French.) 'Now my uncle, my old lady's bro, I have to tell you, is a pen-pusher in the local council administration. And it's His Nibs that does the entries for the Directory, as you might say. So his brother-in-law goes to see him: "Hey! Gus," he says, "got some news for you! Your sis has pupped a boy! The real thing, complete with nuts and a joy-stick." "Listen, Albert," says uncle, "when the same thing happens up the Prince of Wales's neck of the woods, the king of England has twenty-one shots fired from a single cannon. Well, you and me are going to put away twenty-one shots. Down the hatch! Without a moment's delay!" And off go the two brothers-in-law to knock back twenty-one glasses of red. No messing about! Going back to the office, they're a bit unsteady on their pegs. Then uncle picks up his pen to enter me into the local Directory. "We're not done yet," he says, "we need a name for the little blighter." The old man racks his brains. Draws a blank. Then he says, "Remember grand-dad, Gus? D'you remember? Alphonse, he was called. D'you remember? Well, Alphonse is what we'll call our lad. Like granddad!"

'What it is to be susceptible! Next thing, they're blubber-ing, and uncle's snivelling as he writes: A.l.f.o. "Hey, watch what you're doing!" says the old man, "Peeaitch!" "What do you mean, peeaitch?" "Ehelpeeaitch!" Well, blow me!

Scratching out in the register, can't be done, not for love nor money. 'Gainst the law. No way can my moniker be altered. So that's how I come to be called Alfophonse!'

Alfophonse's name made him famous in the army, and then among his workmates. Eventually convinced that his name must be written on the end of his nose, when he finds himself with someone new, he laughs. As others might apologize. He has a good hearty laugh. Of an epidemically infectious nature. He'll live a long life filled with mirth right up to the very last moment.

The Sorry Tale of Théophile Trigou

That blesséd Théophile! One evening he opened up and confided in me. Now I know everything about him!

Nearly twenty-five years ago the young Théophile, a native of Rennes, fresh out of school, demonstrated both a strong bent for classical literary studies and an irresistible leaning towards a career in the Church. His family had to reconcile themselves to letting him enter the seminary. So it was under these circumstances that he visited Paris for the first time, on the occasion of a pilgrimage to Notre-Dame. He took pleasure in wandering through the poorer districts near the Ile de la Cité, and at once responded to their ambiguous charm. A few months later, he returned to the capital as a theology student, but this time to become resident, close to Rue St-Jacques, not far from the place where another 'scholar' once lived: François de Montcorbier, whom we know as Villon.

He must have had the temperament of a missionary or preacher. For not a week went by that our young man was not seen, soberly dressed, wearing a beret, haunting the vicinity of Place Maubert, the least attractive of whose local inhabitants he knew by name, and was able to get them to share their woes and confide in him the most shameful details of their life. Scavengers of fag ends, pickpockets and tramps no longer held any secrets from the man they not unkindly called 'Father Greenhorn'.

The time came when Théophile didn't disdain to go into the lowest dives and mix even more closely with the down-and-outs. He showed a preference for those vagrants who, beneath a stinking carapace of grimy sweat, gave evidence of some education, acquired in 'the days of wanton youth', and they themselves took a certain pride in his friendship.

Little by little, insidiously, the whole neighbourhood became rooted in him; this area, its stones and its people, decided to keep him there for ever, even if this conspiracy of vague wishfulness, in human beings and things, had to achieve its purpose at the cost of some misfortune. Which is indeed what occurred.

Trigou was ordained and yet didn't leave the capital. The young priest became a teacher of French and Latin in a very well-known religious establishment at Auteuil. Uneventful years passed. Théophile fulfilled his duties as teacher and educator to everyone's satisfaction. Every Sunday during the summer months, he observed the Lord's commandments by taking rest. Often he would go out of Paris, by himself, into the wooded countryside, and there, in the woodland solitude, cheered by birdsong, a modern-day Francis of Assisi, he would devote himself to religious texts and meditation.

One August Sunday, even more stiflingly hot than usual, the young priest went to the forest of Fontainebleau. Feeling rather weary after a long walk, he sat down by a big tree, on a mound that seemed to have been placed there specially. He dropped off to sleep for quite a while. When he woke, his hips felt unusually itchy. He realized he had just enough time to get to the station and catch the train. On the walk back, the itchiness, which had spread to the entire lower part of his body, intensified to an unbearable degree. But with no time to spare and perhaps accustomed, in spirit at least, to otherwise painful mortifications, it was only once inside the carriage that he investigated the cause of his itchiness.

This train was composed of old wooden carriages, of the kind still used on provinicial 'slow trains', with no corridors. The priest was alone in his compartment. He immediately discovered the explanation for the 'providential' and extremely comfortable mound he had unwisely sat on: it was a gigantic anthill. His trousers and underpants were full of insects driven to ferocity by having been displaced from their dwelling. It was high time, the priest decided in between stations, to deal with what had become a matter of urgency: he unbuttoned his cassock, took off his trousers and underpants, and began to shake them all out of the window. At one point along the route, the track curves. A powerful gust of wind tore the clothes from the dismayed priest's hands. And the slow train came to a halt.

Waiting on the platform, heaped with wild flowers, singing sweetly, and accompanied by nuns, were some fifty very innocent young schoolgirls from a very Christian orphanage.

The impending danger causing him to completely lose his head, Théophile just had time to dive under the seat. Some of the innocent band piled into his compartment. And the train was off again!

His trepidation, the dust, the wild flowers being shaken about, were a torture to our poor wretched priest. He couldn't help sneezing into one young girl's calves, and she instantly screamed blue murder. Steeled with pious courage, the chaperon nun dared to bend down. A satanic vision met her eyes: a pair of buttocks blue with shame. She fainted and the young girls pulled the communication cord. The train stopped in open countryside while panic-stricken screams spread from carriage to carriage. Stoker, engine driver and conductor all came running, and had the greatest difficulty in dragging Théophile out from under his seat, more dead than alive. On the rail track, he was subjected to countless taunts, insults and jibes to which he was unable to respond, entirely preoccupied as he was with holding together his (much too short) shirt-tails, as a mischievous evening breeze contrived to set them aflutter.

The satyr, as he'd immediately been dubbed, was handed over to two employees of the Railway Company, who marched him off to the gate-keeper's house at the nearest level crossing (several kilometres away).

From there a phone call was made to the police. Théophile

had some difficulty in establishing his bona fides. He spent the night in a cell, and it was only next morning that his clothes were found scattered along the embankment. At Auteuil he came up with some sheepish excuse, not daring to recount his misadventure, and for the first time ever lied to his superiors.

Within the next few days the local press, alerted by the police report, had got hold of the story. The Seine-et-Marne *Progress*, an anticlerical rag, indulged in sarcastic comments, no less humorous than ironic, while the *Independent*, a self-righteous weekly, deplored both the incident and its rival's lack of charitableness. That was enough for a Parisian columnist, Monsieur de la Fourchardière, to seize his opportunity and give free rein to his mordant wit. All mentioned the name of Théophile Trigou, in itself cause for amusement. And that was how from one day to the next this priest of ours was unceremoniously kicked out of the institution where his livelihood had been assured. Moreover, he was so violently traumatized by his experience, he never got over it.

He doesn't talk about the life he led during those subsequent months; but he was soon back in the Maubert neighbourhood, and also seen round the lycées – Charlemagne, Henri IV and St Louis. He's grown a beard. Dressed in a jacket stiff with dirt, he wears a shirt-front and wing collar, but practically never a shirt. For a couple of glasses of wine or a bit of small change, he wonderfully assists school kids and university students with their Latin versification and translations. He's known as 'the Doctor' or 'the Professor'. He accepts his fate philosophically.

At the same time as what happened at Rue de Bièvre, another house in Paris disappeared. It was in the newspapers. A gentleman from Lille – in the prohibited zone – who owns a building in Paris, on Rue Labrouste, put his property up for sale. It was an old dilapidated town house, long abandoned by its inhabitants.

A vet in the southern zone decided to buy the building, with the intention of setting up a dog clinic there once the war was over. A Paris notary conducted the transaction without stirring from his office. But when some sort of quantity surveyor or valuation expert turned up to visit the premises, there was no building.

It was gone. No sign of it. Vanished into thin air. A waste-land where kids come to play ball and piss in the rubble. An action's been brought for 'disappearance of building'. And the newspapers have relaxed reporting restrictions in order to publish the story in exhaustive detail, along with huge photos with nothing to see in them, featuring a house that's no longer there. Even the cabaret singers have latched on to it and are having a field day. Meanwhile, Bizinque is crowing. He now spends his evenings cutting out and filing the articles that relate his exploit.

It's been common knowledge here for the past four months: Bizinque, and he alone, is the roof-scalper, tap-remover, gas-pipe scavenger responsible. He then methodically attacked the woodwork and structural frame of the building. He's never made any secret of it, and he's treated us to a good few drinks. Architect Vergnolle doesn't think anyone will get on to him about this. So much the better.

The Ill-Fated Knees

Yesterday Bizinque turned up with a pretty strange fellow I vaguely knew: it was Monsieur Casquette.

Monsieur Casquette is an undertaker's assistant. Despite his twenty-four years' good and faithful service, he's not a funeral director. His military medal, his liking for 'a job well done' might have won him faster promotion. But he is doubly handicapped: in his, let us say, average intelligence, and his physical appearance. Short and stocky, Monsieur Casquette has an incredibly big flat head.

In the 1920s he had to get his regulation headgear made to measure. This departure from normal practice entailed count-less waivers and signatures at different levels. In the *Municipal Bulletin* the initials of a senior city bureaucrat, later minister, ratified the administration's authority, delegated by an official vote, to equip our man with a custom-made '*casquette*', or peaked cap. The nickname stuck and even he has been known to forget his real name.

Having always remained an ordinary undertaker's assistant, Monsieur Casquette practises his craft in the 5th arrondissement. He carries out the most loathsome tasks with a natural simplicity. Until recently, he was in the habit of playing cards in the evening, in Rue Monge, with some quiet friends.

But Monsieur Casquette is by nature quick to take offence. On one occasion, one of his fellow card-players cheated by way of a joke. Monsieur Casquette took it very badly: after a rather lively exchange of words, he threw down his hand and walked off, cursing. 'Go on, make fun of me while you can. I shall bury all three of you!'

The next day no one gave it another thought. But the undertaker's three mates, all elderly gents, passed away in record time, and the very distressing task of having to bury them fell to their friend. The regulars at the little café were crass enough to remind him of his words, and to suggest perfidiously that he had the 'evil eye'.

In fact, over the course of last winter, he laid to rest so many people of his acquaintance, those around him are upset. Everyone now avoids any mention in his presence of the sick or the very weak and old. It's even whispered that Monsieur Casquette, who is actually a very decent man, is the unwitting and unwilling instrument of fate, and that he's the vehicle of sinister forces. People are cowardly in the face of the unknown. The undertaker's oldest friends have ended up shunning him: he's surrounded by such an atmosphere of wariness, of fearful silence, that he's becoming neurotic and has started drinking.

The Old Man Who Appears After Midnight

The Irish drew up their own map of Old Paris. The one that Dr Garrett showed me. I'd like to do likewise and compile a very specialized map, of 'streets of legend' – which are not necessarily the oldest. There are in a few small areas of the city places where a sense of eternity pervades everything that happens. The simple folk that populate them are the last people to realize what kind of timelessness they represent. Some of them constitute what can only be described as a sheer phenomenon of survival.

At Pignol's, for instance, there are evenings when we experience what I call the 'magic' hour. This word, for me, is fraught with meaning: I use it rarely. I'm wary of it. But I know why I've written it here.

In general it comes the day after a grim day, on which one of us has received bad news: the death of a distant loved one, or the arrest of a friend. Here, we share our sorrows as if by osmosis. We all suffer intensely, dutifully, as if to relieve the person principally concerned. And we only speak of the unhappy event to try and attenuate, assuage, avert what might arise from it. Our silences are filled with suppressed anger. But every time, something unexpected happens to restore the atmosphere, by shifting, rearranging our way of thinking. Often the conversation, desultory at first, revolves round a mythical figure, a curious character, a semi-phantom everyone claims to have met though I still don't know whether he exists in the same way as you and I, or whether he's part of the suggestive fantasy that envelops 'the Village' and sometimes takes possession of it by unhinging the minds of all its nightbirds, simultaneously. We're talking about the Old Man Who Appears After Midnight.

In this most deceptive and secret corner of the capital, many are the bars where the night life, though far from noisy, is in full swing between midnight and five in the morning, during the hours of curfew. Apart from the gang of bohemians of whom I am in some sense the key player and prime mover, it's mostly the dustbin-rakers and wholesale rag-and-bone men who keep these unsociable hours, all shutters closed, all doors bolted, whistle wet and ears pricked. Then, tradition has it – unfortunately, I've so far been unable to check the foundations of this tradition – that when an argument which cannot be resolved sets at loggerheads people of opposing views, whether it's over military operations, black market transactions, or the buying price of non-ferrous metals, the Old Man turns up, without anyone having seen him enter. Huddled in a dark corner, seated with his tall walking-stick beside him, he chips in and with a few words confounds the cocksure or the wrong-headed.

The Old Man doesn't appear to all and sundry. In any case, no one's ever seen him until after midnight, and only in these parts: at Pignol's, Quatre-Fesses, Trois-Mailletz, Dumont's. He takes a mischievous pleasure in making his entrance or exit when people's attention is focused elsewhere. He reveals his presence with a little laugh, a kind of chuckle, or else he says something – a simple truth – that's spot on, and comes just at the right moment, leaving nothing more to be said. Often when there's a quarrel to settle, questions are put to him, but he only answers when both parties are present. And his word is regarded as final. 'God's Honest Truth,' say the old women – Salagnac, Georgette, Thérèse . . .

The old fellow's a good man. It was he who patched things up between Edouard and Bébert, the two junk dealers who fell out over some story about fencing stolen goods of which neither one of them was guilty. It was he who reconciled the Graillot couple, despite the slanderous lies that had been told about Graillot's wife. He saw to it that at the critical moment little Bibiche was kept away because of mumps, and diagnosed Solange's daughter Zouzou's scarlet fever.

I get to hear all this from Pignolette, who appears to have a strange reverence for the Old Man. Her voice changes when she talks about him. It seems to quiver slightly. I don't know what to reply or what to think. I'm living in an unreal world.

The Ill-Fated Knees

Fourteen metres and a hundred and thirty kilos. These are the records held at the Café Guignard, on the corner of Rue Dante, by the bar counter and the *patron* respectively. This colossus has the huge beaky-nosed head of some strange creature. It's impossible not to think of the grotesques on the Pont-Neuf. His bushy brown eyebrows especially lend his face a strength that's both solid and nervy, though somewhat belied by his flabby cheeks.

I'm not particularly fond of squalor, and I don't believe it was the stale smell of sweat, warm sour drinks, and fetid urine that drew me there that sweltering afternoon. Monsieur Casquette was having a quiet tipple. I offered to buy him a drink. He seemed pleased to see me. Perhaps relieved. Everyone was gathered in one part of the room, over on the right. A collective hysteria, a vile brutish laughter had taken possession of this human scum, their shoulders and behinds all heaving in unison. Emanating from this convulsive coagulation of bodies could be heard in snatches the sound of an argument: two shrill voices trading abuse in the most lurid language that it would be pointless and inappropriate to record here.

I overcame my sickened indifference and went over, followed by Monsieur Casquette, to view 'the spectacle'. It was well worth it.

A fair-haired man stood slightly bent forwards with his hands resting on the backs of two chairs. His trousers were rolled up above his knees. The said knees were tattooed. Two faces, two caricatures deliberately made to look alike. On the right, a grim-featured moustached man with dark eyebrows. On the left, a rosy-cheeked woman, with very long eyelashes, heavily made-up eyes, and full lips. The man clenched his muscles, played his tendons; his knee-caps danced, and all his contractions imparted strange life to the two warring faces. For the knees spoke to each other in tortured French, interpersed with Mediterrean pidgin and unidentifiable words, vile expressions: the man adopted different voices, and the scene was of such black comedy that it made me feel a kind of anguish. Monsieur Casquette watched without turning a hair. Admittedly, he's seen a lot worse.

Tiring, the man stopped for a breather, while the baying crowd took the opportunity to relax for a moment. The man downed in quick succession four glasses of alcohol, to which he was generously treated by his audience. He was getting ready to resume his performance; but then the couple came in. About fifty years old, penurious, weary and scruffy. Yet not actually tramps. He was laden with a bundle, one of those rolled-up pieces of black cloth of the kind that painters or some day-labourers carry. The woman was dragging a suit-case. Their features were marked with dejection, as well as immense lassitude.

Meeting the gaze of the man with the knees, they froze. Petrified. For a second, there was total silence. The most befuddled, the most obtuse of the tramps present must have felt a shock. The laughter of the half-drunken women changed in tone and colour. No one dared breathe. Three pairs of eyes confronted each other. They came from another universe, where hatred, hatred alone, serves as the source of energy.

It was the man with the knees who made the first move: he readjusted his clothing, headed for the door, and was caught in sunshine. The couple, very slowly, went up to the counter. They ordered rum and exchanged a few fleeting words in a language I didn't understand.

'Let's go,' said Monsieur Casquette, 'there's a sense of doom here.'

That evening we were at the Quatre-Fesses. A joint so called [Quatre-Fesses meaning Four-Buttocks] because run by two women past their prime, who, disappointed at having found only incomplete satisfaction with their very many male part-ners, now have 'an arrangement' between themselves. To which we have no objection of course.

I'd brought along Monsieur Casquette, to take his mind off things, and asked Cyril to join us. I just couldn't get over that scene with the man and the tattooed knees, and above all the couple that came in. It was really bothering me. I wanted some explanation. I told Cyril the whole story. He showed little surprise. After I described what I'd recently witnessed, Cyril nodded his head and murmured, 'Poor wretch. I think it would have been better if you'd been somewhere else, Monsieur Casquette.'

The undertaker's assistant bristled. 'But what happened's

got nothing to do with me. Besides, there was no harm done.'

Cyril pondered, and weighing his words said, 'Nothing to do with you. Of course, you're utterly convinced it has nothing to do with you. And as for what will happen next, obviously you know nothing about it, it's a complete mystery to you, and there's absolutely nothing you can do about it, is that not so, Monsieur Casquette?'

The undertaker's eyes widened, as if he'd been addressed in Hebrew.

Quietly I asked Cyril, 'Who's the poor wretch you were feeling sorry for just now?'

'Why, Vladimir, of course. You know, the . . .' He pointed to his knees.

'You know him?'

'I'll say! Only too well!'

In 1919, the young Ukrainian lieutenant Vladimir Illine, who had fought in the Balkans alongside the Allied troops, found himself in Marseilles penniless and unemployed. He had gone AWOL from his unit, which was stationed in Corfu and about to be repatriated. Vladimir's legal position was as delicate as that of his finances. On the other hand, the prospect of returning to a country too flat and too monotonous for his liking — solely topographically speaking — was of limited appeal to a spirit hungry for adventure, not averse to a touch of the exotic, and decidedly attached to the people of Western Europe. Trying to make his way to Paris on an empty stomach and, in order to avoid being expelled across some as yet ill-defined border, ending up with the job of digging out bodies from the Argonne trenches or working as slave labour in the war-devastated regions was of not much greater appeal. He had no choice. So it was that he went to the Fort St-Jean and soon found himself under the protection of the red-and-green flag of the 2nd Battalion of the Nth Infantry Regiment of the Foreign Legion, where Cyril, who then went by the name of Petrovich, was quartermaster sergeant.

Vladimir signed up for five years. He adapted without too

much difficulty to the extremely strict discipline of his new unit. And when the regiment sailed for Africa, Vladimir had forged some firm friendships. Moreover, being highly thought of by his direct superiors brought many benefits, in particular greater freedom in his comings and goings, the truth being that the judiciously conceded right to roam some three hundred metres is often a good deal more precious than the right to go round the world with a leash round your neck.

At Sidi-bel-Abbès, Vladimir sealed a pact of 'blood brotherhood' with one of his companions. A very young Bulgarian he'd already singled out in Marseilles and whom he particularly liked, not because of his 'derring-do' but because he was a guy you could count on, his word and all. Actually 'the Bul' had quite a funny story. As an irregular fighting with the Serbian komitajis, he fell into the hands of the 175th French Infantry (at this point in Cyril's story, my ears prick up), at Monastir, that's right, Monastir. And had it not been for the fact he was little more than a child . . .

At this point I burst in. 'They'd have killed him, for sure. But listen, Cyril, I'm going to tell you what happened next. The 175th adopted him. They treated him like a mascot. The kid became a batman for a while.'

'Yeah,' says Cyril, a little subdued, looking far more dismayed than amazed.

'Well, that officer he was batman to was my uncle! And the guy you're talking about ended the war as a cook's assistant.'

'Yes, yes, that's right.'

'Now, listen to this, that cook was my father. I've been hearing this story, at home, since 1920 or '21. Your Bulgarian returned to France with the Dardanelles expeditionary battalion. In Marseilles he joined up. His name's come back to me now. Boris . . . Boris Kazalik.'

'Absolutely right, of course,' said Cyril, almost at a loss for words. 'But how come you're so well informed?'

'It's no big deal. My father and my uncle were together out East. It's only natural I should know the story. I think it's quite amusing. No cause for concern.'

'Ah, but there is cause for concern,' said someone.

And that made everyone jump. It was the Old Man.

It was just gone midnight. Olga, the effective boss, had locked the shutters from the outside. Now she was pulling down blinds to seal the windows from the inside. She to whom buttocks three and four belonged was at the till, checking the day's takings.

The Old Man. We hadn't noticed or sensed his presence. He was stroking his beard in his shadowy corner, pleased with the bit of a stir he'd caused. What struck me most was that once the first moment's excitement had passed, no one seemed particularly surprised.

Many times had I been given a description of his appearance: very small, heavily bearded, long-haired, with a brown hooded cloak and long stick, very beautiful large hands, short misshapen legs trussed up in laces from his ankles to his knees, a quavering voice and a demeanour at once kindly and roguish. To tell the truth, I didn't believe in his existence. I don't know whether, right then, I was disappointed or delighted. Perhaps both. Perhaps it would have suited me better to concede that a well-established, widely-accepted – and admittedly quaint – legend had gained substance in people's minds. And to identify a key symptom in these people: that of the *non-acquired* memory of an occurrence that may or may not belong to the realms of fantasy – there's no way of knowing. For the very first time I had the privilege of experiencing an extraordinary event that was extraneous to me, and the much awaited, much desired thrill, shock, awe didn't ensue. My independent organs, those whose reflexes I couldn't control, that ruled me, that masterminded my sheer terror under dive-bombing Stukas, just accepted it. The old Eyes, Ears, Nerves, Balls were as laid-back and unfazed as any of my mates who were also present: Edouard, Bucaille, old Monsieur Casquette, and even Cyril. Everyone regarded it as completely normal. The Old Man Who Appears After Midnight, and everything uncanny he represents, is just not hooey. Let's face it. And yet . . . There was no way he could have come in: either through the door from the corridor, or the cellar door, because they were right under our eyes more or less the whole time. Or from the street, as Olga had locked up at eleven o'clock. There's no basement window. Could he have been hiding in a corner before we arrived? What an absurd idea! Totally daft. Anyway, that's the score.

The Old Man didn't speak straight away. He quietly let Cyril finish telling the story of the knees.

At Bel-Abbès and elsewhere, legionnaires Boris and Vladimir offered their comrades the most heartening example of pure, practical and devoted friendship. One of them had only to reveal a desire for something and it became the other's immediate and imperative duty to obtain it. The hard school of life in the desert: road-building in the burning heat beneath the frenzied lash of sands whipped up by an apocalyptic wind, an ordeal from which the body only recovers in order to overcome the freezing-cold nights; the manifold elements they'd chosen to brave, with no illusions as to their treacherous hostility, fully aware of what they were letting themselves in for – our two lads successfully surmounted all this, month by month growing stronger, winning ever greater victory over themselves. And becoming ever more close. The exceptionally strong friendship between them being of the kind 'granted' rather than sought.

Cyril knew everything. He was the only possible confidant for the two blood brothers, because he wasn't jealous and was incapable of harbouring any suspicions of so-called 'irregularities', for the sole reason that nothing irregular was going on other than what has just been related.

The batallion was redeployed. It's a dreadful assertion to make that once the war is over, the lesson learned, the conclusion drawn lies anywhere but in the verdict 'slaughter'. The dead are very quickly forgotten. But it's extraordinary – and a good thing too – how we're bested by them in this respect.

What counts, are migrations. The batallion was redeployed. The words 'thousands' or 'millions' of dead, and the word 'defeat' and the word 'victory' have long since become meaningless, and count for nothing one way or another. The batallion was redeployed. War is an unbelievable upheaval, a monster far beyond the grotesque or the contrary, much more coherent, aesthetic, logical, necessary than some of the appendages stuck on our fountains, a monster that swallows its own slaver, throwing up scum cast far and wide. It was with the scum that the batallion was to get embroiled.

From south of Oran to south of Algiers, the Ksour mountains, Djebel Amour and the Ouled Nail mountains were at that time being explored by motley crews that pompously called themselves 'expeditions', even 'scientific missions'.

Acting on behalf of certain captains of industry dismayed by the general armistice in Europe, which had come too swiftly for their liking, groups of so-called technicians, in reality pure adventurers, scoured what they believed to be still virgin territory, in search of some trace of mineral deposits (coal, metal or whatever), or any kind of commercial opportunity suitable for profitably investing – and above all concealing – immense capital assets now lying idle and very soon to be frozen before their eventual seizure.

This duly occurred, to the advantage of other captains of industry . . . (which takes us back to beginning of the preceding paragraph).

The leading lights of African, European and Levantine speculation drove round in motor cars, developing plans as grandiose as they were vague, and trying to live the high life wherever possible. Hundreds of small nomadic businesses, an entire corporation, mushroomed around these conquistadores of sand and road metal. Not the least significant of all these modest but lucrative activities was the sale of cold drinks of a more or less alcoholic nature, tobacco, and hashish, not to mention particular favours granted to the most generous of these gentlemen. This is what Consuelo Quaglia realized.

Born at the turn of the century in Navarre, she came across the border at Hendaye in 1917 and so eloquent were her youthful charms that she continued her advance unchecked until she won her first brilliant and decisive campaign at Bordeaux, within the purlieus of Place Mériadeck. A few run-ins with the vice squad, her unshakeable determination to decline the 'services' of her successive 'protectors', or would-be candidates for that role, forced her to discover another vocation, that of inveterate traveller. Her beauty, extreme avarice, total scorn for everything but her own musky brown-skinned self worked wonders. She'd only just come of age when she fetched up at Aïn-Sefra, alone, with the intention of settling there, equipped with a residence permit, trading licence, liquor licence and a considerable sum of pesetas, francs and dollars in her pocket. When the batallion was billeted close to the town, Consuelo's bar had already become the favourite rendezvous for the entire European population of any means.

Meanwhile, Vladimir and Boris had won their NCO stripes. Cyril had become a sergeant-major. One night all three of them ended up at Consuelo's. There was some brawl – Cyril can't remember why, if indeed he ever knew – between civilians and soldiers; then after the civilians had been evicted, between Algerian soldiers and the legionnaires. The latter carried the day, and Consuelo noticed Cyril's face, Vladimir's shoulders and the elegance of the young Bulgarian. Cyril tells me what happened:

'That bitch. I was the first of the three of us to screw her. I'd have been better off if she'd kept me begging for it. Fabulous body though. But it was as if her head was separated from her crotch by miles, or centuries, or miles of centuries. When you'd spilled your seed, she had a way of pushing you back by the shoulders and looking at you, so blankly and contemptuously at the same time, that all you could do was to pack up your tackle and go and get yourself completely plastered, to provide some acceptable reason for your self-disgust. That was the end of it for me. But Vladimir got hooked. Where I saw the deepest, most utter and foul cynicism, he discerned decency, so he said. I was from Kiev, and he from Kharkov, but he was the more Russian by far! Befuddled, beguiled, bewitched! That made the girl happy. Maybe not so much that he screwed her: or perhaps she held it against him that he made her body react in ways she'd decided not to allow herself any more. It meant she wasn't in control. It was out of revenge that she enslaved him, to the point where she'd only have to lift her little finger and he'd do the most bloody stupid

68

things. Inviting his own death or damnation. Occasionally she'd sleep with young Boris, but less seriously, just to upset the other one. It left Vladimir tormented, devoured with jealousy.

'So one day, mortified with shame, he made up his mind to speak to his mate. He unburdened himself. His Bulgarian pal was flabbergasted. A guy like Vladimir, so crazy for such a whore! But he did what was asked of him: he swore he'd leave her alone. For all he cared . . .

'But then Vladimir started making plans. Civvie Street beckoned: only thirteen months to go. And at the end of it, a French identity card, and his final pay-off, a small fortune. By lucky coincidence, Consuelo was fed up with Africa. She'd wait for him. They'd head off together, each with their own nest-egg, to the South of France, or the Balearic Islands. There they'd build themselves a house with a little hotel. And they'd take life easy. OK, she said. He could already visualize it: and one night he didn't show up for retreat, carried on dozing in his girl's arms.

'That night they woke us at five o'clock, and in no time at all we were on the road, force marching to El Goléa. Vladimir didn't catch up with us until a week later. War-time rules still applied. At least for us. There was no such thing as absence without leave, only desertion. Vladimir was reduced to the ranks. He was court-martialled in Bel-Abbès: six months' jail, six months' extra service. And the long-awaited day of general discharge, he couldn't even shake hands with his 'blood brother', Boris, who was on his way to Oran. But evidently the other guy was hooked. He arranges to extend his stay in Africa. He makes a trip to Aïn-Sefra where the girl's quietly languishing, he gets her to sell up and the two of them sail to Marseilles. They had the nerve to send a postcard to Vladimir, to wish him luck. They shouldn't have done that. Vladimir went ballistic. Even more because of his friend's betrayal than for having lost the girl.

'Now there was no stopping him: bad behaviour, unauthorized absences, brawls at every opportunity. He copped a couple more months in jail, which he served in Algiers.

While he was inside, he had his knees tattooed with portraits of Boris and the girl, by a guy who had known them. He said, "As long as my knees are together, the two of them won't part. But as long as my knees keep giving each other hell, I don't see their life being a happy one." Ever since then he's been entertaining friends with his little party trick. He's become more normal: he even tried to re-enlist, but given his bad record and his health – apparently he contracted TB – he was rejected. I'm the one that helped him out when he first showed up here. He works as a packer for one of the junk dealers.'

Monsieur Casquette had been listening to all this, and now he seemed to understand. He turned to the Old Man, who was gazing at him with all his roguishness.

'Knowing you, you'll be burying at least one or two of the three,' he said out of the corner of his mouth.

This didn't please Monsieur Casquette. 'Now, don't say things like that.'

I took a shot in the dark.

'Of the three? You mean that couple – they were the other two?'

The Old Man shrugged his shoulders.

'What do you think? Of course they were! All we can do now is to wait and see. You can congratulate yourself on having done a good job there. Still, it's not your fault.'

Edouard and Bucaille are the best of friends, but you wouldn't know it, because they spend the whole time bickering. They're both wholesale rag dealers, and they're perpetually at logger-heads over the price of the merchandise. Seeing the Old Man was there, and rightly or wrongly he has the reputation of knowing everything, they tried to enlist him to settle the dispute between them. The Old Man was dismissive.

'Not tonight. Your rags, paper, scrap metal – this is no time to be talking about such things.'

Olga had made some very strong coffee, real black market coffee. We were savouring it, making the most of it, thanking her. Her partner had come to drink at our table. Passing behind her, Olga fondly held her by the shoulders and tried discreetly to kiss the back of her neck, as a man might have done. But Edouard noticed what she was up to.

'Hey, there, lezzies! Don't mind us!'

'We're not bothered,' said Cyril, laughing.

And the Old Man began to chortle. 'There are some scales in which all this weighs very little.'

We were momentarily distracted by a noise outside, where normally there wouldn't have been anyone about yet. It took us a few minutes to realize that the Old Man had disappeared, vanished into thin air, leaving behind his empty cup.

Fernand has a law degree and is currently a police inspector, which is no sinecure for people like him. For he's there, he says – and he proves it – 'for the right reason': to get his man; and he's resigned to being cordially detested by those for whom, without their realizing it, he does the most incredible favours. I know from experience. We're friends. This morning Fernand came looking for me. 'You'll be interested in this. Come and see. It's just round the corner. And if you don't have any, borrow some eau-de-Cologne from your next-door neighbour. Bring at least two handkerchiefs.'

Number 6, Impasse Maubert is familiar territory to me, having recently investigated its history. It was there that three hundred years ago the Marquis de Ste-Croix, the lover of Brinvilliers, set up his laboratory, and it was there that he was found dead among his retorts, in circumstances still disputed by historians.

The stench is overpowering. In his room on the top floor, lying on his bed fully dressed, Vladimir looks hideous. His throat is slit from ear to ear. His whole body is convulsed. His hands clutch the mattress. His knees are drawn up to his chin.

'So?'

'So, nothing. I'm just the local cop. I'm only entitled to make the initial report. The murderer wasn't looking for anything, didn't take anything. This was under the pillow.'

He shows me a bundle of banknotes. He says, 'I'm waiting for the guys from the Crime Squad. The stink in here is really overpowering. Go and treat yourself to a glass of rum down at Pagès. I'll be with you in a minute. I want to ask you a question, for my own information.'

At Pagès, all he asked me was if I thought Vladimir's murder had anything to do with the Germans' being here. I said no, I didn't think so.

'If you want me to forget you're a cop, after all, then don't grill me, even if it's just for your own information.'

He didn't persist.

Vladimir had been dead for several days, and it was because of the smell that the neighbours had broken open the door. The building, which was already squalid, was in danger of becoming uninhabitable. By late afternoon Monsieur Casquette was there, together with two assistants, to do the necessary. No question of taking the body out in a coffin. Impossible to lie him flat in order to get him inside the pine box. He remained curled up. The undertakers pulled and tugged, one holding him by the feet, the other by his armpits. They'd made a kind of cowl for themselves, with cloths soaked in a special solution.

Then Monsieur Casquette took a decision. He grabbed a hammer intended for this purpose, and shattered the body's elbows and knees – the knees! – and then wrapped the corpse, now like a disjointed puppet, in a shroud. So narrow was the staircase, they'd already had difficulty getting the coffin up there. It was the firemen that lent them ropes. They lowered the coffin out of the window, with two hundred onlookers who'd gathered to watch, delighted by this unannounced attraction.

'That sure is a rotten job you've got, Monsieur Casquette.'

'Someone's got to do it. After being at it for nearly twenty years, you don't give too much thought to what you're doing any more.'

'By the way, when you smashed his knees, did you give any thought to the tattoos under the cloth of his trousers that you were blithely destroying?'

'Hmm! No. It's only just now that you remind me of that detail.'

12 September

I ran into Fernand.

'Any news about the stiff at Impasse Maubert?'

'Yes. The Crime Squad didn't take long to identify the assassin: a Bulgarian, a former legionnaire with whom your rag-picker had some falling-out in the past. But he was never brought to trial.'

'Oh?'

'The guy and his wife reckoned they'd soon be picked up in Paris. They went trekking round the outskirts. They were drinkers. One night, over towards the St-Denis plain, they bunked down at the foot of a disused lime kiln that was in the process of being demolished. No one could have suspected they were lying there. In the early morning, they were both hit, more or less simultaneously, by huge blocks of rubble that smashed their faces and crushed their skulls. They were taken to Lariboisière; but they must have snuffed it instantly.'

I related this to Monsieur Casquette. He asked me to help him compose a letter. He wanted to quit his job with the undertakers for health reasons.

Chapter V

Tell me who you haunt, and I'll
tell you who you hate.

April 1943

It had become inevitable.

Here am I, the sceptical, disillusioned, cynical recusant, 'the anarchist' my mates say, not without some justification, placed under orders, of my own free will. A signed-up member of a – military, if you please – resistance unit. This certainly isn't the result of a fit of delayed patriotism. I've good reason not to care two hoots about the fate and progress of the regular army, their backside still sore from the terrific kick in the pants they were given, busily congratulating each other and, in the Vichy zone, pinning medals of the now defunct Third Republic on each other's chests.

But I just couldn't refuse to get involved in hiding this poor parachutist who couldn't speak a word of French and was outraged at not being able to find any American-tobacco cigarettes here. Then one thing led to another . . .

My 'job' consists of directing bombings on to German targets in the Paris region. In other words, to make sure there are as few civilian casualties as possible. That's all! Whatever happens, my conscience will be clear. What more can one ask?

The missions I carry out leave me with a lot of free time; moreover, I needed some sort of 'cover'. Every morning I'm a teacher of French and drawing for the Vocational Education Authority.

Nevertheless, I haven't abandoned my beloved bohemians. But things were beginning to get a bit difficult at Pignol's. We've migrated to a less perilous haven: the Trois-Mailletz, near St-Julien-le-Pauvre. On the corner of Rue Galande.

The 'Oberge des Mailletz' is by far the oldest tavern of which any record can found in the City archives. In 1292, Adam des Mailletz, inn-keeper, paid a tithe of 18 sous and 6 deniers. This we learn from the Tax Register of the period. At the time it was founded, the Trois-Mailletz was the meeting place of masons, who under the supervision of Jehan de Chelles, carved out of white stone the biblical characters destined to grace the north and south choirs of Notre-Dame. Underneath the building, there are two floors of super-imposed cellars: the deeper ones date from the Gallo-Roman period. What remains of the instruments of torture found in the cellars of the Petit-Châtelet have been housed here, along with some other restored objects.

A modest bar counter, a long-haired *patron* who bizarrely manages never to be freshly shaven or downright bearded. A stove in the middle of the shabby room; simple straight-forward folk, less drunk than at Rue de Bièvre, and less dirty. Just what we needed.

Mina the Cat

When she appeared, with that bundle in her arms, we had no more reason than anyone else to be there, Théophile, Séverin and I. A grey fur hat pulled down to her eyes gave her an Asiatic look.

A tatty coat, also grey, with collar and cuffs to match the hat, completed her outfit.

A face of indeterminate age. No chin. On careful consider-ation, a feline cast of countenance. It was only when she was there, with us, that we had the peculiar sensation that we'd actually been expecting her. We noticed her bundle was alive, wrapped in bits of cloth. She just stood there, by the door. The *patron* – Grospierre by name, a decent fellow – observed her patiently, from behind his thick glasses.

Finally, she said shyly, in a shrill and uncertain voice like a squeaking violin, 'You wouldn't have a drop of milk, by any chance?'

'My dear woman, of course not!' said Grospierre. (Milk, these days! Just imagine!)

She gave a sigh. Aaah! And lifted her bundle as though to raise it to her lips. There were in those gestures, the look in her eyes, and that sigh such discouragement, such disappointment and despair that we all felt moved and almost ashamed.

Grospierre gave a grimace of exasperation. 'Wait a moment!'

He came back with a cup, and said, 'Cold? Hot?'

'It's fine just the way it is.'

The woman's eyes shone with contentment, but she'd long lost the ability to smile. She sat down, pulled back a corner of the cloth covering the bundle and revealed the head of a shivering kitten. Grospierre, like the rest of us, was expecting to see the face of a baby. Not at all put out, he just stood there and watched her.

With infinite care, she offered the cup to the animal, which greedily lapped it up. When it was finished the woman said, 'Ah! Thank you!' She hesitated, then added, 'Can I stay here in the warmth for a while?'

The first soft drink, Théophile bought for her. She remained sitting there for a long time in silence. She gazed round fearfully, looking everywhere, especially into dark corners. She left only when she felt completely reassured.

She returned the next day, then the following days. She always carried a cat in her arms, but never the same one. Sometimes she was also laden with a heavy shopping bag full of things she didn't show anyone.

We learned that her name was Mina, that she begged, or worked if the opportunity arose, that she took in stray cats and shared her home with them, in a wooden shed at Gentilly from which she was soon to be evicted.

She was terribly upset about this, primarily because of the animals she cared for and fed, to which she devoted her time and her life.

I don't know which one of us was the first to nickname her 'Mina the Cat'. But it was impossible, yes, impossible, to think of her in any other way.

At the Trois-Mailletz, the regulars ended up adopting Mina

as the symbol of the profound indifference of everyday-life to what most preoccupied the rest of the world. People spoke in veiled terms of the difficulties of the German advance in Russia, of what was going on in Greece, in North Africa and here of course. They harped on about repressive measures likely to be introduced, on rationing to be feared, on the validation of the next fortnight's bread vouchers.

And then Mina would come in, cradling a 'nursling': and no one was worried about anything else any more but the cat's health, the circumstances in which it had been found. And every day all of us would keep aside some scraps of food.

One day we were awaiting Mina with a kind of gleeful impatience. Séverin had found an attic to live in, at Dumont's place, on Rue Maître-Albert, where, if she introduced them discreetly, one by one, she could accommodate her lodgers.

With a few soap boxes, a bit of sawdust, and some bleach – which could be gathered together easily enough – all the requirements of relative hygiene and temporary refuge could be met. Two skylights opened on to the roof, to which the animals would have easy access, and where they could caterwaul at the moon to their heart's content.

In the event of any objection from Dumont, who sheltered – and hid – a good many men on the run, we undertook to square things with him.

The main thing was that Mina should move in.

At last she turned up. She sat down as usual. We broke the good news to her. But she seemed not to give it as much attention as we were entitled to expect.

This time more than ever before, her charge of the day alone claimed her care and solicitude. It was a dreadful little mog, a mangy one-eyed ginger tom. And vicious, stupidly vicious, because it scratched its benefactress when she tried to get it to drink. We advised her to leave to its own fate this ugly and ungrateful beast – dangerous too, for it looked diseased, and was likely to infect its fellow felines. Advice, exhortations were of no use. Mina stubbornly replied that she would devote herself to this animal more than any other, firstly because it spurned her, and also because it was sick and disfigured, and therefore the most unfortunate.

There was nothing left to say.

The next day Mina moved to Rue Maître-Albert. We helped her transport her personal belongings, her cats, and a few carefully wrapped cardboard boxes – what they contained we made no attempt to find out.

Bizinque gave us a hand and lent his trolley.

That same evening, worn out, having taken care of her animals, Mina was able to lie down on a bed made of bundles of newspapers covered with a 'mattress'. The mattress was an oilcloth folded in two, sewn up into a bag stuffed with sawdust.

We really thought we'd done a great deal to put Mina's mind at rest by finding that place for her. Alas! It was from that day her troubles began.

And once again, we weren't to blame.

That ghastly little ginger creature was the cause of it all. Mina persisted in coddling and cherishing the beast, which was undoubtedly afflicted with some dangerous disease we weren't able to identify. Peevish and insinuating, its voice was an amazing, disturbing, raucous snarl.

Mina decided to consult the black vet (the one who'd tried to save the dog at Rue de Bièvre).

Again, Doctor N was circumspect. This is what he said: 'There's more to that cat than meets the eye.' Nevertheless, he cured it. With a shinier coat and a more robust appearance, apparently totally recovered, the beast didn't seem any more grateful to Mina for her patient devotion. Once it was back on its feet again (or rather, its paws) – only its missing eye couldn't be replaced – it escaped through the skylight and disappeared over the rooftops without so much as a goodbye.

For four days Mina was inconsolable. And then . . .

And then there was a new development. Just like every other evening, Mina was spending a few minutes at the bar in Dumont's on her way home to rejoin her menagerie. A cement-worker came in.

A cement-worker: at least, that's what he said. He was looking for somewhere to stay in the neighbourhood. He had ginger hair and only one eye.

Ginger and one-eyed.

His name was Goupil.

Goupil – the old word for a fox. Just as 'Bièvre' is the old word for a beaver.

It would take pages of digression to try and pin down, to define the nature of the immediate rapport that was established between Mina and the ginger-haired man.

Anyhow, that same evening, among the cats and bundles Goupil shared Mina's supper and her wretched pallet. It was simply inconceivable to us that a person like Mina, so different from any normal human being that we regarded her almost as an asexual creature, might be capable of any romantic attachment, even a platonic one.

But there was the evidence, clear and indisputable, and the astonishment it generated in us diverted our curiosity and partly destroyed the interest we took in world events.

From the very earliest days of their relationship Goupil proved violent and hard to please. He seemed to regard Mina much more as his prey than his slave. He worked irregularly, as an unskilled labourer: he said he didn't really care whether he was employed by a company that might have been requisitioned by the occupying forces. As for Mina, she footed most of the expenses of this unlikely household. Nearly every day, laden as usual with more or less voluminous packages, she would head for the banks of the Seine, and indefatigably make her way to where the line of booksellers' stalls ended. Often she would haggle with these people, most of whom were some sort of second-hand dealers. We quickly learned what she was up to: she was 'bargain-hunting'. That's to say, she would seek out certain objects, to buy and then of course sell. All of which had something in common: they were representations solely of cats. In the shape of little figurines, pots, knife handles, unidentifiable tools. There were cats in bronze, porcelain, alabaster, wood, everything you could wish for. We found out a little later that she in turn would pass on these finds, of some curiosity or else of little value, to a wealthy collector. This was a person who, before the war, used to attend the theosophists' meetings at the Salle Adyar. The art dealers on Rue de Jacob know him well. They call him 'the Cat Man'. But the guy doesn't like people talking about him.

This small trade seemed to bear fruit: Mina lived more comfortably, no longer begged, was no longer short of money. She could afford to feed her animals – who'd colonized the roof, now cleared of pigeons – and above all, look after 'her man'. This went on for the few weeks that Goupil had a bit of pocket money, gleaned here and there by grudgingly working for it. But as soon as he ran out of funds Goupil had no qualms about snaffling Mina's savings. He went and squandered these paltry assets in the local bistrots, having made his woman sell every last object she possessed.

Mina could only counter his appalling behaviour with dispiriting resignation. In vain we tried to persuade her to part company with this dreadful fellow. She would shake her head sadly, gaze at us in a peculiar way and say in a dull voice, 'So, you still don't get it?' These words pained us.

Then we couldn't help remembering the cat that had disappeared, the one-eyed ginger, like Goupil. The disquieting mystery surrounding this affair and governing this coincidence inhibited our desire to discuss it with each other. Trigou avoided Goupil like the plague: he wouldn't pass in front of his house, or follow in his wake. He couldn't bear hearing about him. Any evidence of the man's existence inspired him with a morbid horror.

Séverin watched Goupil from afar, made inquiries about what he was up to, solely in the interests of finding out to what extent Mina was going to be persecuted or not.

As for myself, I made a determined effort to overcome my aversion and approach him, sound him out, gain his confidence. I'd already rubbed shoulders with so many monsters. Waste of effort. Waste of time. Waste of money, because in the world of La Maube where everything turns to liquid, the only possible approach consisted of buying him endless drinks. He would down them without demur, other than to make some offensive remark about me once my back was turned. My folly and persistence were beyond his comprehension. Nothing was to be got out of him. The weather? He didn't care. The war, the Germans? 'They're not going to get me for compulsory labour.' That's all he was worried about. To other questions, he would reply with grunts, grimaces, sometimes an evil smile.

Round about Christmas, we had a bad spell. For various reasons, Séverin and Théophile were on the wrong side of the law.

I didn't yet have a steady job, and instead of the payment I was expecting in the form of bank notes, the London end of my network had sent me a cheque negotiable in Algiers!

So far, we'd helped Mina as much as was humanly possible: and yet we knew that Goupil was the first to benefit from what we so willingly denied ourselves.

The latest from London was the extraordinarily rapid delivery of one thousand (yes, one thousand) blank ration cards, admirably copied from the sample I'd sent. But whereas the paper used here is rubbish, the documents they parachuted in are printed on wonderful glossy Bristol board. No comment.

Unable to drink his fill any more, idle and brazen-faced, Goupil turned violent. He would beat up Mina whenever she came home with no money, or very little. And to our distress, there was nothing we could do about it. The period of physical abuse – which Mina endured without protest – was followed by one of calculated cruelty. One evening, not only deprived of his fill of sour red wine, Goupil felt ravenously hungry. Dumont had read him the riot act and threatened to throw him out if he continued to give Mina a hard time. Goupil kept his mouth shut. Without a word, he went upstairs, grabbed one of the cats – the sweetest, most trusting – put it an old bag that he weighted with a heavy stone. And then went and threw it in the Seine.

On learning this dreadful news, Mina displayed such distress, such despairing anger that Goupil flew into a terrible fit of insane fury. Mina had to be dragged out of the brute's clutches and sent into hiding, over in the Glacière district, with a rascally but charitable scrap merchant.

Goupil then began to terrorize everybody. No one dreamt of calling the police. We just put up with the maniac, everyone hoping the inescapable end of the tragedy would come swiftly.

This went on for two weeks. Goupil would return at dusk, fed up with looking for Mina, and drown a cat, sometimes two. He ate the last of them and sold their pelts.

One lunchtime, when Mina unwisely visited Les Halles and was searching through the heaps of rubbish, Goupil ran into her. He beat her up and dragged her back home half unconscious. He locked her in with the aid of a padlock and went prowling up and down the street for hours, without ever letting the entrance to the building out of his sight.

He returned home very late.

A little after the curfew started, the noise of a terrible argument woke the neighbourhood. A ruthless battle had begun between Goupil and Mina. Fearfully, people gazed up at the roof from their windows.

The disturbance ended with a long drawn-out howl.

Old Tacoine, who lives opposite, said he caught sight of a yellow creature – he couldn't swear to its being a big cat – escaping through the skylights.

In the morning, Dumont, accompanied by Séverin and myself, broke open the door. Amid the incredible clutter of smashed boxes, tattered rags, rubbish of every kind, we found neither Goupil nor Mina.

Just a stiff grey she-cat that had been hanged from the window frame.

In its contracted claws, there were tufts of red hair.

I carefully gathered up these hairs. I handed some of them over to my childhood friend B, a local furrier. On first inspection, he told me, 'It's fox hair.'

I met him the day before yesterday. 'By the way, that tuft of hair – it was pulled out of an untanned skin. In my opinion, it came from a living creature.'

I've tried several times to relate this story. Some sort of reluctance, some unconscious but irresistible rule of silence made me transpose it and recast it as a story of the Middle Ages. Nor can I say what prompts me to write it down now, without rereading it. That would be too painful.

I nearly forgot: I told all this to Doctor N, the black vet who knows about such things, the one who said of the vicious tom, 'There's more to that cat than meets the eye.'

The kindness of that man, especially towards animals, is legendary. He fixed his eyes on me with an expression at once wary and regretful. Thowing his door wide open, he said, 'Just mind your own business.'

Chapter VI

I'm very pleased to say that, since my enrolment in the fighting forces, extraordinary good luck has protected my companions and me. We're not any of us 'spies' exactly. We're all quite incapable of that. I run a mapping and transmission centre. The others are radio operators, liaison agents, coders – all technicians. Not double-dealers. With our makeshift means, we daily defy detection by German direction finders. Danger lurks all around. I can always smell it. I am then extremely self-possessed: all senses keyed, capable of any miracle, 'supercharged'.

I've learned that, just as a war between men is not a human-scale phenomenon, danger that assumes a human form and a human quality is much more related to time and place than to its extremely unwitting vehicles.

Keep-on-Dancin'

Yesterday, at Quarteron's, in Rue de la Montagne, I made a complete fool of myself and aroused suspicion. I must learn to curb my friendly impulses when they are rather too spontaneous.

I was taking round this young Pole, who arrived from London the day before yesterday, and has been entrusted to my care. He has a radio transmitter. On Tuesday, two Wellingtons piloted by compatriots of his will come and photograph the Brétigny airbase, which I 'monitor'. He will guide the mission by radio telephone from the ground at Marolles-en-Hurepoix. He speaks very little French, very good German, not bad English. I've provided him with an air-raid warden's identity card – this has become child's play for me: his name is now Watsek, he's an engineer working for the

Jerries on the Belgian border. We're all set. But between now and then he has to make contact with the 'wireless group' of my network, and take part in a broadcast from Paris. The risks are enormous, and I think it's stupid to put this boy in danger almost needlessly. But those are our orders.

I can't help being extremely worried about him. So I wanted to take him on what I call the 'salutary tour' whose twists and turns are familiar to me. A stop here, another there, and elsewhere if necessary: he will, without knowing it, be infused with hopefully protective energies that will also rid him of all kinds of burdensome, paralysing and, if one's not careful, possibly fatal handicaps. It's his pointless death I'm afraid of. I daren't say, I have this feeling about it. It's high time to take the matter in hand.

Gérard, the bearded painter, was with us. These days he looks devilishly unkempt.

Evidently on edge, old Quarteron was rummaging through a pile of bills. He kept glancing apprehensively at a stout fellow sitting at a table, doing some calculations, with a bottle of bubbly to hand and three empty glasses. Two officious-looking individuals, their hands in their pockets, raincoats flipped behind, hats tipped back, were nervously pacing up and down. Quarteron seemed pleased to see us. However, he said, 'Sidonie came by this morning. She says hello.' Which clearly meant, 'Watch out. I don't know these geezers, or not very well. Better be careful.'

I gave him a reassuring wink. Of the three blokes, I knew two of them: Joseph Brizou and Tricksy-Pierrot. Gangsters, the worst kind of ruffians, but no squealers, not at any price.

The stout fellow looked up, saw Gérard's beard, and said, 'They've got class, these guys!' I was offended. I take the most infinite pains so that my dress and appearance attract no attention, wherever I might be. My Pole, in his narrow-shouldered coat, has the harmless appearance of a fast-growing schoolboy. But I didn't say a word.

'Not so bad,' said Brizou.

'How are you doing?' I replied in time-honoured fashion: it's our little joke.

Brizou set up three more glasses and filled them up with what was left of the bubbly in the gold-topped bottle. Tricksy-Pierrot relaxed, came over and shook hands. But he had other things on his mind. Abruptly he turned to the big fellow.

'Have you worked this one out? You know what the risks are? You know what the score is?'

Unfazed, the other guy says, 'You just keep on dancin'. I'm an old hand at this game.'

This tickled me. I burst out laughing and the tension eased. Quarteron took me aside for a moment to tell me that Keep-on-Dancin' was a very dangerous crook (why should I care?), that every police organization was after him, and it was all very well this whole gang being good clients, but as long as they were here, he, Quarteron felt nervous, and he didn't mind admitting it.

When I rejoined the others, Keep-on-Dancin' gave me a sidelong glance. 'Now you've been briefed. You know what the score is, right?' Quarteron looked uncomfortable and bent down to pick something up off the floor. I burst out laughing again and ordered a bottle.

Keep-on-Dancin' gave me a slap on the left shoulder that made me stagger. And we exchanged one of those bone-crunching handshakes that take their toll on your finger joints.

Well, he sure made me sit up and listen, that guy! The others couldn't keep up with us. They went to bed. I gave my key to Watsek. He slept in my bed, tanked up with schnapps. At six o'clock in the morning, Keep-on-Dancin' and I end up at the bottom end of La Mouffe, near Les Gobelins, sitting in front of two bottles of nicely chilled white and a steaming lobster, just out of the pot, that was still alive half-an-hour ago. These days, it's almost a crime. It's offensive to the other fellows in the bar. Who aren't complaining. Keep-on-Dancin' told the bartender, everyone that comes in gets a drink on him.

All night and all morning, we talked about him and Paris, Paris and him. They're inseparable. To be more accurate, there's a certain Paris and a certain aspect of him that are inseparable.

I've seen it before, and it's always amazed me: when men who've met by chance realize in the course of their conversation that they both have the same mistress and, instead of adopting the dignified, cold and constipated attitude appropriate to such a situation, laugh heartily and shower often liquid attentions on each other, whispering into each other's ear, swopping risqué confidences and getting emotional. Well, it was just like that with Keep-on-Dancin' and me, with regard to our city. Not an ounce of jealousy between us. We complement each other. Men are so isolated, prisoners of their own wretched selves, that they can be unbelievably sociable.

Leaving Quarteron's, he sniffed the fresh air from La Montagne, listened to the tentative strains of an accordion that unknown hands tried their skill upon behind an open window somewhere in a block of darkness. And then he breathed in deeply, and said something very commonplace: 'Ah! Dear old Paris! There's nothing like it.'

He dragged me off to Rue Descartes. Perhaps out of professional idiosyncracy, I took it into my head to relate, for his sole benefit – and what a first-class audience! – the history, the anecdotal history mostly, of the already hushed streets we wandered. Walking past the Quatre-Sergents café-tabac awakened memories in him. 'I know that lot well,' he said. 'You might say those four guys were mates of mine: Goubin, Pommier, Raoulx, Bories. When I was a kid, the *patron* would point out a big old table in which they'd supposedly engraved their names with a knife that was hanging on the wall, alongside a handgun dating from the same period. There was also a colour picture in which the four of them held their glasses raised, with the sea and the sun in the background, and even on the sun they'd stuck a red cap.'

'Yes, but that's not the only establishment in Paris operating under the aegis of the four sergeants from La Rochelle: there's another one on Boulevard Beaumarchais.'

'Sure. And the other?' (He was expecting to catch me out.)

'The other? Good Lord, yes! Rue Mouffetard, Olivier's . . .'

'Olivier's, that's right.'

'The carved and painted tavern sign used to hang outside. But they did well to move it inside and mount it on the wall . . .'

'Yes, and do you know why?'

'Why what?'

'Why they moved the sign inside.'

'Because of the rain?'

'Like hell! It's because it serves a purpose. A purpose that you don't even suspect. It's closed now, but we'll go there in the morning, as soon as it opens. I'll tell you about it when we get there.'

I'd passed this hovel in Rue Thouin a hundred times, never dreaming there was a clandestine canteen in the backyard where you could eat your fill of excellent charcuterie smuggled in from Brittany. Keep-on-Dancin' is a valued customer here; they call him Monsieur Edouard. He spends lavishly. We regaled ourselves. And Keep-on-Dancin', who was in expansive mood by then, was determined to describe to me his harrowing youth.

'It wasn't really my fault. I was a strapping lad, and unruly, and I'd had a succession of "fathers" – five or six of them. They'd thrash me, but I could never conform, never be told what to do. When I was seventeen, a lousy NCO deserter shacked up with my whore of a mother.'

'Don't say that. You can't, you mustn't say such a thing. Even if you think it. Even if it's true.'

The table must have been solid, he would have split it otherwise. He shouted, 'It's true, true, true. And I'm entitled to badmouth her, because here, *here*, that's precisely the one thing you can't do and that's bullshit.'

'Now, just calm down.'

'I couldn't stand the bastard. And most of the time, it was yours truly who was the breadwinner. So one day I decided I'd had enough. The bozo tried to throw his weight around. I was in a foul mood. With a single punch, just one, with this fist here' (he gazed at his huge hand as if it didn't belong to him),

'I clocked him, right on his temple. He fell badly. Died of concussion. I ended up in reformatory on Belle-Ile. I was with guys who had nothing left to lose, guys with eyes that burned too bright . . . You get the picture?'

'Yeah, I get the picture.'

'After that, there was no going back. Maybe I could have taken advantage of the 1939 war to straighten myself out: but I was in prison. And now I'm as tough as they come. I'm a hard man in my line of work, but basically there isn't a more miserable wretch than myself. Understand?'

'Of course I do. I really wish I could help you, and it's quite possible that one day I might be able to. Anyway, there's something I find reassuring about you.'

'Tell me.'

'I've taken in everything you've told me, I understand your predicament and I deplore it, but try as I might I don't feel the slightest hint of what's called pity. I think that's just as well.'

'I'm glad to hear it.'

His thoughts ran on.

'It's all down to Paris. You see, it's because of Paris, the city without its inhabitants, that I'm not serving life. I'm really lucky that Paris has a soft spot for me.'

'I'd like you to explain what you mean. I'd also like to know why here more than anywhere else you can say what you like but you can't bullshit.'

'Madame Rita, you wouldn't have a street guide?'

'But of course, Monsieur Edouard.'

'I'm pinching it from you. Here, buy yourself another one in the morning.'

He handed her a bundle of small bank notes.

He tore out the folded pages – one for each arrondissement – and began to lay them out on two adjoining tables.

He marked with his pen reference points corresponding to central squares, crossroads. And rapidly, confidently, he drew two, more or less straight, parallel lines: one on either side of the Seine. And two lines running across them. Finally, an irregular curve that clearly traced the route of the old city wall, dating from the thirteenth century. 'That's the circuit. Within that circuit, everything's deadly serious,' he said.

This was getting fascinating.

I said, 'Go on.'

He took his time.

'You know the Vieux-Chéne, of course.'

'Of course.'

'And how much do you know about it?'

'A fair amount. The old washhouse . . . Casque d'Or, Leca and Manda, the brawls . . .'

'What else?'

'Periodically, it's as if fire starts to run in people's veins: knifings over the merest trifle, even murders . . .'

He chose his words for effect.

'Listen. *Every seven years*: a pitched battle or bloodletting, and not just some pin prick, it's got to be serious, the blood has to flow. And *every eleven years* — it's a fact, there's evidence to prove it — murder, with loss of life. There *has* to be at least one death. It's the street, the place that dictates it. You know the Port-Salut?'

'With the railing, Rue des Fossés-St-Jacques? Sure.'

'What happened there during the Revolution?'

'Save your breath. It's been a breeding ground for conspiracies since the year dot.'

'And is it any different now?'

'I don't want to know.' (Honest to goodness!)

'Fine. What about this place?'

He shows me on the map. It's near the Seine. I laughed.

'Oh, my! It's an old bistrot that functions as a bit of a brothel on the side, just for the odd customer, so word doesn't get round too much.'

'Since when?'

'Are you kidding? Since the days of St Louis, at least.

> '*Dames au corps gent, folles de leur corps*
> *Vont au Val d'Amour pour chercher fortune.*'
> [Fair wanton ladies go to Val d'Amour
> In search of fortune's favour.]

90

'That figures. So listen to this. Do know what La Mouffetard was before?'

'Before what?'

'Before all of this. Before there were any houses.'

'The Via Mons Cetardus, a graveyard where the Romans who occupied the City allowed Christians to be buried. In fact, even today, from time to time a sarcophagus turns up. It was the Aliscans of Paris.'

'Right. The Christians at that time . . . they were sort of outcasts?'

'Well, they were regarded by others with some suspicion . . .'

'Did you know that since forever the Mouffe's been a place for saying phoney prayers?'

'Phoney prayers? What do you mean?'

'Prayers that are different from everyone else's. Not the common currency. Ma'me Rita, you wouldn't have the last few days' newspapers?'

'Indeed, Monsieur Edouard.'

And Keep-on-Dancin' starts going through a dozen or so papers. His attention is completely devoted to this. He produces a flick knife with a blade as sharp as a razor. Every now and again he cuts out a very short paragraph, without any headline; and he puts the cutting in his pocket.

In its pure form, suppressed anger, that builds up because it can't find any conductor through which to discharge itself, has a potentially huge destructive power. From Keep-on-Dancin', silent, preoccupied, his teeth clenched, there emanated a raging storm of terrible humours. Anger, anger alone consumed him, permeated him, had become his entire being's sole reason for existence. Though he strove to contain himself, nonetheless I dreaded an imminent eruption. Unseen by him, I picked up one of the articles he'd cut out. It gave notice, without any comment, that one Armand B, condemned to death by the Criminal Court of the Loire, for a double murder, had 'paid his debt' to 'society'.

'It won't be long before the inevitable happens,' he said. 'We've got to get to Olivier's by first light.'

I said, 'It's a beautiful night. There's something of Villon in the air.'

Keep-on-Dancin' gave a start. 'Villon! Did you say Villon? François Villon?'

'Well, of course.'

'Hang on. I've got something to show you.'

In his gun pocket, he had a luxury leather-bound edition of Villon's *Testaments and Ballads*. But with him, nothing could surprise me any more.

'He's my man, my hero, if I'd known him, we'd have made a curious pair. I should have had a brother like him.'

He wanted to trace the poet's footsteps. 'So how far up the Rue St-Jacques did his uncle Guillaume live? And where exactly was the Pomme-de-Pin located?'

I answered his questions as best I could. We recited to each other under our breath 'The Ballad of the Gallows-Birds'.

'No, your pronunciation's wrong. It's much simpler than that.'

He meekly corrected himself. After which he heartily slapped me on the back. 'You're a great pal, and no mistake.'

I'd forgotten that since midnight, it was Sunday. On the stroke of five, we went out for a breath of air. At the very same moment, two hundred gnomes, goblins, elves or witches, clothed in rags, carrying enormous bundles, harnessed to trolleys or hauling improvised carts, emerged from the shadows like maggots out of a cheese, and coughing, belching, yawning, jostling, arguing, hurried in the direction of St Médard. These were the 'owners' of the first stalls of the famous Mouffetard Flea Market, on their way to fight over the best places on the pavements of Rue St-Médard and Rue Gracieuse. A very ancient concession permits the rag-pickers and anyone else who wants to come here, every Sunday morning, to trade their goods on the pavement, without having to hold a licence, or pay any fee.

At Olivier's, the small smoky room 'decorated' with old colour covers of the *Petit Journal Illustré* was already filled with a chilled, damp, acridly steaming rabble.

The shop sign, of imposing size, brightly coloured and

freshly revarnished, is affixed to the wall, to the left of the entrance.

The bas-relief figures of our four conspirators, each with a glass in hand and fired with enthusiasm, stand out against a seascape background overcast with pitch-darkened clouds. The naive skill of the craftsman who made this piece, a real jewel of popular art, betrays the exact date of its conception and completion: some time during the course of the year 1822, this jobbing-sculptor was in the grip of emotion, the generous indignation of a population incensed by the absurd beheading on Place de Grève, of four very young prankish insurrectionists. I ask you, what NCO in his cups has never made up his mind to save France – or some other country?

Keep-on-Dancin' nudged me with his elbow. A man stood motionless in front of the sign, which he seemed to be examining with close attention. He was not in the least affected by the increasing rowdiness. It was dawn. Revealed against the light was a sharp profile set off by a narrow fringe of greying beard. I got as close as I could to this man. I'm sure I'm not mistaken: he was praying with unusual fervour, I could *feel* it. This went on for some minutes, very long minutes. Almost imperceptibly, the man bowed his head three times. And then he turned and approached the counter. Keep-on-Dancin' went up to him and with easy familiarity placed his arm under his elbow. I thought they knew each other. But not at all. Keep-on-Dancin' signalled to Olivier, with his thumb, to serve the fellow a drink, whatever he wanted. And then my newfound friend drew from his wallet a large sum of money: several thousand francs. Discreetly, he offered them to the guy. 'For the family,' he said, in an undertone. The man thanked him with a knowing smile and a handshake that spoke volumes. He went off without having uttered a single word. Keep-on-Dancin' produced one of those cuttings he'd taken from the day before yesterday's newspapers.

I said, 'Thanks. I'm beginning to understand.'

'Maybe, but you don't know the whole story yet,' he said.

And he whisked me off once again. He pointed to the

Vieux-Chêne. Between the two first-floor windows were displayed the old oak's twisted branches and sturdy roots.

'Could you say how old that tavern sign was?'

'No. All I know is that it was already there by about the middle of the seventeenth century.'

'What's it made of?'

'Wood, with several layers of plaster mixed with alum, to protect it.'

'What kind of wood?'

'How do you expect me to know that?'

'I'm going to tell you: ship wreckage. The wreckage of a vessel that sank in the Seine estuary in 1592. I repeat: fifteen ninety-two.'

'Where did you learn that?'

'Here and there, but mostly at Melun where I was doing time.'

They sure as hell know a thing or two, the guys that graduate from Melun!

Keep-on-Dancin' went on, 'And do you know where its sister sign is?'

'Yes, on Rue Tiquetonne, there's one that resembles it: the Arbre-à-Liège. Old La Frite's place.'

'Right. To begin with, you'll realize they're both cut from the same wood. But apart from that, you don't notice anything?'

'Straight off, no.'

'I'll fill you in. First, we're going to have a bite to eat.'

And that's how we came to buy the lobster.

Keep-on-Dancin' lifted a corner of the veil for me. In simple words, commonplace expressions indicative of the fundamental honesty and profound goodness that inform this veteran villain, he led me to discover my City from a wonderful perspective. I would never have dared to imagine everything he told me.

'Yes, my friend, ship wreckage was once the wood of a tree, nothing special about it – just like any other kind of wood. Men cut down the tree. They sawed and worked and planed and shaped and polished and caulked and tarred it. They made

94

a ship out it, and they celebrated the birth of that ship, they christened it like a child. And they entrusted themselves to it. But the men were no longer very much in charge. The ship too had its say. A ship's a being in its own right, like a person, so to speak, that thinks, and breathes, and reacts. A ship has its own mission to accomplish. It has its own destiny. So it sinks, this vessel, it founders because it was meant to founder, on such a day at such a time, on account of this or that, and in such a place. Maybe it was already written in the stars. And then long afterwards, other men discover the wreck, they refloat it, they bring to the surface the bits of wood – and you should see with what respect they do this. And you think a piece of wreckage like that doesn't know anything, doesn't remember anything, isn't capable of anything, that it's as senseless as it is hard, that it's . . . as thick as a plank? I'll tell you something worth remembering, that sailors well know: wood from a shipwreck is "back-flash" wood. Whatever takes place under the auspices and under the sign of even the smallest fragment of a shipwreck cuts more than just one way. One swinish deed is multiplied a thousand-fold; one flower', (he meant, a kindness), 'will bring you a field full of flowers, an entire province, tulips, cyclamens, take your pick. For instance: there's shipwreck wood in the base frame of the sign of the four sergeants. That's something "the likes of us" know. Well, once that guy was through,' (he meant, the man who'd been praying), 'I guarantee, the judge, every member of the jury, the prosecutor, the warders, the hangman, his assistants, the whole damn lot of them are going to get their comeuppance, and how! From now on they're jinxed. Seriously jinxed. And for a long time to come.'

'In other words, it wasn't, as in the usual way of things, for the repose of the soul of the departed that guy was praying?'

'No. It was not a well-intentioned prayer. And believe me: to take that risk, the guy must have had some courage. Luckily people like him exist. Otherwise how could the rest of us defend ourselves?'

'You say, "the rest of us". There may be charges against you, but you haven't actually been sentenced to death, have you?'

He shrugged dismissively.

'Uh! Not quite. But as I was saying, the Vieux-Chêne is the only place in this part of town to have "declared itself". Whatever you do, or say, or even think here is deadly serious, and fraught with repercussions. It's the start of the circuit that has no place for bullshitters. Now, wait, I'm going to show you something else.'

He insisted on clearing the table, and again devoted himself to his game of patience: piecing together the map of Paris, the bits of which he'd stuffed into the pocket of his raincoat, folded up any old how.

I helped him.

Then he asked me, straight out, 'What would you say was the true centre of Paris?'

I was taken aback, wrong-footed. I thought this knowledge was part of a whole body of very rarefied and secret lore. Playing for time, I said, 'The starting point of France's roads . . . the brass plate on the parvis of Notre-Dame.'

He gave me a withering look.

'Do you take for me a sap?'

The centre of Paris, a spiral with four centres, each completely self-contained, independent of the other three. But you don't reveal this to just anybody. I suppose – I hope – it was in complete good faith that Alexandre Arnoux mentioned the lamp behind the apse of St-Germain-l'Auxerrois. I wouldn't have created that precedent. My turn now to let the children play with the lock.

'The centre, as you must be thinking of it, is the well of St-Julien-le-Pauvre. The "Well of Truth" as it's been known since the eleventh century.'

He was delighted. I'd delivered. He said, 'You know, you and I could do great things together. It's a pity I'm already "beyond redemption", even at this very moment.'

His unhibited display of brotherly affection was of childlike spontaneity. But he was still pursuing his line of thought: he dashed out to the nearby stationery shop and came back with a little basic pair of compasses made of tin.

'Look. The Vieux-Chêne, the Well. The Well, the Arbre-à-Liège . . .'

On either side of the Seine, adhering closely to the line he'd drawn, the age-old tavern signs were at pretty much the same distance from the magic well.

'Well, now, you see, it's always been the case that whenever something bad happens at the Vieux-Chêne, a month later – a lunar month, that is, just twenty-eight days – the same thing happens at old La Frite's place, but less serious. A kind of repeat performance. An echo . . .'

Then he listed, and pointed out on the map, the most notable of those key sites whose power he or his friends had experienced.

In conclusion he said, 'I'm the biggest swindler there is, I'm prepared to be swindled myself, that's fair enough. But not just anywhere. There are places where, if you lie, or think ill, it's Paris you disrespect. And that upsets me. That's when I lose my cool: I hit back. It's as if that's what I was there for.'

God knows what maelstrom I've got caught up in on account of Keep-on-Dancin'. I certainly didn't need this, but I won't do anything to impede the unfolding of all that's to follow.

Yesterday, apart from Brizou and Tricksy-Pierrot, his sidekicks, and bodyguards when necessary, Keep-on-Dancin' was accompanied by a badly-dyed blonde. Not a young woman. Dumpy and loud-mouthed. He introduced us: Dolly-the-Slow-Burner. She was, he said, his 'orderly-in-chief'. She receives his mail and when the gang wants to spend the night locally she takes care of finding them some discreet hangout.

They were all in a pretty foul mood, angry with some Corsican who'd crooked them in a rather complicated-sounding deal involving tungsten steel drills. Having been summoned, the Corsican had failed to appear. Keep-on-Dancin' was seething.

'This is the last time that bastard puts one over on me. When I next see him, even if he shows up now, I'm going to twist his ears.'

I knew these were not just empty words. I wished for an

easing-up of tension quite impossible to achieve. Fortunately Alexandre arrived.

A rag-picker. A little too fond of the bottle. Harmless-looking sort of guy. Known round here as a bit of loony. No one pays much attention. Everyone has their little foibles.

'Ah, police officer,' said Keep-on-Dancin', suddenly relaxed, good-natured. 'Have a drink, that's an order.'

'Thanks, boss, to your good health, boss, ladies and gentle-men, one and all,' the fellow belched, downing two large glasses of rough red, one after the other.

Brizou laughed outright, but Tricksy-Pierrot and Dolly-the-Slow-Burner, she especially, eyed him with distaste.

A great many things have been said about Alexandre Villemain. Complicated, disturbing, not very nice things. The truth is more straightforward. I heard it from Quinton, his main 'buyer'. Here it is:

At forty-five years of age Villemain was called up and drafted into the territorial army to take part in the very con-fused phoney war of 1939–40. Impossible to get this dosser to do anything. Incapable of marching in step, but canny as hell, and a source of amusement to everyone. One day it became apparent he couldn't read. He was redeployed to a different company – without being entered on the roll of his new unit – given a fake commission covered with bogus stamps, a Gras gun, some Lebel cartridges, provisions for three days, a bucket of red wine, a litre of brandy, and installed in a roadman's hut by the side of a road just above Senlis. An NCO tells him, 'You police the road. You stop every vehicle, military or civilian, check their papers, and only let them through if they're in order. Otherwise, you call the gendarmes. Understand? Dismissed!'

And the regiment went off, leaving Villemain behind. An obliging soul by nature, he lent a hand here and there to the farmers, repaired bicycles, and set about scrounging from wherever he could food, wine, tobacco and, when reduced to rags, even clothes.

Locally he was known as 'the freak'. But during his regular working hours – from six thirty am to five in the evening –

he carried out his duties conscientiously, frowned over the documents of motor vehicles, allowing them to pass with a big wave and a patronizing smile. On the stroke of five from the nearest church bell, he would lay down his gun, close up his hut, and go foraging. His policing of the road made hundreds of people, including several generals, weep with laughter. And this went on until the exodus. Then there were just too many people: Villemain granted himself leave, and took a rest. Two days, two nights of silence, no other sound but that of aeroplanes in the distance, and above his head the crows . . .

And then a Panzer division turned up, in the most orderly fashion. It's quite true that Villemain stopped the motorcycles riding ahead. Amazed by this apparition, they disarmed him, put him in a sidecar and took him with them 'to show them the way'.

Arriving ahead of schedule, the division camped out to the north of Paris for two days. Alexandre was kitted with Kraut fatigues, rewarded with a pair of boots, and made officially responsible, at a *Kantonsstandort Kommandantur*, for the distribution of petrol to fugitive Belgians returning to their country.

This extraordinary adventure addled his already feeble wits, and ever since then poor harmless Alexandre has a way of buttonholing people. A gabardine in his eyes is a kind of uniform. Every time he sees someone wearing a raincoat, he sidles up to them, nudges them gently and says, very mysteriously, 'I'm like you . . . I'm with the police . . .'

After Alexandre left, tight as a tick, the better off for a hearty snack, with a little money in his pocket, Keep-on-Dancin' and Brizou joked light-heartedly. 'Ah! isn't he a laugh? If only all cops were like him!' This clearly didn't go down well with Tricksy-Pierrot, and Dolly had her say: 'I don't find him funny, that tramp of yours, no way. So what if he's bonkers? Even if he's got nothing to do with the fuzz, like this jerk who can't even write his own name, any guy that imagines he's a cop isn't to be trusted. On principle. It's in his blood. No need even to bribe him to grass. And, shall I tell you something, I wouldn't be so sure this fellow wasn't a bit of squealer.'

And Tricksy-Pierrot chimed in. 'The poor sod must be deranged. Otherwise, being a local lad, he'd know that, here, there's a price to be paid for everything, especially anything you say out of line. But it's not me that's got any reason to be scared of him, I'm lucky, he's a problem for the big guys. Besides, you've got to have some fun from time to time. "You just keep on dancin', I know what I'm doing . . ." '

Keep-on-Dancin' wanted to take everyone to eat at some place run by a Chinaman he knew, when the Corsican turned up. It would have been better if we'd left five minutes earlier.

What a ugly mug! I've come across him two or three times before. He's revolting. He calls himself Sacchi or Saqui or Saki. He says he's from Calvi, but I'd swear he belonged to that rabble of the voluntarily stateless, reprobates from all over, those oily, greasy, creepy-crawly, stinking human cockroaches that infest some Mediterranean shores. They're not features on his stupid face, but rather disfigurements. Along with loose bags under his eyes and great flapping lugholes. Sick-making.

They immediately got down to business. I vaguely understood that the deal involved selling off to some German purchasing agency a consignment of drills made of metal that was hard to come by, all of which had been rejected as faulty. They were to be sold at full price, and Sacchi was willing to take care of that. But in order to keep most of the profits for himself, he was claiming the unverifiable existence of countless middlemen who naturally had to be bribed. The guy's deviousness was patently obvious. Keep-on-Dancin' held himself in check. Finally, with deceptive calm, he went up to the cringing Sacchi and said, right in his face, 'You frigging Corsican. I gave you a chance. You can forget the drills, I'll flog them myself. But you screwed me over that deal with the vices, and the one with the copper wire. You're going to bugger off and stay away from this neighbourhood, right now. But before you go, I've got something to settle. Not with you, with my patch. This here is my patch. I swore I'd twist your ears. I can't go back on my word here.'

And my giant friend grabs the other by his lugholes and sends him flying through the air over a rattan chair. It was a terrific stunt! The Corsican flailed about, whimpering cravenly. Quarteron did well to intervene. Sacchi was bleeding, both ears practically torn off.

He made a dash for the door, and pointing an angry finger at his torturer said, 'This time I'm levelling with you: my ears will bring you bad luck. Do you hear? Bad luck they'll bring you!'

Keep-on-Dancin' spat in his direction. 'Come here and say that, I'll cut them right off,' he said, drawing his knife.

But the treacherous Corsican was gone.

'Let's make a move,' said Dolly. 'We shouldn't hang about here. That guy's evil, now you've given him a beating he's capable of anything.'

We went off to the Chink's place, and of course didn't get back until dawn. Clearly obsessed with what Sacchi had said, three times that night Keep-on-Dancin' swore he would slice off his ears and dry them out to keep as lucky charms.

He wasn't at all drunk.

Yesterday I was at Brétigny with Watsek, the Polish radio operator. Everything went extremely well. Very clear weather, almost no cloud. The two Wellingtons, after circling above for a few minutes, dived twice, braving the flak. The Jerries in a panic ran for shelter. Unfazed, Watsek transmitted his messages. I can breathe freely now. But tomorrow's going to be difficult: we have to radio from Paris and our transmission centre, near the Gare de Lyon, has fallen into the hands of the Germans. Fortunately without causing us too much pain.

At lunchtime I heard that ten minutes after we left Quarteron's the other evening four police inspectors, tipped off by a phone call, came to nab Keep-on-Dancin'. In charge of the operation was my friend Fernand. I wish he'd turn his attention to something else.

I said nothing of this to the Corsican who, to my great surprise, was waiting for me at the Trois-Mailletz. Ingratiating, smarmy, devious as ever, he tried to pump me for information.

He wanted me to arrange one last meeting between him and Keep-on-Dancin'. He said everything could be straightened out and there was a lot to gain. Of course I refused, with the excuse that I didn't know where to contact any of the gang, and that their affairs were of no interest to me. At which point the guy showed his hand. He bears a terrible grudge against Keep-on-Dancin'. That punishment session the other night has made a mortal enemy of him. With me, giving the impression as I do of being absolutely neutral, he feels the need to boast. Even though he hardly knows me, he wants to regain some sort of credit in my eyes. He inflicts stories on me, with no truth in them for sure, of cruel revenge in which he's always cast as the leading light, and to which he adds crudely sadistic details as he goes along.

I let him talk because he twice said to me, 'My ears', (they're both covered with dressings held in place with sticking plaster), 'my ears will bring him bad luck.'

'But why your ears rather than anything else – your entire self, for instance?'

'Just my ears. Then I won't need to do anything else.'

'But what are you going to do?'

'Damn it! I'll have them magicked. You don't know about that?'

'No, I'm afraid I don't. And I'd be very interested to hear about it.'

'I can give you the low-down, but nothing's free. Fair's fair, eh? A thousand francs.'

The little shit. I paid him half in advance. We arranged to meet on Friday morning, at the Gobelins intersection.

Géga is the most unbelievable guy. These days he's always broke, yet he always manages to do the most unexpected favours for the wanted men that happen to end up in my care. He finds us shoes, decent clothes, food, places where they can sleep easy – it's as well not to be too particular on this score – and even bicycles that he buys piecemeal, as the parts turn up. Now he's the owner – or manager, no one knows for sure – of a little café he's just opened in Rue de Bièvre, next to the vacant lot where old Hubert's house used to stand. As Géga is completely skint – being the person we know him to be, this won't last – and he has almost no supplies in stock, his customers pay in advance when they come to him for a drink. Then he goes and gets the glasses filled at the bar across the street. He doesn't make anything out of this, which everyone finds killingly funny, he most of all. This afternoon we held a council of war at the Eye – the name of Géga's new bistrot – with two radio operators from the wireless group Hunter, and Watsek the Pole. We have a problem. The messages that are supposed to be transmitted in twenty-four hours are so important that we must at all costs, whatever the risks, immediately find some place to send them from. Until the last few days there were two rooftops we could use to set up the aerial. The motorcycle direction finders located them. So that's that. Transmit from the outskirts? We'd run the risk of interfering with transmissions from a friendly network based locally, and jamming everything, their messages and our own. Reluctantly, Cap'n Brochard, head of the group, had to come to a decision.

'Too bad. We'll transmit from the wine market, where the guy who lends me his shed has no idea what we're going to do there. It's almost certain there'll be trouble. All we can do is ask for our cover to be increased. It can't be helped, we have to go through with it.'

He's right. Maybe several hundred lives depend on just one of our messages getting through: what must be averted is the bombing in the station, in a very densely populated area, of a train carrying a much greater quantity of explosives than London has been led to believe. The convoy is travelling south. A ground attack would destroy it in open countryside. That's where I come in.

The guys looked at each other. They know what lies ahead. They nodded: OK. Watsek didn't turn a hair.

Keep-on-Dancin' is really playing with fire. He only has to be seen by some nark and he's done for, simple as that. Well, there's no reasoning with him: he insists on making his appearance in the neighbourhood.

Quite by chance he came into the Eye and on seeing me he said, 'It seems I've sniffed you out.'

This didn't amuse me, but there was nothing I could do but introduce him to Géga and the boys. They talked for quite a while. About what, whom, I ask you? About François Villon. Keep-on-Dancin', who's practically illiterate, almost hero-worships him. Géga, a well-read fan, was in seventh heaven. I was watching the door. You never know.

It was in 1940, in a cat-house in Lorraine. Some guys from another company were with me. Being responsible for the 'good behaviour' of the detachment, I had to look out for them like a mother hen.

The colonel had told me: 'The 10th goes into attack at four in the morning. There's no telling what they're going to have to face.' (He dared not come right out and say that in his view it was completely futile, but you could work it out for yourself.) 'These guys deserve a bit of a good time. Just make sure they don't get drunk. Try to get them to write home. And bring them back before midnight.'

And then the old boy turned his back to me and let drop the words, 'Poor kids!'

I shall remember for the rest of my life those hours spent with four jaded tarts, so worn out and disenchanted they didn't even bother with make-up any more. They were expecting to have to evacuate the area at any moment. They were much more interested in getting some sleep than in turning a trick, and none of my guys was in the mood for any fun and games.

They sat there quietly drinking Moselle wine. There was a general air of melancholy, which even affected the madam, who out of despair stood her round. Everyone was isolated with his or her own memories. And it was at that moment, as though through a mist, a greenish cloud which does not deceive, that I saw four of the ten faces turn a pearly grey, become attenuated, spare, translucent, then blurred. I even scribbled on the tablecloth some fragments of a poem:

> 'Yes, I see you marked out beforehand
> My brothers on this last morning . . .'

The following evening was soon enough to find out I'd not been mistaken in my forebodings.

But what happened just now, in the presence of Keep-on-Dancin' and the radio operators, was quite different. My sixth sense, more edgy than ever before, authorizes me – no, compels me – to assert there are two prospective dead men among us. Two imminent deaths. Which two? I don't yet know. It's almost as if it were up to me to decide. An inexplicable sense of responsibility oppresses me. With all my might I project onto Watsek my will to see him survive this.

Keep-on-Dancin' went off once darkness had fallen. Before leaving, he took me aside.

'You know that bastard Sacchi? He tried to shop me. Now, he's finished for sure.' And he made three slashing gestures – two at his ears and one across his throat.

Friday evening

As was only to be expected, it was not plain sailing. At five to five everything was in place. At five-o-four they linked up with the relay transmitter flying over Normandy, halfway from the English coast. Five nineteen: tranmission completed. Five twenty-three: raid by roaring motorcycle radio-detectors, immediately followed by Feldgendarmes, and straight after by a truck-load of SS.

The equipment was left behind. Brochard, in his shirt-sleeves, rolled an empty barrel down to Rue St-Bernard, managed to reach the embankment and hide on a barge. He's safe, as well as Watsek: but there's one dead, a guy from the protection group – and two slightly wounded who've fallen into the hands of the Jerries. Even if they tell all they know, we won't have anything more to worry about: once again the warning system has worked. One dead. Just one. I know that's not the full score. I'm relieved about Watsek, but can't help thinking of Keep-on-Dancin'. It's no good telling myself that whatever happens doesn't depend on me, I can't shake off this awful anxiety.

This morning Sacchi was waiting for me as arranged. First of all he hit the bottle, and demanded his five hundred francs, swearing me to silence with regard to what I was going to see and hear.

I thought this district, essentially bounded by Boulevard Arago, Avenue des Gobelins and Rue Croulebarbe, was one that I really knew like the back of my hand. Why did it have to be this unspeakable creature, reviled by his fellow men and the very buildings themselves, who revealed to me the secret of this happy hunting ground?

Away over there, the Gobelins Factory, Collège Estienne, the metro shunting yards. A little closer to hand, the furniture warehouse. And here, the streets lined with low buildings, with their reassuring names: Rue des Cordelières, Rue des Marmousets, Passage Moret. The stones are light-coloured, the courtyards deep and spacious, from which outside staircases of mahogany wood give access to the first floors. Many artisans seem to have inherited – and continue to practise – skills of bygone days: skinners, bookbinders, illuminators, lithographers. The pace is slower here than elsewhere.

The faces of the people express a quiet and industrious patience. Now what have we here? That's curious: this wall overlaps its neighbouring wall by some fifty centimetres, with at most a foot between them. For the locals, who are more of a late-to-bed than up-all-night crowd, this is a perfect 'natural' urinal. A thin man has to edge his way along the narrow space, which I manage to do without difficulty in the wake of Sacchi, to find himself at the end of a long curving passage-way, unknown even to the kids from round here who would have used it without shame as a *buen retiro*. Forty, maybe fifty metres long, running between two blind–deaf–mute walls, one of hollow brick, the other of unrendered limestone. We veer right: and suddenly there's an indentation on the horizon, revealing a patch of miserly sky, above a miniature Venice of the North. I was unaware there was a stretch of the Bièvre, in Paris, that flowed above ground. It's cold. The windows over these black waters are closed. With your right arm you have to grab hold of a rope hanging from the wall and haul yourself on to a narrow suspended walkway that comes halfway up your thigh. Having negotiated this feat with difficulty – it's a standing jump – you edge your way along the wall, until you reach a Lyon-style wooden blind: and you're there. Jump inside, on to not very solid ground, a floor still softened by a layer of sawdust. You're in the home of Monsieur Klager, right in the heart of a sorcerer's lair. I recognized him straightaway: it was the bearded man engaged in 'unholy prayer' at the Quatre-Sergents on Sunday. He gave me a pleasant unassuming smile, but his expression froze when his eyes fell on the Corsican. He spoke to him harshly, treated him brusquely, unceremoniously. So much the better.

'Did you bring what I told you?'

Cowed, cringing, sheepish, Sacchi said, 'Yes. Here you are. It wasn't easy to come by. And it cost me.'

'That's your business, keep it to yourself. You'll never pay enough for what you're up to,' growled Monsieur Klager scornfully. 'Let's see what you've got.'

Sacchi removed the lid of an ordinary round cough-sweet tin. It had been filled with a substance that shared a likeness with him: dark, dirty, greasy and smelly. Monsieur Klager examined the contents of the tin in the daylight, and sniffed at them.

'That'll do,' he said. 'Let's get on with it. Stand straight. Don't move.'

The other obeyed.

Monsieur Klager, who was wearing a grey overall, rolled up his sleeves. He seemed to meditate for a moment. Then he turned his attention to working some of the disgusting paste between his fingers, and smeared it over Sacchi's ears, rubbing them with his thumbs. He followed this up with a series of strokes, that became ever less slow, from the back of his neck to his parotid glands, and along his jawline.

'There you are, it's done. Don't wash it off before tomorrow. I suggest you go straight home: you stink.'

Discomforted, Sacchi drew Monsieur Klager out of my presence into a neighbouring room, to hand over the fee for his 'intervention'. Which must have come at a high price, to judge by the prolonged rustle of large bank notes, which have a distinctive sound.

They returned.

'Now, I just have to get the bastard to pull my ears again. But his days are numbered,' sniggered Sacchi, his eyes screwed up, his mouth ugly.

'All the same, you'd better watch out,' replied Klager. He turned to me, and in a decidedly more friendly tone said, 'For you, sir . . . well, now that you know your way here . . . At your service.'

He obviously didn't want me to say anything about my own affairs in front of his other visitor. We took our leave before climbing out of the window. Sacchi tentatively extended his hand, which Klager ignored.

I stayed with the wretched Corsican a while longer, in order to find out two things.

'What are you intending to do now, about Keep-on-Dancin'?'

'Get two tough guys to come along with me, meet up with him and provoke him. He has to touch my ears once more. But only touch them, mind: I don't want to take a beating like I did the other day.'

'And then what happens?'

'One way or another, he's in for a hard knock.'

'Yeah, but tell me, what was in that tin of yours that smelt so bad?'

'Don't talk to me about it. It's disgusting. All I can tell you is that in order to obtain it I had to get a grave-digger from Bagneux involved.'

'You mean, that was the smell of putrefying flesh?'

'Maybe.'

Having parted company with the skunk – ugh! I felt like vomiting! – I rushed back to Klager. I couldn't help myself, I wouldn't have been able to sleep. He greeted me without surprise.

'That guy . . . you know him?'

'Very vaguely. I don't like him. He intends harm to a person I've not known for very long either, but for whom I have a certain regard. That aside, not much to recommend him.'

'The one who was there on Sunday?'

'Precisely.'

'And you've come here for . . .?'

'I couldn't exactly say. Originally, I think I'd better admit straight away, though I'm sure it's not what you'd like to hear, out of sheer curiosity. And now because I must learn more about things I was previously completely unaware of.'

'But who exactly are you?'

From what I told him, just a technical education supply teacher, curious by nature, passionately interested in everything related to Paris as it used to be, and whatever survives of its old traditions.

'A journalist?'

'Not in the least, especially not right now.'

That made him smile. We understood each other. He ushered me through the door at the back of the room.

Our conversation lasted two long hours. I cannot report it in its entirety, here or anywhere else, now or later. I'm bound to secrecy, and it's much more out of respect than fear that I hold my tongue and stay my pen.

If by any chance, however, I happen to speak of Monsieur Klager, or write about him, I'm entitled to reveal what follows.

First of all, Klager's real occupation doesn't in any way consist of ensorcelling his fellowmen or casting spells on this or that part of their anatomy. Nor engaging in occult and baleful prayers. Klager is a brass-worker. He makes metal objects – bowls, goblets, vases, buttons, brooches – in repoussé. Right now, the shortage of tin and copper, either as sheet metal or in any other form, means that Monsieur Klager has been forced to do something slightly different: he makes all kinds of lanterns and light fittings. With consummate skill and very good taste, he uses whatever materials he happens to come by.

But this man, whose life should have been free of any care other than that of his very profitable livelihood, had not always known days of plenty and reliable friends. While still young, in order to avert a disaster that would have compromised his peaceful existence for ever he felt constrained to resort to a magus from Lorraine. The latter died suddenly of a stroke during a particularly serious and delicate 'operation'. Ever since that day, Klager has been the involuntary heir to an enormous complex of forces – good and evil, to put it in very elementary terms – that he administers like a banker, according to his conscience and depending on the opportunities that arise to 'unload' – as he puts it – an 'accrued glut'.

'But why do you allow your power to be used both ways?'

'Do you think that the bad people who come to me would behave any better if they didn't know me, and would do less harm?'

'But you take money for what you do.'

'Don't worry. I haven't kept a centime of that money for myself: it ends up in deserving hands. And that's not exactly charity.'

And am I any different? I try to anticipate the points of impact, simply in order to limit the damage, but there's nothing I could do to reduce the hail of bombs.

Chapter VII

We're under the full sway of uncertainty, indecision, flagging defiance. Every Frenchman has pinned to his kitchen cupboard a map, bought from a street hawker, of 'The Theatre of Operations in the East'.

Every midday and every evening at nine o'clock, with a pencil or if he's patient with the aid of little pins, he amends his 'front line' as he listens to the news from Radio London.

This is as far as his worries extend, his fighting spirit is confined to this. There's increasing acceptance of the idea this endless conflict is just a huge con that we French can hardly complain about, for compared with all the rest of Europe we seem to be spoiled little darlings.

The producers, directors and stage-managers of future wars should have learned by now that a war, just like a film, cannot sustain periods of tedium. If the rearguard gets fed up and bored, the front-line combatant feels the effect, and this has an enormous influence on the quality of his output (fighting, that is).

As for me and my friends, whose information comes from sources not at all propagandistic, we know this will end sooner or later with the already orchestrated defeat of the German forces. We're on the winning side. But I tell myself that if I were capable of holding any convictions and these drew me to the other side, I'd be no less blithe a loser, and I'd have no apprehensions whatsoever. Anyway, I congratulate myself every day on being in permanent contact with a select group of people who are no more in the business of altruism than anyone else – each man is primarily pursuing his own personal adventure – but who bring to bear an edge of danger, risk, violence, excitement without which dying of boredom would be only our just desert. All the same, if one day we hear talk once again of 'authorities' being entitled to some respect from a population that has regained its citizen status, the restored institutions – republican or otherwise – will have considerable difficulty in getting themselves taken seriously.

Fortunately the City is vigilant. It too has its secret weapons. Since the summer it has released safety valves that form part of a wonderful mechanism, known only to itself. For the past three months we've noticed the most heartening appearance all over the place of eccentrics, more or less raving lunatics, cranks, and reinvigorating crackpots. The most modest lay claim to securing only the well-being of France, or Europe. But the majority take on the whole World with a capital W, if not our poor little planetary system in its entirety. We already had our established comics: the ineffable Ferdinand Lop, about whom the most ignorant purveyors of anti-semitic, anti-democratic (as if that still had any meaning), anti-whatever shit prose vent their indignation at ten francs a line in the appalling *Pilori*. I've long been convinced that our national institution Ferdinand isn't as crazy as he likes to appear, and I think there's something courageous about him. He lets the wolves howl and continues to receive a succession of contradictory messages announcing the arrival under the Pont des Arts of the submarine that will eventually pick him up and take him to the North Sea to negotiate a settlement between the warring parties. So what's so stupid about that!

There's Raymond Duncan, on Rue de Seine. Olympian, hieratic, cunning, superficial, he feels the need to dress like a character in an Aristophanes' play adapted for Barret's circus. He ignores the kids who make fun of him in the street. He continues to preside over 'Socratic dialogues' attended by frightful old trouts wearing huge hats, fantastic creations in which stuffed birds frolic among French-style gardens scattered with candied fruit. Duncan has managed to outwit the very naive Occupying Authorities: although an American, he's not subject, as the rest of his compatriots who remained in France are at this time, to the regime of concentration camps, with all due honour, respect and deference owed to the shareholders and co-owners of many a steelworks, armaments factory and other bauble-manufacturing plant located in Hitler-controlled territory. There's Fèvre, the booted, jack-eted, pensioned-off soldier, with his long straggly hair under his bell-crowned hat, his wan face typical of the persecution maniac, his eunuch voice, his corkscrew cane. There's Praying-Dodo, in a perpetual state of ecstasy, who, blessed with amaz-ing suppleness, falls to his knees every ten paces, with his hands held out before him, and touches the pavement with his fore-head, grown calloused as a result. And a few others of lesser distinction and interest, but no less longstanding members of the cohort of everyday eccentrics who will leave their mark on this quarter-century. They've been categorized, accepted, included once and for all. Only a country bumpkin would be prompted to raise an eyebrow.

And now we have the new ones, the unsuspected prophets, messiahs, krishnas, those 'we'd always been waiting for'. There's no part of the city that doesn't pride itself on its own preacher.

Montmartre has its 'public astronomer' who for forty sous will show you the Moon and its craters through a gimcrack telescope, and treat you to a bonus tirade: 'Ambassador of the stars, in the name of the billions and billions of galaxies' (which is not greatly compromising), 'I protest against the war and I see the way out . . .'

Auteuil has Baptiste the tramp, a veteran, of the 1914 war of course, who predicts the imminent self-destruction of human-ity, and the conquest of the world by horses, sea horses, land horses, the ressurrected ghosts of all horses killed in all battles of all ages.

At Grenelle, there's the raving Ben Derrer, who by special favour is in constant communication with Mohammed. A third sex has come into existence, henceforth responsible for perpetuating the species. From now on it's a mortal sin to put to normal use whatever bits of human plumbing we may have at our disposal. The future belongs to abstainers, masturbators, paedophiles and lesbians. So there you have it!

In Parc Montsouris, it's a more serious business, because there's a whole gang of them. Two gangs rather. What am I saying? Two sects who very decorously meet in the Marron-niers temple, above the waterfall, and very politely indulge in absurd discussions. They are the 'Radiant Vectorists' and the 'Perpendicants'. They've repeatedly baffled the guards, who must have thought they were using some sort of private language and left them alone. But when some police informers got to hear about them, they organized a raid. Apparently, it all came to nothing. They were just a bunch of low-grade clerks, very junior employees, harmless pensioners quite incapable of explaining why they felt the need to talk a lot of nonsense for at least an hour every day.

Yes, there's a wind of madness blowing these days – and this is no random choice of metaphor. No one's immune from the collective enervation that's affected people's minds. Everyone considers himself a bit of a hero. Including – and this is the real disaster – the genuine heros. Those who ought not to see themselves in those terms for some time yet. I'm thinking of the guys I rub shoulders with every day, who, having been parachuted in, are being hunted down, and face the prospect of violent death if not the most dreadful torture. They're well aware of what the slightest folly, the smallest departure from the very strict and very basic rules of caution might lead to. It makes no difference. They're all capable of picking a fight with the most insignificant *Feldwebel* they might happen to run into at the wrong moment.

At Place Maubert, where their carefully fostered – this is one of their secrets – physiological plight keeps my tramps in a permanent state of nirvana, a universe of soft light and muffled sound, a weightless, insubstantial world, life's an orgy of ultimatums and melodramatic gestures. A request for a glass of brandy on credit is met with a tirade that would have done Corneille proud.

Imagine the literary buff, steeped in his beloved classics, rejoicing in a memory that sings, prepared to dispense kilowatts of goodwill, who fetches up at the Odeon on an off day. There are days like that, when everything rings hollow, and even the hollowness is unconvincing. There's nothing to be done about it: the inspiration's not there. He's left with a terrible sense of disappointment, resentment, against whom he doesn't exactly know: the playwright or the actors? All he can do is curl up in bed, alone, all alone, and console himself with suitably wrought alexandrines.

With the tramps it's different. The one who swears to God he'll soon make his fortune solicits a miracle. For he knows that miracles can happen. You have to prop yourself up or sit down in a quiet corner, make sure you don't attract any attention, close your eyes if you can – and listen. The fellow talks to himself. He lays out his gems. 'On the head of Geneviève who had a little girl that died at the age of seven . . .'

This is way past the point of melodrama. This is high drama, the real thing. An event is never just what it is in itself and nothing more. It's what goes on around it, at the same time, that makes it – potentially – a tragic situation.

You have to have been exposed to this, at least once, to understand it.

The responsibilities, day by day more serious, that I'm taking on constrain me to be always mentally alert.

So I'm now quite incapable of dozing as I used to, of devoting quite as much time to day-dreaming and doing sweet nothing. My investigations, my research take up all my leisure time. I would eventually like to publish, among other things, a glossary of French words that owe their origin to the lesser-known aspects of Parisian life. I've already con-ducted some very curious analyses and made some unexpected discoveries.

St Patère

There is an ordinary, respectable, and equally unpretentious noun that nevertheless derives from the most Rabelaisian earthiness: the word '*patère*'. You know, that thing that causes you to forget your raincoat, on which people who still wear them hang their hats.

The word also means (according to Larousse) 'gadgets' fixed

to the wall that serve to support curtains. *Patère* supposedly derives from *patera*, a Latin word that means something completely different. Well, far from it, as it turns out.

The Roman *patera* was a vessel ressembling a shallow saucer, used for libations. Its shape was reminiscent of our present-day wine tasters. On the grounds that these receptacles were usually embellished with engravings, they've been likened to the decorative metal heads sometimes attached to the ends of *patères*, or hooks: all this in order to justify a far-fetched etymology. You are mistaken, gentlemen of the Sorbonne. Once again, Paris has the right answer.

Now, in olden days, on Monkey Island, a spit of green beyond Les Gobelins that divided our old friend the Bièvre in two, there used to be some constructions of wood and branches. The land belonged to everyone, and riverside dwellers with time to spare liked to come and relax now and again in this quiet and shady place.

Now, during a period I believe I can date to around 1350, a priest whose name posterity has not bequeathed to us went into retreat on this island in the summer season. An early Robinson Crusoe, he lived austerely in a hut built by his own hands, and devoted himself to strict and profound meditation. When the weather was hot, he was not above devoting himself to pious ablutions in the waters of the river. Few human beings lived in that place. And the pure-hearted priest, having nothing to hide from his Creator, would bathe in nature's apparel although, as a mark of the utmost respect, he would keep his hat on.

Brambles and brushwood formed tufted promontories, and the shores of the island were thus fringed with charming creeks where a person could feel at home, in the trustful privacy of earliest times.

One day the priest ventured a little further out than the curtain of foliage allowed. The water only came up to his mid-thigh. And there he found himself face to face, so to speak, with two adorable naiads – it might have been Eve with her twin sister. Surprise transfixed our sirens for a while. And perhaps a touch of curiosity . . .

The ways of the Lord are impenetrable. Was not this vision one of the temptations the Gospels warn us against?

The priest was in a quandary: wanting to observe the basic tenets of decency, and also to beseech God not to let him succumb to temptation and to deliver him from all his impure desires.

In great agitation he removed his hat, which he placed where eternal laws dictated, joined his hands above his head and in all humility recited: *Pater noster qui es in coelis . . .*

Then the miracle occurred: O, the Lord in His omnipresence is ever mindful of His servant! The hat remained in place.

Adveniat regnum tuum . . .

The marvellous efficacy of the Paternoster recited in such dramatic circumstances confirmed the priest in his edifying beliefs.

With his own hands, he built a chapel on that very island and adorned the front of it with the face of a young woman radiant with divine purity. And the chapel was dedicated to St Patère. No one held against him the addition of this newcomer to the ranks of the blessed.

Even among the Elected, there should be a 'Company of Irregulars'.

I've come across late 16th-century references to the remains of the St Patère chapel. I have a special fondness for this little saint. I think of her every time I hang up my raincoat.

I've run into the Gypsy, of Rue de Bièvre fame, on several occasions. He continues to occupy the site of the demolished house. Despite his actually very weak denials I haven't concealed from him my conviction that the whole series of disasters connected with this place was his doing, and due solely to his ill-will. But leaving that aside, I don't presume in any way to pass judgement on him or his behaviour: I confine myself to my very self-centred remarks. Fascinating as they are. He smiles, without ever compromising himself.

However, one day, he said to me, 'I shan't be staying in Paris all the time. I've two things to ask of you: if you run into me anywhere else but here,' (his circular gesture was intended to include La Mouffe, La Maube, and La Montagne), 'act as though you'd never seen me before. There'll be time enough to renew our acquaintance, if you so wish.'

'All right. I give you my word. What else?'

'You very likely have contacts . . . among architects . . . city officials . . .'

'Very likely indeed. So what?'

'So, do as you will, say what you like, but make sure that no one decides to build anything you know where, for a long time, a very long time.'

'Why not? What would happen?'

'Catastrophes . . . unimaginable . . . there's nothing more I can do about it . . .'

'I'll see to it, I promise. One day I'll even write about it.'

'That would be better still.'

Dolly-the-Slow-Burner, who's out looking for me, stops me crossing Rue de la Huchette. She's covered kilometres of paving stones and asphalt before catching up with me. With a firm grip, she drags me off to St Séverin. Into the church. There at least no one bothers you.

'Has something happened?'

'Yes . . . No. Yes and no.'

'Keep-on-Dancin'?'

'Lying low. There's trouble brewing. He's got to go into hiding.'

'What's he done now?'

'The Corsican . . .'

A discreet but nervous gesture, indicating that I'm not going to be given any details.

'And what can I do?'

She comes right up close. A whisper: 'There's no one but you that's to be trusted any more. We've got to get something to him . . .'

She draws out of her bag a brown paper parcel tied with string.

'What is it?'

118

'Two million.'

'Right. Where?'

An address, or some crazy joke? Rue des Terres-au-Curé. There's actually a street in Paris called that? The Street of the Priest's Estate?

Yes. At Porte d'Ivry. On the outskirts. Low-built houses. Very few Germans. No cops. Keep-on-Dancin' greets me in this simple little restaurant with the kind of deference and courtesy I'm not really used to.

Stuffing the parcel into his pocket, he asks: 'Is there anything you need?'

'Not right now,' I said.

'So much the better. We'll talk later. But don't ask any questions.'

We went for a walk. In that quiet neighbourhood too, a lot of people make their living dealing in second-hand goods. We went into a shop with an earthen floor, a kind of storeroom, an Ali-Baba's cave filled with the most disparate and apparently most useless objects. The owner is a Polish Jew, a jolly little chap whose French vocabulary comprises not more than fifty words. He's contrived to instal a bar in a corner of this retreat. He pours us some excellent plum brandy.

'You see, Papa Popovitch is one of the best,' declares Keep-on-Dancin'. 'Seeing it was me that introduced you, you can ask him for anything. Even dangerous things, which is something good to know.'

The guy has his own way of concurring: with a burst of laughter. I'm amazed this old fellow doesn't seem to be affected by the raids and all the kinds of persecutions with which his community is oppressed.

'He's registered at Gentilly,' explains Keep-on-Dancin', 'but he lives round here. Nothing to fear. You see, this area lies outside the zone I marked out for you one day. But you'll be able to complete the map, draw a line from Place d'Italie. Because Paris is expanding, little by little. It takes a lot of time and patience before it embraces a new village.'

Keep-on-Dancin' made it clear he didn't want to share any more of his problems with me than he had already.

'My affairs are my own look-out, it wouldn't serve any purpose to get you involved. I've got to get away from the City. It's getting too hot to stay here.'

I said, 'What about your Corsican? Have you seen him again?'

The look in his eye said it all as he calmly replied, 'If by chance you meet him in the street and you don't like ghosts, cross the road.'

Keep-on-Dancin' put into an envelope two pages of notepaper covered with his neat upright handwriting. These are addresses, practically all of them of drinking establishments, telephone numbers, names like Swindle-the-Hat at Les Tonneaux between eight and midnight; Redhead-Dora, Passage Ramey at five o'clock, etc. All these people, on the sole recommendation of my friend, are to provide me in case of need with unhesitating and unqualified assistance. This is extremely valuable. But that's not all. Keep-on-Dancin' mounts his hobby-horse and is determined to pass on to me his final tips, for we'll probably never see each other again. He tells me, this time in extraordinarily abundant detail, where best to go in Paris to instigate, discuss, conclude an affair of this or that nature. And above all, the places to avoid. It's a kind of initiation into the mysterious fluxes that pulse in the darkest secrecy of the City's veins. Keep-on-Dancin' also told me a number of astounding things I'm forbidden to divulge. Especially his last remark, a matter of eight words. And suddenly he leaves me there, shakes my hand and is off, into the boulevard outside without a backward glance.

The 'Bohemians' and Paris

I had for some time felt I was being followed, tailed to be more exact. No matter how much I resorted to the ploys used in such circumstances – abruptly turning round, stopping in front of shop windows that reflected the traffic in the street – I saw no one. Yet I cannot be mistaken. Finally my mind was put at rest: it was the Gypsy, who came up to me with a smile on his lips after Keep-on-Dancin' had left.

'I wouldn't have spoken to you. Remember what you made me promise . . .'

'Oh! I remember. And that's valid from this evening. But before that I wanted to see you one last time.'

'How did you know I was in this area?'

'When I want to find someone, I know how to go about it.'

'What's up?'

'Well, I'm leaving Paris for a while. I have to change my name.'

'Because of the police?'

'Not at all. It's a family matter. I may tell you about it one day.'

'So you want some false documents?'

'No need. We have our own ways and means.'

'Money?'

His smile broadened.

'No, no. I've chosen you as my godfather: you're going to tell me what my first name's going to be for the next seven years.'

What he told me, I shall be able to reveal later.

Yesterday, between eleven and midnight, at a time-honoured location in Rue St-Medard, as instructed by the Gypsy, I played my part in performing the rites of his tribe. We had a glass filled with wine. With the aid of a razor, we each made a small incision in our left wrist. A few drops of blood fell into the wine, which we drank in four mouthfuls – two each. The Gypsy will henceforth be named Gabriel.

I already knew quite a lot: I've often had the pleasure, when a rare document has come into my hands, when my eyes have fallen on the forgotten pages of a three-hundred-year-old book, of realizing that what I'd just read confirmed intuitions that didn't even need any external proof to become certainties. But Keep-on-Dancin' and the Gypsy, the latter especially, opened up new horizons to me, when I was far from suspecting they were so vast. I couldn't help going and prowling round Rue de Bièvre once more, by myself. Having paid my respects to the wretched place, I found myself walking past the railings of the archbishop's palace, and my footsteps led me to the Ile St-Louis, 'isle of my misty delight . . .', that enclave of trusting peace, that vessel of dreaming stones with which, at certain times, on certain nights, I feel I'm communing. As I crossed the bridge it occurred to me that the Gypsy was not the only one of his race to have cast an evil spell on a site of Parisian wrong-doing.

A chronicle of 1427, in the middle of the Hundred Years' War, tells us that on 17 April of that year, twelve 'Penitents' arrived in the City: that's to say, 'a Duke, a Count, and ten men on horseback that describe themselves as Christians of Lower Egypt driven out by the Saracens who having come to the Pope to confess their sins were told as a penance to travel the world for seven years without lying in a bed. Their retinue was of some 120 persons, as many men as women and children remaining of the 1200 they had been at their departure. They were lodged at the village of La Chapelle where crowds flocked to see them. They had pierced ears from which hung a silver earring. Their hair was black and curly, their women very ugly and witches, thieves, and fortune-tellers . . .'

These 'Bohemians' were summarily banned from the City, where they intended to commit themselves to 'spectacular devotions'. Faced with the intransigence of the mounted police, they tried to stir up the ever-generous crowd of onlookers. They were rounded up and forced on to the ferry, then landed in batches on the shores of the Ile Notre-Dame, which now forms the prow of the Ile St-Louis, until they could be repelled further. This swift banishment was not to their liking. At which point the penitents revealed their true selves and put a curse on the branch of the Seine they'd been forced to cross.

Since when, at that very place, things have happened.

In 1634 the Wooden Bridge, built by Marie de' Medici, was no more than 'an eight-yard span, with railings on either side'. It was inaugurated with a jubilee procession. When three par-ishes rushed onto the bridge at the same time, it collapsed. Twenty drowned, forty injured. In 1709 what remained of the bridge, badly damaged by ice-drifts in the Seine, had to be demolished. It was rebuilt in 1717, and painted red; hence the name 'Red Bridge', perpetuated by the tavern that stands at the corner on the embankment. This structure soon began to display signs of inexplicable weakness. It was closed to carriages. In 1819 the arches had to be rebuilt. By 1842 the accursed bridge was again in danger of collapse. A provisional metal bridge was erected, then the stone-built Pont-St-Louis . . . which completely collapsed in December 1939.

Since then, we have this dreadful makeshift structure of wooden planks and iron crossbars linking the two islands.

'Where my horse passes . . .' as Attila was wont to say.

For all that, I don't think Gypsies ought to be likened to birds of ill-omen. They return evil for evil, and good for good. One hundredfold. Their powers seem to exceed them. I knew some in Spain who could read the stars; in Germany, who could heal burns; in the Camargue, who tended horses and could lessen the birthing pains of both women and beasts.

There are some human beings who are not bound by human laws. The sad thing is perhaps they're not all aware of it.

Meanwhile, here's an idea I volunteer: the day when the borders of Europe and elsewhere become, as they once were, open to the movement of nomadic tribes that some regard as 'worrisome', it would be interesting if researchers qualified in astronomy (yes, indeed), with calenders and terrestrial and celestial maps to hand, were to examine the routes travelled by wandering Gypsies.

Maybe they'll discover that these slow and apparently aimless journeys are related to cosmic forces. Like wars. And migrations.

The Gypsies were persecuted, in France and elsewhere, with cyclical regularity in a vicious, inept and stupid manner. Almost as much as the Jews. In Paris for century after century they were corralled outside the successive boundaries of the City. In 1560 they were banished by the Estates of Orleans, on pain of being sent to the gallows or the galleys if they dared to show themselves again. Tolerated in a few regions riven by heresy, driven from other places as the descendants of Ham, the inventor of sorcery, nowhere were they regarded as anything but a menace.

Only people with a yearning for the supernatural dared to reach out to them, beyond walls and barriers. Nowadays, there are some who have become 'respectable', 'assimilated' – a dreadful word! – who take pains to conceal their origins, except from those whom they know – or sense – to have an intuitive sympathy towards them.

I can't resist the pleasure of relating at this point a fifteenth-century legend. It relates to the effigy of a virgin that once adorned the choir of the chapel of St Aignan, the remains of which are still to be found in the City, on Rue des Ursins, very close to Notre-Dame.

At the window of a low-built house, a young girl sewed and mended her family's clothes. Outside, children played beneath her gaze: her own younger brothers, and the neighbours' sons. One hot afternoon a Gypsy minstrel was making his way to the parvis of St-Julien-le-Pauvre where, as was the custom, singers, musicians, storytellers, animal exhibitors, and contorsionists came to give an open-air demonstration of their talents and to hire out their services to the stewards of castles near and far.

The Gypsy stopped in the middle of a little square lined with squat houses. Attached to one of these houses was a well-head.

Women stood chatting round it. The Gypsy drew a viola from his green canvas bag. He patiently tuned it.

Attracted by the appearance of the bronze-skinned young man, by the bright colours of his unusual style of dress, by the strange shape of his instrument, the children came running.

The Gypsy took up a position near the young girl and observed her at length.

The maiden's hair was braided and pinned up beside her cheeks in the fashion of the times. A white veil framed her face of such perfect beauty that its sweetness, refinement,

124

oval purity were already legendary: had not a monk drawn inspiration from it to paint the virgin above the choir in the St Aignan chapel?

The Gypsy began to play. And the melody that filled the air was so captivating, so appealing, the sound of his instrument so ravishing that, stilled and reduced to silence, everyone there was caught in its spell: for spell there was. But it was not intended to affect the children or the women rendered speechless with wonder and admiration. The young girl realized the Gypsy was playing for her, and for her alone. The departure of the musician, who against all expectation solicited no payment for his playing, left her overcome with blissful languour. In her innocent mind unfamiliar dreams began to flourish.

On the following days, the Gypsy returned at the same time to play in the same place. His gaze grew bold enough to meet that of the young girl. He must have beheld there so much admiration, gratitude and amazement mingled with a desire at once fierce and ill-defined that the magic stratagem he was pursuing seemed to be favouring him. When he was sure of having won the fair child's heart – to what demonic end? – he began to play a bizarre tune, at first heart-rending, disquieting, and then obsessive; ever faster but always dwelling on the same motif, one that seemed to want to sweep up in a frantic saraband houses, stones, sun and people.

He concluded abruptly, on a shrill note. Then off he went, very quickly, without looking back, and disappeared into the narrow streets that led towards the cathedral.

It was impossible for the young girl to conceal from her family how deep – and strange – an impression the Gypsy had made on her heart and her feelings. And her father had taken exception to the street musician's insistence on playing his bewitching tunes outside her window. He was about to chase him away when the Gypsy left the square.

That very evening the young girl, succumbing to a sudden fever, began to shiver and grow delirious. Her mother sat at her bedside.

'Mother, the Gypsy's calling me. He draws me to him with

his violin. He plays as he walks and people come running, people of many colours . . .'

'Those are the colours of the lingering clouds. It will be dark soon. Go to sleep.'

'The Gypsy, the Gypsy, he's calling me! Everyone's dancing round him. There are so many people! I can't see their faces. I'm going, I want to join him! I'm leaving. He's calling me, he's calling me!'

There was nothing to be done but to send for a priest. Even before midnight he was reciting the prayers for the dying.

No one ever knew what became of the Bohemian. Once again all foreign nomads were driven out of the City, with the intention they should be banished from the realm.

Many people believed that during the requiem mass they saw the pure-faced virgin above the choir in the St Aignan chapel stir, and her complexion darken.

And who was the German poet's inspiration for the legend of the *Roi des Aulne*s (*Der Erl-könig*)?

Here, I must yield to the voice of the great Kostis Palamas:

'Music becomes flesh and thrives in a new world, a new man . . . He, the last-born, son of music and love, shall arise in triumph over an ample land, prophet of a soul yet more ample . . .

'Take me in your arms, o great virgin forests,' he said, 'and listen! And we embraced him in our dream and the voice of the singing lyre consumed everything, became an abyss, a dream and an incantation: we became a temple, and he a bard, a prophet, a god of harmony . . .'

O Bohemians of my Bohemia! Happily the curses and anathemas heaped on you for centuries have not shaken the vigilant fraternity of your true bards.

Every day the words that Keep-on-Dancin' and the Gypsy imparted to me – theories, observations, advice and warnings – are substantiated and acquire deeper meaning.

'It's not for nothing there are so many bistrots in Paris,' Keep-on-Dancin' asserted. 'The reason so many people are always crowded into them isn't so much they go there to drink but to meet up, congregate, come together, comfort each other. Yes, comfort each other: people are bored the whole time, and they're scared, scared of loneliness and boredom. And they all carry around in their heart of hearts their own pet little arch-fear: fear of death, no matter how devil-may-care they might appear to be. They'd do anything to avoid thinking about it. Don't forget, it's with that fear all temples and churches were built. So in cities like this, where forty different races mingle together, everyone can always find something to say to each other.

'But this is something you need to know: when you find a place that suits you, where you decide to go back to often, to meet your pals there, if you want to feel at home and not discover some snag at the wrong moment, sit yourself in a corner, write letters, read, try and eat there, and watch what goes on for a whole day. At least twice during the day, and three times if the place is open at night, there's that moment of "temporal void". It happens every day, at the very same hour, at the very same minute, but it varies from place to place. People are talking, letting their hair down, having a drink together, and all of a sudden, the moment of silence: everyone turns stock still, with their glasses in the air, their eyes fixed. Immediately afterwards the hubbub resumes. But that moment when nothing's happening – it can last five, ten minutes. And during that time, outside and everywhere else, for other people life goes on, faster, much faster, like an avalanche. If you're prepared for it, and take advantage of that moment not to be fazed and to have your say, you're certain to be heard, and if necessary even obeyed. Try it. You'll see.'

It's absolutely true. At Les Grilles Pataillot, on Rue Frédéric-Sauton, the first 'temporal void' is at 12.36. I happened to be there three weeks ago. There was Jean the mattress-maker, a very simple decent sort of fellow, and among some dozen regulars two young housewives everyone knew, Jeannine and Thérèse. They're great friends and usually do their shopping together. The 'vacant moment' came. And during that pause Jean, looking at the two woman and voicing what was passing through his mind – normally not a great deal – said, 'Oh,

127

look! Coquette and Cocodette.' That was all. Just a couple of words. Anyone could have said any other words. But the moment of their utterance invested those words with such weight, such resonance, they prospered. From that day on, throughout the entire neighbourhood, they were no longer Jeannine and Thérèse, seen together doing their shopping, but Coquette and Cocodette.

No one will shake my conviction that those leaders of men, who are in the nature of carbuncles, of semi-conscious abscesses, who draw feverish crowds to them like noxious humours, have an innate knowledge of arrested time. They play with those vacant moments as though at a game of chequers. A fraction of suspended, frozen time, of inert time, jammed like a wedge into the most wonderfully oiled cogs of the most lucid of minds: and the whole mechanism is brought crashing to the ground, prepared to accept any authority, to endorse the most monstrous aberrations, especially collective ones.

You have to have been present, as I have, at one of the *Licht-Dom* ceremonies to understand the Nazi phenomenon, to experience its sterile grandeur and to appreciate its real danger, which will not cease with the defeat of the Wehrmacht.

Cyril is devoting himself to developing his 'receptive' faculties. He now claims to be capable of distinguishing, more or less at a distance, a true Nazi from an ordinary German soldier. It's mostly in the metro that he indulges in this little game. He picks out a Jerry with his back to him. He tries to get close. Puts out all his feelers. Makes his assessment. Then all he has to do is check. Those who were members of the Party or belonged to the Hilter Youth before 1939 wear a black-and-purple badge. Apparently he's never wrong.

What I've been doing until now is not 'adventurous' enough for my taste. There is a danger, of course – it's all about not getting caught – but it's just the work of a clandestine bureaucrat. So I no longer take any notice of strict instructions that preclude me from any other activity apart from my official missions.

I distribute false papers as freely as handbills to anyone who asks. I hide escapees, parachutists. I've arranged for Austrian deserters to slip into the southern zone. Now I'm taking really big risks. But my luck never fails: my City's taking care of me.

However, I did go a little too far in giving my address to Oscar Heisserer. He's a guy from my regiment. We recognized each other in the street. He's Alsatian: another five hundred metres and he'd have been German. He speaks French without an accent, but his mother tongue is the language of Goethe. I recall that he was not very keen on the phoney war. Once he was taken prisoner, he immediately became very friendly with the Jerries. A little more perhaps that was appropriate. His comrades – for whom he acted as an interpreter and 'right-hand man' – didn't like him, and among themselves referred to him as a turncoat. Freed as a German national, he doesn't fancy putting on a German uniform and being sent off to the Russian front. I made up a set of papers for him in the name of Lagarde. Census certificate, work permit, the lot. Yet I know he's very impressed by the German 'order', very influenced – perhaps since before the war – by Nazi propaganda. He's exactly the type to be wary of. I've been insanely reckless. But he's tortured by doubt and I like to play on that.

Zoltan the Mastermind

I also have 'my' cops. These guys are pure gold. The most valuable, and he's also a really decent bloke, is Jean Lecardeur. This enormously fat man has been out of uniform for at least fifteen years. He acts as an inspector at Les Halles, where he has the power to allocate 'medals' – the licences for authorized porters. He lives at Ste-Geneviève-des-Bois, near Brétigny, and every morning he brings me my liaison agents' reports, as some of them actually work on the base there. Lecardeur takes care of my 'babies', as he calls them, providing them with fruit, vegetables and sometimes meat.

The other day he told me he had a problem on his hands.

He's got mixed up with a stateless person, a Hungarian called Zoltan, who has once and for all signed his own separate peace with whoever's fighting, Axis or non Axis, and has little desire to go and swell the ranks of Admiral Horthy's troops.

His long and eventful wanderings through central Europe had reached their logical conclusion when in 1938 Zoltan settled in Paris, where he intended to lead a quiet life free of surprises. Twenty years of adventures and mixed fortunes had furnished his mind with enough memories to fill the three or four hours of blissful daydreaming Zoltan allowed himself every day, regardless of how convenient this might be.

Employed in a circus in his native Budapest at the age of twelve, Zoltan Hazai became successively an apprentice pastry-cook in Belgrade, the proprietor of a disreputable eating-place in Saloniki, a docker at Tulcea on the Danube.

He embarked on a Russian vessel and for two years stacked crates on the wharves of Odessa. After that, he travelled through Poland, northern Germany, and was in France when the phoney war broke out. He fell under the suspicion of the police authorities – no one quite knows why – and it was only thanks to the confusion following the German attack that he didn't enjoy the hospitality of our own concentration camps (which, since the flight of the Spanish Republicans, will never be any credit to our country – far from it).

Since the Occupation, the situation has changed. Zoltan keeps to himself, lies low, plays dumb. But a man has to live. Being of very muscular build, he finds work now and then at Les Halles.

Which is how he came to be taken under the wing of Jean Lecardeur, whose duty was to hand over this 'maverick' to the Police Aliens' Department, that's to say, the Germans.

'He speaks German, Russian, all the languages of the East. We should give him some false papers. He could be useful to us.'

Yes, but I can't pass him off as a Parisian when he still speaks so haltingly. In France he's mixed almost exclusively with Jews, Poles and Gypsies. Besides, his physique won't allow him to pass unnoticed. We've found him a job as a labourer with a timber merchant, at Clamart. And it's turned out well. According to Lecardeur, the Hungarian feels the need to get rid of so much physical energy that, in addition to his job, he seeks out and cheerfully performs the most arduous tasks. I went to see him twice. I was pleasantly surprised by his evident intelligence, his knowledge of men, his patient indulgence towards those of a pig-headed or fanatical disposition. To enable him to improve his French, I lent him the series of novels by Panant Istrati: *Kyra Kyralina, Uncle Anghel* . . . He devours them and in just a few days has already made astounding progress.

The Old Man Who Appears After Midnight

It was raining outside. All day long a persistent drizzle imbued garments, faces, even the walls with a kind of chilly dampness that seemed to seep from within. We'd met up, all the artist crowd, at the Quatre-Fesses.

Feeling dejected and chilled, we'd unadventurously ordered for ourselves, each man for himself, some pretty poor quality drinks: thin red or acid white wine.

When Olga, a brunette with her hair cut very short, pudding-basin style, had reassured herself that none of us was in any mood to misbehave, she said, 'All right. This evening, drinks are on the house.' Thereupon she opened a litre of punch and immediately set it on the stove to warm up.

The atmosphere soon improved. We all had something to say about the rain and we started chatting. During the course of the evening Gérard gave Olga one of his canvases.

I gave her friend Suzy some engravings I happened to have with me. And Paquito – a new recruit – offered to go and fetch coal from the bunker at the back of the yard the following morning. Olga and her companion were so touched by these demonstrations of generous goodwill that the glasses of punch were succeeded with a pretty good Beaujolais, accompanied by a rustled-up snack.

Outside the rain grew bolder. Now less furtive, it drummed

down fiercely, and occasionally a vicious gust would drive it horizontally against the windowpanes. Olga asked us to help her lower the shutter and bolt the door, so we'd be more cosy. Who could possibly be expected to turn up at such a late hour in weather like this?

It was then that she appeared in the doorway, breathless from running, dripping wet, with her hat in her hand. Very beautiful. Really very beautiful. She gave the impression of having fallen with the rain, and as she wiped her face, of swallowing childish tears.

Her name was Elisabeth. She stayed, not in too much hurry to leave, waiting for the rain to stop. She stared at all of us in turn. She was probably surprised that, having asked her name, none of us felt the need to pose any further questions.

It was for fear of being disappointed, of finding out she was stupid or not at all virginal. We were satisfied with her just as she was. Her wet hair and pale face lent her the charms of a water-sprite.

Olga had taken off her shabby coat and hung it to dry by the stove.

The rain intensified, we could hear it pelting on the asphalt and roofs. We'd turned off the light that could be seen from outside. Huddled in the semi-darkness, squeezed up next to each other, we were about to take it in turn to recite in hushed tones one of the poems that haunt our memories.

At that moment brakes screeched outside the door. There were two sharp knocks on the iron shutter, then two more with a greater interval between them. 'It's Edmond,' said Olga. 'I'll go and let him in.'

She went down the corridor.

'It's no joke getting in here!'

My chum Edmond and his inseparable companion Bucaille jigged about, shaking themselves dry. Naturally they ordered drinks – all round, would you believe it!

We really liked Edmond and Bucaille. Nevertheless, they'd broken the incipient spell and we were disappointed. I was certainly annoyed with them.

True to form, after cracking a few coarse jokes, though not

too obscene on account of Elisabeth being there, these two cronies got out their notebooks and pencils, and started settling some business between themselves. Within two minutes they were shouting and hurling abuse at each other as though about to come to blows.

Edmond had put down in front of him a pile of old books that had been saved from pulping. The boys and I started to look through them. The argument between the two rag-pickers went on interminably. It's all beyond me, but I think I understood that one of them was accusing the other of having sold him some copper more dearly than the going rate. They ended up shouting figures at each other. 'A hundred and eighty!' 'Two hundred and five!' Then from behind the stove, behind the rest of us, a shrill quavering voice said very calmly, 'A hundred and eighty-eight! It's dropped six francs since the day before yesterday!'

I had plenty of time to notice that the Old Man's hair and beard were unruffled and completely dry as if he were immune to the weather, or had emerged from some underground tunnel whose outlet nobody knew of.

He asked for some warm milk and gazed at us good-humouredly.

'So, my friends.'

He pointed to Elisabeth.

'Who's this young lady?'

'A friend,' said Gérard.

'Elisabeth,' said the water-sprite with a smile.

The Old Man Who Appears After Midnight stroked his beard with that familiar slow gesture.

'Elisabeth . . . mmmmm . . . yes . . . pretty.'

The rain drummed its fingernails on the lintel outside.

'Where does the young lady live?' asked Edmond.

'Rue d'Ulm, beyond the Pantheon, with my aunt.'

'I've got the van. No point in getting your feet wet. At five o'clock I'll give you a lift. Until then, you might as well relax . . .'

Edmond, Bucaille and Paquito started a game of cards.

Olga and Suzy dozed in each other's arms.

Gérard found a sheet of canson drawing paper and began to sketch a portrait of the girl.

As usual I offered round my packet of cigarettes. The Old Man thanked me with a meaningful smile, a smile that said, 'You don't seriously expect *me* to smoke?'

Yet he drinks milk and, on other occasions, wine. So why not?

There's no way of getting him to talk. I know he never answers direct questions, especially about himself. But that's no reason to be so timid and unenterprising. I've known fear before now – but not fearfulness. With the Old Man, that's how I was, tongue-tied and pathetic, and I felt the total absence of radiance, projections of warmth or any other emanation that might have issued from him. I was intimidated by a moving stone. The Old Man could read me like a book, and he smiled. He doesn't know how to chuckle, he can't possibly know. It was he who broke the ice.

'What became of that Pole you brought along to Rue de Bièvre one day. You seemed very anxious about him.'

I notice he addresses me as '*vous*'. I had the impression he normally used the familiar '*tu*' with everyone. His question throws me into confusion. The number of times I've thought about that moment when I felt death lurking, taking stock, as though quite at home. I try to respond. 'But that was during the daytime. You weren't there. How could you . . .?'

To silence me, a wave of his hand, and the same meaningful smile, which this time said more or less, 'You don't seriously expect me *not* to know something?'

I yield to his authority. 'The lad survived. He's not in France any more. He's keeping himself in training somewhere else, until he can get back to work.' And I made a noise, 'Bzzz . . . bzzz . . .', pointing at the ceiling.

The Old Man looks at me intently. 'No news of Keep-on-Dancin'?'

'No. Because I don't want to hear any. I know he's alive and that's enough for me. Why do you ask?'

'I don't know which of the two would have been better off

134

not spending so much time with the other. But you were bound to meet.'

These words were spoken in a tone of voice that removed any suggestion of slight or offence that might have been detected in them. They mostly conveyed a strange regret. Could the 'powers' of our old after-midnight visitor be so restricted?

I've had plenty of time to relive that awful moment when, sensing Watsek to be a marked man, I exerted all my energies to try and save him, this time at least, from a fateful end. As others would have prayed with the most concentrated fervour.

Watsek made it. Only the young gunner was killed. There should have been two corpses. That claim was outstanding, and death wants its due. Which of the others?

If I learn of Keep-on-Dancin' 's death, even in twenty years' time, I shall feel partly responsible.

The water-sprite was tired, the light too poor. Gérard put away his drawing and decided to finish it another time: the girl had promised to come and see us again.

I borrowed a sheet of paper from Gérard and a charcoal pencil. I did a fairly elaborate sketch of the Old Man – he complied with good grace – which I carefully put away in our group's portfolio until I could fix it. Watching me strive so hard to capture his features, especially the detail on one of his hands, seemed to delight the Old Man. He didn't say why.

We made some coffee. Notre-Dame struck five o'clock. We all got to our feet. In the confusion that preceded and followed our farewells, the Old Man melted away.

The next day I bought some Lefranc fixative and borrowed Gérard's aspirator in order to preserve my portrait of the old boy, which I considered quite successful. I hunted through the portfolio in vain, I couldn't find my drawing. In the end we took out every single item it contained, one by one. I recognized my sheet of paper, carefully laid flat on a piece of white card. The drawing had completely disappeared, as though it had been rubbed out. We had to clean the bottom of the portfolio, for the cloth was blackened with charcoal powder.

Elisabeth came back to see us now and again. And then it became a habit. Very young, newly arrived from the country. No other family but her aunt, a prospector for old books and rare documents.

Funds were low: 'the black flag flew over the cooking pot'. The girl had no work experience, and certainly didn't have the face or the hands of a domestic servant or waitress. We wanted to help her out.

Gérard eventually sold a few canvases. Paquito received some pretty meagre funds from his family, but they came regularly. Séverin survived, by falsifying foreigners' passports when their visitor's permit expired. For this, he used my own fake ID materials. As for myself, I put everything I earned into the kitty, as well as my allowance from the network budget. For everyone it became easier to get by. Meanwhile Doudou Landier, born in Tahiti, an excellent painter and sculptor, was allowed to 'join the club'. And Clément Dulaure, a sign painter, decorator – wood-graining and marbling – who thought that because he occasionally copied a postcard with the skill of a good craftsman it was only natural he should be included in our group. Much younger than the rest of us, and 'not one of the lads', he was soon Elisabeth's lovesick suitor. A very pure, shy, romantic suitor. Apart from the poet's cape, all he needed was the balcony, the guitar and the knotted climbing rope.

One day we hatched a scheme amongst ourselves. We'd get Elisabeth to pose for a few hours a day in Doudou's room, which was spacious. We'd pay her, and it would be too bad if one of us didn't manage to produce a saleable piece of work out of it.

Dressed up in more or less bizarre costumes, the girl posed with a guitar, a child, a bandoneon, and a large earthernware oil jar that we chose to see as an amphora.

The lovesick Clément didn't get back till the evening.

Our canvases, gouaches and drawings found favour here and there among the local metal traders. Géga especially became something of a patron.

On one occasion Elisabeth agreed without any problem to

pose with a bared breast. It was with no ulterior motive, and certainly with great tactfulness that we asked her to give us a few quick full-nude poses every day. To show her how natural, commonplace, necessary and uncomplicated it was, we took her to the Grande-Chaumière one day.

She agreed, on condition we kept it a total secret. And above all, above all, 'Don't tell Clément! He'd be really upset.'

Ah! That body, that line, that pearly whiteness! For the past two months we've felt akin to the artists of classical antiquity.

Chapter VIII

*England. That peninsula
is connected to the Continent only by the sea-bed
because of the wariness of its inhabitants.*

Pierre Mac Orlan

London, February–March 1944

Exploring London in wartime, a city with stiff upper lip, gritted teeth, clenched fists, makes you realize that Paris is a bit of whore.

Every day and every night for weeks now, London has been bleeding and hiding its wounds with impressive dignity. A *'don't show off'* attitude prevails. From time to time a sputtering doodle-bug (a V1) shatters the torpor of the overcast sky. One second, sometimes two . . . at most three . . . of silence. Visualising that fat cigar with shark fins as it stops dead, sways, idiotically tips over, then goes into a vertical dive. And explodes. Usually it's an entire building that's destroyed.

Apparently the Civil Defence rescue teams observe a very strict rule of discretion and restraint. You never see any panic. In this impassive city detachment is the expression of panic.

I'm obliged to keep secret what's happening in Paris, and above all the nature of the mission that brings me here for a short stay. At a barracks in the south, beyond Morden, a model of the base at Brétigny has been built, partly on the basis of my information, on a scale of one to a thousand – which is huge. The teams that are to be sent in to plough up the runways and destroy ammunition depots and magazines at this important transit camp study the topography of the terrain in minute detail. Every two days accurate reports come in – *Secret Urgent* – on the location of new flak equipment. Good work if ever there was.

I'm kitted out with the blue uniform of a flying officer, although my original service branch is the infantry. French circles here are dismal: in commenting on events, no one demonstrates any nobility of sentiment, let alone the most basic sense of History. At Patriotic School, in Duke Street, where we meet to attend lectures devoid of interest, visitors cannot but be dismayed by the extraordinary mediocrity of those who fully expect one day to become prominent figures. It's less demoralizing at the St James's club where men of action dine and clink their jars of stout, play bridge and talk of nothing but the weather, literature (detective novels!), food and women.

The East End, Whitechapel in particular, has lost the essence of that somewhat perfidious charm that seems calculated to bear out Mac Orlan.

Admittedly, at Old Berlemont's in Dean Street, there are evenings when you can enjoy a good dose of hearty laughter and a rather inane, self-confident unconcern redolent of the boulevard or the banks of the Seine. But it doesn't happen very often. Frith Street has the Mars, a Greek restaurant where a congenial group of French-speaking intellectuals gather. None of them admits to angling for a job above the level of under-secretary of state in the future French government once the country's liberated. This modesty is entirely to their credit. But I'd like to see their faces if they had to get through a French-Gestapo police raid at St-Michel or anywhere near a Paris railway station, with their pockets stuffed with incriminating documents.

I had only one thing on my mind: to track down Dr Garrett. And I have. This energetic old man is a Major and teaches, at West Norwood Hospital, foreign doctors and nurses recruited to the Home Guard.

He recognized me straight away – after nine years! – and his evident delight gave me great pleasure. He asked me how much time I had to spare, and whether I'd recently flown over Paris. He must have understood from my embarrassed reply that I wasn't free to talk, however much I would have liked to satisfy his curiosity. Garret made no secret of his intention to monopolize my every available moment.

I eagerly consented: spending time with a man like him is the most wonderful escape. Garrett lives in Harold Road, not far from the Convent Hill Catholic School, recently hit by a flying bomb. He lives by himself in a small bedsit converted into an improvised laboratory – which is something of a collection of curiosities, and not at all common in England. Mrs Garrett, also a doctor, runs a department at the hospital in B, a town in Wales where the couple have their family home.

Normally, Dr Garrett is not involved in therapeutic medicine. An ethnologist and biologist, he gives the layman the impression of dissipating his energies in strangely divergent areas. To anyone familiar with his work who has been following his progress, it all makes complete sense.

Garrett is of Scottish origin. He speaks every one of the Highland dialects, as well as Welsh, Gaelic, and the different Breton languages. But he's absolutely impervious to French.

He brings me up to date with his most recent research, which the war has to some extent interrupted. For a few months every year he scours not only the South of England but also Scotland, Ireland, the Isle of Man and as far north as the Shetlands, in search of rare objects that are all used for a particular purpose: magic rituals, which apparently persist to an extraordinary degree in all these parts of the country.

Some of his finds he keeps, right here in fact: chalices of hammered pewter, elaborately-wrought goblets, bracelets of bone or ivory engraved with runic symbols; pots of every shape; books, parchments, very ancient documents in which geometric figures are scattered throughout texts in foreign languages, some in 'English-style' Latin, others in Gaelic and even Friesian.

It's Garrett's ambition after the war to set up a museum dedicated to witchcraft as once practised, and indeed still practised, throughout northeastern Europe.

When I expressed surprise at the fact that Garrett should compromise with systematic quirkiness the more 'pragmatic' concerns with which I associated him, the doctor launched into a long explanation in which he stated that human knowledge was now ridiculously circumscribed, that for thousands of years occultism had been crucial to the most extraordinary instances of scientific 'revelations' to mankind, and he put forward the hypothesis that the great civilizations of Memphis, Nineveh, Carthage and Babylon were perhaps not solely the product of millions of brutalized slaves ruled by a mindless elite.

He argued strongly that the study of paranormal phenomena ought to be pursued in depth, especially during times when serious upheavals such as this present war were afflicting the planet.

A siren interrupted his monologue, which was almost like a sermon.

I don't really think I betrayed the Allied cause in revealing to Garrett that I'd come from Paris and was returning there shortly. He hasn't been back to France since 1919. He asks me if the mausoleum erected near the Arc de Triomphe still exists. He overwhelms me with questions about my ancient city, and especially the St Séverin neighbourhood, which seems to interest him more than any other. I assume it's because of Huysmans. I think I exceeded his hopes by relating in detail all the strange events I've witnessed in the last few years. He was extremely interested in my account of the jinxing of the house in Rue de Bièvre by the Gypsy. He asked me to describe in the most minute detail the wooden statuette that turned up in old Hubert's cellars.

'I've been postponing my honeymoon every summer for the past twenty-five years,' he said. 'I'm longing to show my wife round this Paris of legends. I want to get over there as soon as possible.'

'I look forward to making you welcome.'

Rue des Maléfices

He talked about St Séverin. I seized my opportunity.

'What became of the document you once showed me: a

map of the City and the Sorbonne district, with place names in old English?'

'It's in my library, in B. It's one of the most precious items in my collection.'

'You remember that Rue Zacharie, marked on your map with the name Witchcraft Street – Rue des Maléfices?'

'Of course I do, I remember your amazement, and your interest in researching the history of that ancient district. Have you come across any further information on Witchcraft Street?'

'I know that for just a few years it was called Rue des Trois-Chandeliers, and towards the end of the thirteenth century Rue de l'Homme-Qui-Chante.'

'And do you know why?'

'I think the three candlesticks commemorate an exorcism. According to the ancient ritual for pronouncing the Great Anathema and exorcizing the evil spirit attached to a man or an object, three priests dressed in their ceremonial stoles, after reciting the sacred words, must hurl to the ground three candlesticks, each bearing three lighted candles. The nine flames are supposed to be extinguished simultaneously. Holy water is then sprinkled on the ground or on the object now freed from demonic possession. As for the name Rue de L'Homme-Qui-Chante, I don't know what the explanation for that is, much to my regret, because it must relate to a very ancient and probably very splendid legend, now lost for ever.'

Garrett was rinsing glasses with a smile. From a cupboard filled with books and journals, on the door of which hung a helmet, a ration box and a gas mask, he produced a whisky flask.

'Sit back and make yourself comfortable. I'm going to recount that legend to you. I myself am not allowed to commit it to writing for it belongs to the oral tradition perpetuated since the fifteen century by members of an extremely exclusive secret society, which I agreed to join, more out of curiosity than intellectual need. With my express authorization, you a foreigner will be allowed to record it and add it to your archives.'

Dumbfounded, I lit a pipe and waited, 'wet with anticipation', as Keep-on-Dancin' would have said.

'First of all, you need to know – to remember, rather – some historical facts that regrettably tend to be forgotten in France. The fact that Paris was for many years an English capital. The fact that when "our" king', (I started to smile), 'Henry V made his entry into "your" capital on the first of December 1420 – what on earth are you laughing at?'

'You talk of "my" capital, which is fine by me, as long as you don't blame me for what my compatriots were up to five hundred years ago. But "your" king Henry V . . . Where were your ancestors at that time, Dr Garrett? Are you quite sure they were his subjects, and if so, were they willing subjects?'

'That's the least of my concerns. I was saying that when he entered Paris, Henry V, King of England, was acclaimed by the populace.'

'It requires only the slightest sense of mystification to get anyone acclaimed by any crowd. These days . . .'

'If I may continue: Henry V was proclaimed King of France and England at St Denis. He was later crowned at Notre-Dame to great rejoicing.'

'In other words, you're justifying the Hundred Years' War.'

'More or less. For it enabled our two peoples to become deeply interdependent, allowing the most fruitful of intellectual exchanges.'

'You mean, the French are "anglicized" without knowing it.'

'And the English have assimilated their Continental experience from that time much more than you think. But this is what I was leading up to: the Englishman is essentially a mystical being. And, because he's scrupulous, he's apprehensive. And therefore susceptible to everything that might be interpreted as a superhuman manifestation, whether it be a legend of esoteric significance – as in this case – or an event of peculiar resonance. Don't forget, all the official bodies in Paris – parliament, clergy, and especially the university – were in favour of the English at the period I'm talking about.'

'Of course!'

'And that your University had such influence here that it attracted the elite of our own faculties' future members. Now, the English, Scots and Irish who stayed in your Latin Quarter must have fallen so much under Paris's spell that they've left us with the most stirring collection of tales, legends and fables connected with the City's stones. Here then, is the story of the Man-Who-Sings, orally transmitted by the descendents of a Welsh officer who heard it there.'

A man was dying. And he knew it. He was beyond suffering, at the utmost limit of his strength. His final steps were numbered. As were his final moments and his last wishes. In deep and quiet contemplation, in which were mingled love of the poor and forgiveness of the wicked, he'd already taken leave of the living, with whom he would no longer concern himself.

It only remained for him to bid farewell to non-living things, the silent and familiar witnesses of an arid, dull and joyless life. The man had overestimated his capabilities. For while bustling mankind that passed by him in Rue Sac-à-Lie took even less notice of his presence than ever before, the things that loved him – and had never told him so, perhaps they realized too late – were loath to see him depart for ever. They tried desperately to detain him.

The dying man thought he had just enough strength to make his way to the end of his street, from St Séverin, the church under whose porch he'd so long been a beggar, to the banks of the Seine – at that time the embankments were gently sloping.

It was twilight. Exhausted, the man leaned against the wall as he walked. People called out to each other, children ran about and shouted, creating a disturbance. And these excessively loud noises danced in moving colours before the man's eyes, who thought he would collapse.

At the place where the street narrows, a lantern hanging above a pile of rubbish winked at the man and reflected back to him as a blazing ball a fragment of the setting sun. And the man was wounded by this light, and the purple and gold that caught the roof-edges bruised his pupils, and the farewell fraught with unspoken regret that the stones, and shop signs, and the dancing, grimacing marmousets on the corbels bade him, wrang his poor heart. Utterly exhausted, the man was about to sink to the ground, like an empty wine-skin. But the woman kept him from doing so.

She too had that look in her eyes of those who are dying. She was walking up the street, making the same slow progress as the man trying to reach the tree on the riverbank that he had chosen to lie down beside, where he would die, gazing up at the stars. The woman turned and came back. She slipped an ice-cold hand under the man's arm to support him. Then as the dying couple, already detached from all life on this earth, covered the remaining distance, darkness instead of falling rose from the earth.

Darkness rose from the shadows, stones, gloomy crannies, like a living ink. And as this dense and opaque darkness, welling up from below, engulfed the town, the woman gained strength and her grip became assured. She held her arm around the man and led him firmly to the fateful tree, where they lay down on the riverbank as night filled the sky and blackened the contours of the stars' eyes. No one understood exactly the nature of the contract that bound these two beings.

But the following day there were no bodies found beneath the tree.

Who that woman was, no one ever knew, nor what became of her.

As for the man, suddenly filled with renewed vitality in which he revelled with robust joy, he sang in the street. He sang in a high, clear, warm voice abounding with all the light of the world.

But he was now blind.

Chapter IX

Paris, May 1944

It's Sunday. It's very sunny.

I left England at midnight on Thursday, and here I am dawdling along the Quai de la Tournelle, with a Dunhill pipe in my mouth, and my hands in the roomy pockets of a raincoat to which the Thames' fogginess still clings.

Whenever I pass a German, or even just people-who-don't-know, I've the childish impression of having played a good trick on them, and I chuckle to myself.

My goodness! He must be tough, this *Oberleutnant*. Although an infantryman, he's wearing his iron cross pinned to his collar. He's kitted out with the full paraphernalia of an artist and is quietly painting a canvas – not bad, not bad at all: the succession of bridges, and in the foreground some broad-beamed barges that have been tied up for months, straining at their moorings.

He's given it the commercial artist's treatment, the colours too bold with that I.G. Farben look. He must be Bavarian. This romantic with his long slender hands, insensitive to the slate-grey shimmerings on the water this side of the island, will never be able to appreciate the subdued subtlety of the flickering light on this branch of the Seine.

Inside my pocket I roll into a ball a very unwisely preserved London bus ticket. I flick it into the water with an inner guffaw.

To the regular stroller along the embankment, the book-sellers have grown so familiar, by their silhouettes, their voices, their little ways – their choice of merchandise and how they display it on their stalls – that they awaken obscure needs, no less strong than unacknowledged.

If one of them moves, shifts his boxes, his stall a hundred metres, a whole slowly-established equilibrium is disturbed. The entire riverbank has to be 'rethought'. All the more so, if he crosses the bridges, migrates to the other side of the river: the disruption is comparable to that which would be caused by the relocation overnight of the Sainte-Chapelle to Montmartre.

I have a lot of bookseller friends. In particular, on the right bank, Fallet, father and son, and Borel-Rosny, a novelist when the fancy takes him. But on the left bank – the Favoured One – we might as well say all of them.

Pierre-Luc Lheureux sells books to make a living, but he's a poet, and far from being the only one in that situation. He holds court, from a bench facing his boxes, at the corner of Pont de l'Archevêché. With jet-black hair and a fastidious concern for a certain sartorial elegance, he's apt to make declarations of faith that reflect the most uncompromising pacificism. From whatever distance he catches sight of me, he treats me to a broad smile: and it's not because you're easily pleased that this is something you appreciate.

'A sophisticated tippler disdainful of swill', Pierre-Luc shares my own liking – which, it will have been noticed, and this I readily concede, is considerable – for Cabernet served at the right temperature, in other words, ice cold. So when a new delivery is advertised in one of the local watering-holes, we usually go along together to sample the quality of the nectar. Sometimes we find ourselves heading for the Ile St-Louis, but more often than not we walk past Notre-Dame and make for Desmolières, on Rue des Ursins. To get there, you have to cross the Pont-au-Double.

And it's a sight worth seeing. A little bit of sunshine is all it takes.

The tramps, begging, sitting, standing, lying down, or collapsed in a heap, are legion, despite having the police on to them, anxious to keep the city looking like a village fair *à la* Breughel. Hunchbacked, one-armed, one-eyed or legless, whatever: but freshly shaven, well-turned-out, and certainly not drunk. Your destitution mustn't be taken any more seriously than the painted and bewigged destitution of the characters in a Boris Godunov production at the Opéra. To tell the truth, for anyone well acquainted with these guys – they

147

are none the less worthy of interest – the local cops, often good-natured, do have some justification in this instance. At least in being a little chary of credulity.

For if the days are past when charlatan beggar bands, the so-called '*Rifodés*' and '*Malingreux*', substituted for their sound limbs the horribly distorted or disjointed ones taken from hanged men, the tradition still persists of offering the much despised passer-by such a sorry spectacle that giving money is an instinctive reflex.

There are to my knowledge two schools of thought at which novice beggars – duly authorized to operate on a specific site to which they've acquired, often very dearly, usufructary rights – take lessons from their elders, the latter being remarkable practitioners who demonstrate extraordinary psychological insight. I suspect those masters I've had the privilege of observing at work of being former actors steeped in the art of mime.

They're the experts. They demand of their pupil that he be sober; that he pay close attention to the advice and comments meted out to him; that he display total obedience towards his master. Otherwise, the two 'schools' call for different techniques; it's easy to distinguish the adherents of one or the other.

All the same, the bosses are very good friends; they're not rivals.

'The Guv'nor', d'Aubervilliers, is tall with a bushy beard. Under his cape, which he knows how to drape artfully, he carries a guitar slung over his shoulder on which no one's ever heard him play. He doesn't deny rumours that he was once either a very great violinist, deprived of the use of his left hand in an accident, or a celebrated tenor whose voice was ruined in a shipwreck or carrying out some other act of heroism: it all depends on the imagination of the person talking, who's never the man himself. He never answers questions. When photographed, he behaves like a coy maiden caught in flagrante, and pockets the tip with lordly disdain. The punter addresses him as sir and feels the need to apologize. He told me one day that he'd based his character on that of Vitalis, one

148

of the heroes of Hector Malot's *Sans Famille*. 'The truth is,' he said, beating his thighs, 'I've never been able to sing, I don't know a single note of music . . . I've been a conman all my goddamned life!'

(This too was a lie, I know. But he was being dishonest with himself this time.)

The Guv'nor studies his new disciple closely. He works out, from the thinness or imperfections of the face, the infirmities, mutilations, wounds or malformations of the raw recruit's body, the best use to be made of them. And he assigns two, at most three, poses: one, propped up – against a pillar, a wall, a garden-square railing – the other, sitting on the ground. His pupil's then on the rack. The Guv'nor circles round, checking details that all have their own importance.

He's well acquainted with Callot's paintings, but seeing what he manages to get out of his protégés, I'm compelled by the pathos of their attitudes to cite the early masters. I think of Mantegna's stark, spare, heart-rending depictions of silent suffering. Once the pose has been conceived, determined, vetted in the smallest particular, the pupil has to return several days in succession, take up his position and under the master's watchful eye remain absolutely motionless, until he's capable of turning himself to stone. Only at that point does he 'qualify' as fit to take over a spot that provides a guaranteed income and not to let it depreciate in value.

'The few centimes from the regular patron who passes by every day at the same time from one year's end to the next are worth a great deal more than the ever possible hundred francs from some future passer-by,' the Guv'nor maintains. 'I demand of my guys that they hold their poses like statues. The patron who has once given to them must never more be able to act otherwise.'

The Guv'nor is against the flaunting of stumps or skeletal limbs. 'There's no need,' he says, 'to overdo it.' In this, he is at odds with his crony All-by-Myself, who runs a school at Nanterre. He trains a lot of women, whereas the Guv'nor won't have anything to do with them. Those that All-by-Myself takes in hand, he instructs to adopt an exaggeratedly moronic look: staring eyes, half-open mouth. All-by-Myself's people are mobile and active, unlike the Guv'nor's. Nearly all of them have to feign some nervous complaint, unless they actually suffer from one: the constant trembling of a limb, the face, even the whole body, spasmodic convulsions, but it's the eyes that really count. The beggar accosts the client in motion, head-on. She stops dead in front of him. She stares at him with frantic insistence, holding out a trembling hand. The victim, seeing his way barred, has no alternative but to delve into his pockets. Woe betide him if he should try without discourtesy gently to move aside the importunate nuisance. The latter takes a tumble – she knows how to fall – and mobilizes the local begging fraternity who are duty-bound and only too pleased to raise an outcry. This is how good old traditions survive. The Middle Ages had the '*sabouleux*', harmless acrobats who chewed saponary, better known as soapwort. The froth they produced looked like the foaming at the mouth of falling sickness. These fake epileptics would throw themselves into contortions that upset no one. People paid out depending on how spectacular the performance was.

The Sleeper on the Pont-au-Double

So, that glorious Sunday when the uncertainty of the morrow seemed to cast scarcely a shadow over anyone's face, Pierre-Luc and I crossed the Pont-au-Double, having observed the row of tramps slumped on the ground, stupefied with red wine.

At the corner of the bridge, on his folding chair, with his walking stick between his legs, was the Sleeper. For years I'd noticed this motionless creature, but vaguely at first, without paying closer attention. He doesn't beg, strikes no pose: he sleeps, that's all.

The raincoat he wears in all weathers is threadbare, but scrupulously brushed. He has a beret on his head. The uppers and soles of his shoes – the soles being of decent thickness – still hold together. He sleeps.

He's not bad-looking, his face bears no indelible marks of vice or illness: he sleeps peacefully, calmly, from morning till evening – if it doesn't rain. I've never been there to see him arrive or leave: I know nothing of the sound of his voice, the way he moves, the colour of his eyes: all I know is, he sleeps.

Nor had I ever spoken to anyone about him. Today, however, I said to Pierre-Luc, 'How strange. Whenever you go anywhere near all these dozy wretches, you sense their presence, you know there's a stubborn life lurking within those slumped bodies. I get a completely different sensation from this sleeping man: it's as if he, or some part of him, were very far away. As if he were hollow, empty, and this emptiness – how can I put it? – sucks in whatever goes on outside. I'd find it very difficult to stop here for any length of time. I feel as if I'm relinquishing a little of my own substance.'

Pierre-Luc gave me a peculiar look.

'There's something in that,' he said, 'there's something in that.'

'But who is this man?'

'I thought you knew him. It's Lancelin. So, are we still on for Desmolières?'

I noted with surprise that Pierre-Luc, who usually had quite a lot to say for himself, wasn't at all happy to talk about the Sleeper, quite the opposite. This only intrigued me all the more. I pressed him.

'He lived for some years in Africa, then South America. Some people say he's a chemist, others a former missionary. I don't rightly know. He contracted a terrible disease in some insalubrious country, which has left him half paralysed. His movements are very slow. He sleeps all the time. But his brain's unaffected. Fortunately, there's his brother.'

'Ah! He has a brother?'

'A twin brother who looks after him, feeds him, puts him to bed, as a nurse takes care of a patient. It's the brother that brings him here around mid-morning, and comes to fetch him at nightfall.'

'I'm glad to hear it . . . But what does the brother do?'

'They "work" together . . .'

'Why the sarcasm?'

'I'm not being in the least sarcastic. But I'd prefer to explain some other time. I don't know why, I can't face telling you about the poor wretch today.'

Once we'd spoken of him, circumstances conspired to bring us back to the subject. Yesterday, Pierre-Luc and I were taking the same stroll. As if he hadn't stirred since the day before, the Sleeper was at his post. But this time he was the butt of laughter from passers-by. Three pranksters – probably students – had placed a placard at his feet reading DEAF-MUTE FROM BIRTH, along with an ancient phonograph they'd set up to grind out that well-known old song:

> '*C'est la femme aux bijoux*
> *Celle qui rend fou*
> *C'est une enjoleu-se . . .*'
> [It's the bejewelled woman
> Who can drive a man insane
> With her seductive wiles . . .]

Admittedly, the effect was comic. Our three lads were having a good laugh – with not the least malicious intent. But Pierre-Luc took great exception to this. He flew into a rage of which I'd never have thought him capable, tossed both phonograph and placard into the Seine, and harangued the trio, who cleared off, vexed and a bit shame-faced.

'You still don't want to tell me what it is that he does with his brother?'

'Go and take a walk round the flea market at Bicêtre one Sunday. Now, can we talk about something else?'

That's all I could get out of him.

Bad news. Two of our agents, who were cycling to the Swiss border with documents of considerable importance, have been stopped on the road between Dijon and Lyon. No other information has reached us but this undoubted fact: they are now in the hands of the Germans. It's absolutely imperative this mission is repeated and, no matter what, that someone else is sent. Aside from that, we've had no news from our auxiliary network in Bordeaux. The Gestapo is wreaking havoc. And we've never had so many, or more urgent, messages to transmit. It will be like this to the end, which the more gung-ho among us hope will come soon. Peace or an all-out battle. But no more of this life of dissimulation that we're not cut out for.

I've rented an apartment near Châtelet, right in the heart of Paris, on the sixth floor under the roof. A roof I can get out onto without leaving my own home, and put up an antenna, ten metres high or more if necessary, without any problem.

From here, every evening at five o'clock, the radio operators make contact with London and transmit for ten minutes. As well as the refrigerators at Les Halles, there are in this district so many goods lifts, machinery and electrical equipment that the continuous interference makes the detection of radio signals extremely difficult for the direction finders. But I'm wary of every possible setback, and the moment has come to go and check out the contacts Keep-on-Dancin' gave me.

Keep-on-Dancin'

I started with the place closest to my new home: the Gobelet d'Argent, in Rue du Cyne, on the corner of Rue Pierre-Lescot.

A curious-looking little bistrot, a triangular-shaped recess whose frontage, aiming for a neo-Gothic style, is decorated with a variety of ornate mouldings. There are whores at the counter. And two somewhat unprepossessing fellows playing dice.

Pastis served in a cup to make you think that customs and excise don't know what's going on.

A busty tart scenting a potential client gives me a deeply meaningful, heavily masscara-ed look. I acknowledge it by offering her a cigarette. I convey my refusal with a world-weary smile. And, following Keep-on-Dancin's instructions:

'Is Solange around?'

'Which one?' says the tart. 'The new one or the old one? Tall or short?'

'I don't know . . . a friend sent me. The new one, has she been here long?'

'Oh, no . . . She came out of the slammer three weeks ago . . .'

'Then I think it must be the other one. Will you have something?'

Her black satin–corseted boobs wobble like jelly. She pulls the door handle towards her and yells into the empty street.

'Mimile!'

A lazy voice answers from upstairs.

'Yeah . . .'

'Go and fetch Solange, and hurry up about it!'

'All right! All right! I'm going . . .'

A German walks in. The tart comes over all kittenish. A Persian kitten, on account of the possum fur wrap she's wearing. Overcome, sinking on to a stool too small for her large buttocks, she says, 'Rascal!' The Hun glances at her, steely-eyed. He shouts, '*Weg da! Weg!*' Furious, outraged, he takes off without even finishing his beer.

The girl gets indignant.

'What's wrong with the guy? Honestly, they're all poofs . . . If this carries on, I'm going back to working in a brothel.'

I have to fork out ten francs to get rid of the guy in a flunkey's jacket who's brought Solange. She's very, very pretty. Like a Dresden doll. She offers me a slender hand, questioning me with her big bright eyes that have no need of any make-up.

I say under my breath, 'Keep-on-Dancin' . . .'

'Ah, right! Come with me.'

Her voice isn't in the least bit rough. This girl, a tart? I don't get it. She walks quickly, with me on her heels, sweeps into a hotel on Rue Pierre-Lescot, takes the stairs four at a time, calls out in front of the glassed-in office on the mezzanine, 'It's Solange. I'm going up to number eight.'

'Well, what happened?'

'What do you mean?'

'With the Corsican?'

'I don't really know. I don't ask questions.'

She's surprised.

'Really? What's your name?'

I give her the agreed alias. She seems delighted.

'Oh, that's great! My, did he go on about you! You've sure got a friend there, one in a million! So, what can we do for you?'

'Nothing right now. I just thought I'd make contact. If there's trouble, I might have to show up at any old time, unannounced. And when that happens, I'll need . . . absolutely everything.'

'Don't worry, worse things have happened. Going by your own name?'

'Yes.'

'Ever done time?'

'No.'

'No problem then.'

We chatted about the war, the long-awaited landing, and Keep-on-Dancin', especially about him, for whom Solange has the most touching admiration.

'Guys like that, they don't make them any more. Not since the last war. Today's young lads, they're wimps, I'm telling you.'

That's it: she's dropped the formality. We're on familiar terms now. The ice has been broken. And I found out a few things I didn't know!

'Yes, it was Tricksy-Pierrot that told us. Sacchi didn't play straight. Keep-on-Dancin' beat him up in a bar . . .'

'I know, I was there.'

'. . . and told him to stay away from La Montagne and not set foot in this neighbourhood – in fact, anywhere they might have run into each other. Sacchi, the little creep, was determined to betray the gang to the cops before making himself scarce. He tried twice: the first time, everyone got away. But the second time the cops had some informers in place: they caught Brizou red-handed.'

'Ah, so Brizou's been arrested.'

'Joseph Brizou, yes. And he won't be out for a while. There were a hell of a lot of charges outstanding against him. Keep-on-Dancin' was livid. It didn't take him long to track down Sacchi's address: he'd gone to ground in a villa on the main road near Melun. One fine morning Keep-on-Dancin' and Pierrot went to pay him a visit. Sacchi knew he was done for. He wouldn't open the door. They climbed over the gate and found our Corsican friend telephoning the police. Well, they didn't mess about. Crrr! Crrr! Crrr! His throat and both flappers. They made their escape through the garden as the fuzz arrived from the other direction. They managed to shake them off and cut across country. They filched clothes they found in barns. Disguised as yokels, they legged it to Mormant, where they caught the train. That was a fair old distance they covered!'

'What about the ears? What's become of them?'

'Keep-on-Dancin' wanted to keep them both as lucky charms. He was obsessed with the idea. But he dropped one as he scarpered. It wasn't a good moment to go back and look for it . . .'

'I don't know where Keep-on-Dancin' is now, and I don't want to know. But if you get a chance to send him a message, tell him not to keep it, tell him from me.'

'Not to keep what? The flapper?'

'Yes, the flapper.'

I describe to her what happened at Klager's place, the Bièvre, the ointment, the smell. She gazes at me with a reproachful expression.

'Seeing as you claim to be a friend of his, that was when you should have killed the Corsican.'

'There's no guarantee that would have settled the matter. And you have to understand, not everyone's free to do as they like.'

Solange asked me if Keep-on-Dancin' had told me about that psychic circuit – those uncanny places – he'd identified, running through the streets of Paris. I described my enthusiasm the night my new friend had expounded his ideas on the subject of cyclical events and fateful whereabouts. Solange went into raptures.

'He's a smart guy, there's no one smarter. You know, it's because of him I'm in this room. He identified the place, just like that, without knowing anything about it. He came with some newspapers, really old and all yellowed, that referred to the house way back in the past. I think he even asked an architect for the plans.

'He said, "It's number eight I want." He got himself introduced to the owner and talked him into it. He paid a year in advance, a whole year! They moved the previous tenant next door, and here I am.'

The building isn't new. The walls are thick. The solid doors have old grilled hatches in them. There's an enormous beam running across the ceiling.

'And have you noticed anything special about this place?'

She rests her hand on my arm, confidingly. 'Listen, my friend. Most of the clients I bring up here – the ones I have now are almost exclusively regulars – it's not even for sex. They want me to listen to them: they come, a long way even, to tell me the story of their life, in minute detail, in every particular, and to share with me whatever's on their mind. So I give them advice, when I'm confident of not getting it wrong. They nearly all want to be comforted. What do I do? I cosset them. You've no idea how sweet they are. And stupid. But I'm the sentimental type. The more stupid they are, the more I like them. It's just the way I am.'

She had a tear in her eye.

'And Keep-on-Dancin', is he . . . protecting you, then?'

'Oh, I'm not his girl. He's a pal, a real pal, like no other. As long they know that, no one's going to give me any trouble.'

'Tell me, is it you or the room that encourages your clients to bare their souls?'

'Both. Anywhere else doesn't have the same effect on them. Or on me. Keep-on-Dancin' told me, "You'll hear all sorts of things here. But no one will ever be able to put one over on you." And it's true: there are punters who'd like to pass themselves off as their boss, as someone more successful than they are. Not that it matters, mind. But no way is there any bullshitting within these four walls. They all come clean. When I see Keep-on-Dancin' again, I'll get him to give me the lowdown on what happened here before. I'm interested now. He mentioned some Russian and his girl . . .'

Good Lord! I've just twigged. I knew it was Rue Pierre-Lescot, but I didn't know it was in this building, and probably in this very room. April 1814. The Empire was in its final death throes. A few Cossak cavalry squadrons with the Prussian regiments, having entered the capital through the gate at Clichy, bivouacked for a day and a night on the Champs-Elysées. After a dismal parade at the end of which, if contemporary historiographers are to be believed, the Parisian 'upper crust' behaved with a certain lack of dignity, the troops were granted furlough and had to be divided up into different sectors. The officers were billeted at the Palais-Royal, the men quartered in the Great Fleecery. Rue Pierre-Lescot, it was said at the time, cost the Russian army as much as a battle.

'An unfortunate girl,' it was later reported in *The Constitutional*, 'seduced and abandoned by her seducer, and who had subsequently fallen into the abyss of prostitution', happened to end up spending the night with a Cossak NCO. Among the jewellery that her vanquisher, like a real barbarian, dangled before her eyes, she recognized a family medallion that her brother, a sergeant in the National Guard, always wore over his heart. It couldn't have been taken from him without first killing him. So the girl was obliged to yield herself to her brother's murderer.

Resistance was impossible, but not revenge. While the sated Cossak slept, Judith took one of Holophernes' pistols and blew his brains out. The next day she made a full confession of what had motivated her to do this. The French police, obliged to incarcerate the culprit and inform the Tsar's representatives, during the night substituted for the prisoner some poor wretched woman who had died at the Hotel-Dieu.

And Judith continued to pursue elsewhere her career as a prostitute driven to despair.

Solange was keen we should spend part of the evening together. But I didn't have time. She said as we parted, 'If by chance your work gets you involved with some dubious type, a guy you don't trust, bring him to me, he'll lay himself bare, just like the others. You know, I can be a real bitch, if I want to.' I kissed her with genuine affection. It's the first time I've ever felt this way about a whore.

I gave Solange's offer serious consideration. I'd like to know what Heisserer (alias Lagarde) is up to. The other day he tracked me down at the Quatre-Fesses, where I thought I was safe. His fake ration card needed to be stamped, to make it look as if he'd collected his quarterly allocation of coupons from the town hall. For the police even check up on that.

But I have the feeling that was just an excuse. Heisserer told me that since he has no regular job at the moment, he was prepared to help me out if there was anything he could do. If necessary, he would travel.

I need liaison agents for Paris: our best cyclists have gone to the South, or Normandy. I gave Heisserer some money – in fact he didn't seem to need it particularly – and put him in the hands of the secretaries at the operations centre, promising to take him on 'officially' later if he proved satisfactory and providing he liked the work. It's only now that I have some misgivings – very vague, actually – about this guy.

It was as easy as anything. Yesterday the four of us had dinner together: Heisserer, Solange, and Paulette, my former neighbour. We parted company at half past eleven, just in time to get back to our respective homes. Heisserer lives too far away. He seemed delighted that Solange should carry him off, on the grounds she'd find him a place to sleep in a more 'civilized' part of town. They must surely have gone to bed together.

The Sleeper on the Pont-au-Double

This morning, acting on Pierre-Luc's suggestion, I went and wandered round the Bicêtre flea market.

There, tramps even more wretched than in the centre of town, most of them very old, flounder among chaotic piles of scrap iron, chipped crockery, faded garments, all kinds of objects whose purpose has long been forgotten. I applied myself to reconstituting a Breton spinning-wheel, buying separate bits here and there from different traders. Two men walked very slowly among the busy junk dealers and rag mongers. The Sleeper on the Pont-au-Double and his brother, who looks amazingly like him, dressed identically, wearing the same kind of hat. I followed them. I was lucky, for they headed over to the snack bar where I'd left my purchases. They sat down. The Sleeper was served a big bowl of tapioca with milk, which his able-bodied brother fed to him with a spoon. Now and again he wiped the paralytic's lips, tidied the collar of his shirt. It was touching and very sad. After the tapioca, the Sleeper drank a few sips of wine.

'That feels better,' he said in a lifeless voice, with a heart-rending smile.

People looked on sorrowfully. They all seemed to be waiting for something. I heard them say, 'What a pity! He's such a good man!'

How could this half-untenanted carcass, quite incapable of harm or of being good for anything have created such a reputation for himself? I soon found out. The brother – they call him Monsieur Frédéric – cleared the bowl and glasses off the table and laid a notebook on it. And the procession began.

A man in blue overalls came and sat down between the two Lancelin brothers: he unhooked the top of his garment, lifted up his shirt and uncovered his hip.

'It's here that I get it,' he said.

'How did it start?' asked Monsieur Frédéric.

'Lifting a pig of iron. I went at it the wrong way; it wasn't the right position. I must have twisted my back.'

'Show me the movement you made.'

The man stood up, mimed the action of someone lifting something very heavy from the ground.

'You're not straining. Do it again and put some strength into it.'

The patient did so, but without following all the way through with it: he grimaced in pain.

'I see what the problem is.'

Monsieur Frédéric bared a little more of his hip and a bit of his back. He sat the guy down in front of the Sleeper, whose hands he took hold of and placed on the painful part of the injured man's body. Some twenty people observed the scene in total silence. The *patron* came out from behind his counter so as not to miss anything. The Sleeper, whose face, contrary to what you might expect, displays a lively intelligence, appeared to be lost in thought. He remained like this for a long while.

And then his brother said, 'That's fine. That's enough.' Monsieur Frédéric picked up his notebook. 'Your name?' he said to the patient.

'Portal. Xavier Portal.'

'Fine. Not before Tuesday morning . . .'

'Tomorrow's not possible? Really and truly?

'No. We've got Chopitel all day Monday and Thursday . . .'

'And how's he doing?' asked the *patron*.

'Better. He'll get over it. But it'll take a lot of effort and patience. Whose turn next?'

It was a pregnant woman who complained of pains in her ribs. The Sleeper's hands were applied over her clothes.

'Tuesday afternoon,' Monsieur Frédéric decided, writing in his notebook.

People queued up: cases of rheumatism, persistent migraine. An asthmatic. Monsieur Frédéric always asked such pertinent questions that he might have been a doctor. And he covered his notebook with jottings that looked like appointments for the following week. There were still people waiting.

'With the best will in the world,' he said, 'next week's fully booked.'

161

A woman groaned.

'What about my lumbago, couldn't you sleep it for me this session?'

I didn't understand. This was the first time I'd ever heard the verb 'sleep' used transitively like that. I was wondering how to get into conversation with one of the people present, and buy them a drink in order to obtain the key to the mystery, when I caught sight of Armand Lassenay.

I met him two years ago. He was a sapper involved in mine clearance. At that time he had four limbs and two eyes like everyone else. Now, he's half the man he was. A badly defused shell devastated the right side of his body. It's a miracle he's still alive. He's become a pedlar: he sells corn-cure and lighter flints in the marketplace.

We have a drink together.

'You're intrigued by the Sleeper? The fact is, you've good reason to be. The way he operates is very curious, but extremely simple in itself. As you witnessed, he applies his hands to the part of the body requiring treatment. Just for a few moments. At that stage he's not yet trying to cure anything. He calls it "connecting". He says he feels whatever the patient is suffering, the same ailments, symptoms, pain. But only for as long as the laying on of hands lasts. Then he files away the memory of what he's experienced, as you might place a book on a shelf. And he passes on to the next person. When the time comes to treat this case or that, all he has to do is recall it, and think about it as he sleeps. Think about it in a certain way, of course. After each "operation", his brother reminds him who's next on the list. He wakes him up and "connects" him to the following case.

'In the absence of the patient?'

'Yes. The patient could be five kilometres away, it wouldn't make any difference.'

'And he cures everything?'

'No. He can't mend fractures, or arrest the progress of an infectious disease once it's taken hold. But he's remarkable effective with rheumatism and anything that relates to the nervous system. And when the patient's very feeble, when a weak constitution's not doing very well, it gives you a terrific boost to have him sleep for you. I know what I'm talking about: if it weren't for him, I could hardly move the arm and leg I've been left with.'

'And does he charge a lot?'

'He never asks for anything in return. He accepts little kindnesses people might want to do for him – the odd snack, a bit of coal in winter, old clothes . . . Those two brothers are the benefactors of the poor. They could live like kings.'

'They've never been given any trouble?'

'I'd like to see anyone try. Even the medics get themselves treated by them, or call on their services for their own patients.'

Solange is the great love of my life at the moment. I took her for a walk round her neighbourhood, behind Les Halles, which she doesn't know very well. I told her all about the Truie Qui File, Traverse Philis, Cul-de-Sac Corydon. I described the Carrefour de La Coudrette, the greasy pole in Rue aux Oües, the Panier Fleuri . . .

She said, 'You know, I like you. So much, I could never go to bed with you.'

'What about on a desert island?'

'Even with all the time in the world, I'd never be able to enjoy it. I'd be too busy thinking what a pity it was.'

'And what about that guy Heiss . . . I mean, Lagarde, what do you make of him?'

'Ah, he's got me under his skin. He comes to see me every evening. I'm not too happy about it myself. I do it to please you.'

'You think there's reason to suspect him?'

'I couldn't really say. Not yet. He's a real hard nut to crack. But I'll get there. He's already told me that the Germans are going to bring out a secret weapon soon. Something first-rate. He sounds as if he can hardly wait. You must give me an address or a phone number, so I can get in contact if there's anything new.'

This fellow Heisserer bothers me. I was really too rash, too trusting, for once. I can't get rid of him now. Besides, it seems he's very good at the job. Intelligent. And doesn't lose his nerve. At the Gare de l'Est he got through a police checkpoint by showing them a fake Civil Defence card.

All the same, I'm going tell the others they must keep their eyes open.

Chapter X

I'm in a bad way. Fragments of the German grenade that knocked me out for the count, in June 1940, have reawakened. They roam about, in my side, my hip, my neck. They tickle, prick, scratch, throb, and sometimes leave me prostrate with attacks of absolutely unbearable convulsive pain. The only remedy against this is morphine injections, which I want to avoid at all costs.

For the past nine days – since the great drama – I haven't taken anything solid. I'm living on my nerves. I stink of bleach, creosol, formalin, any disinfectant I can lay my hands on. Despite the fact I spend all my time rubbing it into my body, I'm haunted by that smell of fresh cadaver, warm blood, steaming entrails. It's horrible. It's fortunate my life is not my own any more. I'd have committed suicide. I say, 'it's fortunate', but who knows?

At nine o'clock one morning Solange had come rushing over to my place in a panic. I'd already left. My old mate Bourgoin was there, coding messages for that evening.

'You've got to get in touch with him right away, at once: you've got to warn everybody. That Alsatian guy of yours, he's a Kraut, with the Gestapo, a traitor. Now he's got the address of this place, of your operations centre and your letter drops, he wants to round up the entire network in one go, and take charge of the raid himself in order to get the reward. He's a real bastard!'

While they were searching for me in all the places that I might be, I was watching the unloading of phosphorus bombs and their transfer from the railway station to 'my' camp. Bourgoin carried off everything that needed to be moved somewhere safe: maps, documents and codes. The codes especially. But he left behind the revolver hidden in a guitar that had no back to it, hanging on the wall.

I arrived at the Gare D'Austerlitz at about four o'clock. Bourgoin was waiting for me there: Solange was posted at the station on Place St-Michel.

It had been a relatively easy job to clear out the operations centre. They sent a kid up to the floor above, to ring a doorbell and then go away, apologizing for having made a mistake. The kid spotted some guy studiously polishing the parquet on the landing right outside the door of our office. In the caretaker's lodge, a fat guy smoking cigars was sitting by the door and had the caretaker trapped.

Our guys, having worked out in detail what they were going to do, went into the next-door building, terrorized a bewildered pianist who'd been taking a nap and couldn't understand what they were doing using regulation Civil Defence pickaxes to break through the wall of his bedroom. They were able without difficulty to rescue the mailbag, documents, money and even the two typewriters.

But as far as I was concerned, it wasn't such a picnic. I had fifty minutes to tip off the radio operators who were due to arrive just before five. Bourgoin positioned himself downstairs on the café terrace. I went up at four thirty. Debrive was already out on the roof, setting up the aerial. I signalled to him to get down between two chimney pots and wait to see what happened.

Just in case, I handed him one of my two bakelite grenades that look like sticks of shaving soap.

The only clothing I kept on were a pair of underpants and a dressing gown. I set up my amateur painter's easel, and scattered about my tubes of paint. With some fresh stuff smeared on my palette, I started having another go at some wretched still-life I'll never finish. Too bad for posterity.

Ten to five. A knock at the door: it was Heisserer.

He seemed cheerful, all spruced up. He'd brought along a half-bottle of brandy.

I said, 'Pity there's no ice here.' I went to fetch some glasses and a carafe, and ran some water from the tap.

Heisserer boasted of his prowess.

'Three times now I've been stopped in the street, and once in the metro, and each time I've avoided being searched. I think I've proved myself. But in case I get caught, I'd really like to be taken on officially. It could be useful. Later on.'

I say, 'Absolutely. Do you have a pen?' And I hand him a form to fill out his personal details. 'You'll be RJ1682.' (That's my own code name.)

He sat by the window, placidly writing.

There was a string hanging down from the roof which I was supposed to pull in case of emergency. Debrive, sitting above my head, was holding the other end of it.

I walked over to the far side of the room and took down the guitar. Without raising his eyes, Heisserer lit a cigarette.

'Heisserer.'

He leapt up, caught off guard. His eyes dilated in the most amazing way. My 92 cylinder, held close against my hip, said it all. Nevertheless I spoke.

'You've got fifteen seconds. If you behave. Look at Notre-Dame.'

He knew there was nothing he could do. The smallest movement and he'd have lost this respite.

Notre-Dame is in the background: nearby is the tower of St Jacques. You can see the top of a horse-chestnut tree between two gables.

I aimed at his lower back.

It wasn't me, it was a machine, an automaton, a remote-controlled robot that walked over to that repository of sapped life, painfully collapsed on the badly polished wooden floor thirsty for his blood, and finished him off with a bullet in his ear.

The two Jerries that paid me a visit a quarter of an hour later didn't really know what they'd come for. Their mates were searching the building, they were doing the same. They'd divided the task between them, floor by floor. I delayed them for a while. When they came in, they stepped over a rolled-up linoleum lying in front of the doorway into the main room.

Inside it was Heisserer. As I had paint on my fingers I asked them to help themselves to my papers from the inside pocket of my jacket. I opened the brandy and offered them a drink.

One of them went over to the window and said, 'You didn't hear two shots fired?'

'Sure I did. It came from the stairwell. I don't know how your submachine-guns are designed but I think you need to be careful the way you handle them. What's going on round here anyway?'

They made an evasive gesture, the Lance Corporal asked me how many neighbours I had on the same floor – I've still no idea – and wanted me to go with them and act as their inter-preter. I said I didn't really want to do that, I wasn't a police-man and I didn't really want to make myself unpopular in this building where I was a new tenant. They agreed I had a point.

They didn't check the roof.

I was told they conferred at length on the ground floor with their commanding officer: they couldn't work out how their informer had disappeared.

Once they'd left, Debrive was able to climb down from the zinc roof guttering where he'd been perched. We searched the body. The bastard wasn't even a member of the SD, merely accredited at Avenue Foch: all he had was a *Dienstausweis* [service pass]. He wasn't armed. Even the Germans didn't trust him. He had only six hundred francs on him. In the end we spent five on a wicker basket and a poor quality cardboad suitcase. I sent Debrive home. Although he'd knocked back what was left of the brandy, he was spewing his guts out. He took away the dead man's clothes and shoes, with instructions to destroy them.

I'd actually once taken courses in anatomy, dissection even – and my mind was extremely clear. But I acted like a totally inept child. Instead of disjointing my stiff neatly, at the hip and shoulders, I set about cutting him into pieces the way you'd saw up a treetrunk. I thought it would be quite simple. The butchering, packaging and cleaning took all night. Pensive, with one eye half shut, the severed head watched me take care of the rest. I'd placed it on a brass platter that I bought at Bicêtre.

The upper part of the body, that made the suitcase bulge slightly, has been deposited at the left luggage at Gare Montparnasse. The lower part at Austerlitz. We'll see what happens.

> Better beware of the newly dead
> Of the white-handed ghost
> And the brightness of these lamps . . .

wrote Luc Berimont in 1940, in *Reign of Darkness*.

I've always felt the greatest reluctance to go anywhere near, to touch, a fresh corpse. For me, it's an unseemly thing. Useless. Hostile. Cunning. Dangerous. The 'presence' is much stronger, more perceptible one hour after death than one hour before. By my observation, this was not the case with Heisserer.

He was entirely absent from his head, his hands, his quivering body. He was gone instantly, unburdened of his absurd life, released.

It's no good my friends telling me the execution of Heisserer was a remarkable feat, trying to persuade me it averted a whole chain of disasters; this mental obsession, my shame and distress are beyond, beneath, the judgement of men. I don't need to reflect, calculate, weigh up my rights and obligations, to find myself guilty of an offence against human nature itself. I shouldn't have taken part in this battle, got bogged down in this mire. I'm stricken with remorse of a melodramatic kind: I think of his aged parents waiting for their weekly letter. Of course, it's ridiculous. But no argument, no logic will pacify me.

It's the act in itself that's vile. I should have left to others the task of carrying it out. What's excusable for anyone else, I myself can never be forgiven for.

The next evening I went over to see Solange. The tiredness, delayed shock, disgust had caught up with me.

I threw myself on her bed fully dressed. She sat beside me on a low chair and took my hand.

'You see, he spent his last night here, lying where you're lying now. He hardly slept. He was dreaming out loud, making plans. He said he'd soon have lots of money, that afterwards he'd go to South America, he'd take me if I wanted to go with him. And then all this (gesturing with both hands, she indicated the walls and the ceiling) must have got to him. In the morning he talked, he got it all off his chest. Then he fell asleep for an hour. When he left, he was worried, he couldn't remember exactly what he'd said to me. I told him, "When you started snoring, we were in Brazil together." That reassured him. You shouldn't let it prey on your mind so much. I know it was no joke having to bump him off, but that's Paris taking its revenge. Think of Keep-on-Dancin'.'

The Sleeper on the Pont-au-Double

July

I was now in increasingly acute pain all of the time. In desperation, I turned to the Sleeper, having got myself an introduction from Lassenay the sapper. The brother examined my torso with probing fingers, asked me some questions so pertinent that I suspect he's pursued some extremely serious medical studies.

Then he said to me, touching his forehead, 'Things don't seem to be quite right in there. You must be very stressed.'

If he only knew.

He placed the Sleeper's hands on my painful side and on my head. I'm down for the third session on Sunday. I'm amazed to feel the real benefits of this mysterious therapy. It was high time I returned to form: we're overwhelmed with work.

September

Phew! The Germans have left. Without too much devastation, which is a miracle. I'm working as both journalist and

170

officer – in uniform, at last – redeployed to military security. I'm on celebratory duty at the paper every evening. More specifically, I've been given the task of retelling in instalments the epic story of the liberation of Paris.

If I wrote down what I really think, I'd be hacked to pieces. I saw a body gathered up at Les Halles – a kid in short trousers, fifteen years old at most. He'd attacked a Jerry truck that was flying a white flag. The kid was armed with 5.5 pistol with a mother-of-pearl grip: a 1924 lady's handbag accessory. The real criminals weren't in the truck.

My old neighbourhood's been invaded by blacks from the plantations. They're nice guys when they're sober, terrible when they're drunk.

Léopoldie and her girlfriend, Alice, are making up for lost time. They're having a ball. Every night, at one of the gates of Paris, they smuggle themselves into the precincts of a car park, and make love with the blacks under their trucks. They're doing so much 'work', they're getting blisters on their buttocks and their shoulderblades. They're buying everyone drinks. Pépé the Pansy regrets the departure of our former occupiers: the Yanks don't appreciate his charms. One of them told him he smelt too bad. He's been dousing himself with violet perfume ever since, which is the reason the Pignols decided to throw him out. He was making the place stink.

At Place Maubert, the worst scum have taken advantage of some quieter moments to get themselves photographed on the barricades, dressed up like buccaneers, striking the most heroic poses.

I cut a sorry figure in my uniform: I display my usual rank of lieutenant. Here everyone is at least a major. Only the under-twenties are mere captains.

The cops – whom we now have to glorify – have even arrested two six-pip 'colonels-in-chief', on Rue Monge. One of them was Armenian.

I've noticed that the flash-points in the old part of Paris have been the same since the Middle Ages. The first barricades that sprang up corresponded to only very vague strategic objectives: Rue de l'Arbre-Sec, for instance. But, it was there, it was on Rue Pernelle, Rue du Fouarre, Rue de la Huchette, Le Petit-Pont, true to its age-old traditions, that trouble broke out in the City.

My bohemian friends more wisely kept out of harm's way on the first floor at the Quatre-Fesses, where Elisabeth prepared meals for them. No change has entered their lives, except for Théophile, who has returned to the priesthood. He wants to go to Black Africa as a missionary.

December

Marius Labadou, known as the Commander, was a comic character in his fifties, a house painter by profession, fond of fruity-flavoured beaujolais.

Between the wars, Marius Labadou belonged to that glorious band of reenlisted NCOs who carried to deprived populations in different latitudes the message of Sweet France, and asserted with hobnailed-booted conviction the universal brilliance of our culture.

Marius Labadou returned home with the rank of sergeant-major.

Marius Labadou, whom the military authorities, doubtless under pressure of other concerns, had neglected to consult before negotiating the armistice of June 1940, was foaming with rage at the sight of the Teutonic hordes who came streaming inside our walls. And Marius Labadou was one of the first to found a resistance organization within occupied Paris. He set about it in a prudent manner: he gathered together a group of five or six Hitler-phobic wine-lovers, people who could be trusted. And for four years the private back rooms of Rue de la Huchette became familiar with the regular presence of some eminently patriotic figures: Doudou the Gentle Verger, Lucien Domaom and his pal Collard, known as Teddy Bear, a few others, and Fralicot, nicknamed Les Eparges because of his truly epic 1914–18 war experiences. Under the enthusiastic but circumspect authority of Marius Labadou, these honest folk held a daily reunion, during which they would bring each other up to date with the latest rumours to have reached their ears that day. A discussion would follow. Bottles of increasing rarity were cheerfully drained – yet another one the Germans wouldn't get hold of!

Domaom, who set great store by reaching firm conclusions, would grab each of his mates, one after the other, by the lapels. 'So, tell me, *d'homme à homme*, man to man [hence his nickname], that you haven't lost hope?' It's partly thanks to the Labadou group that the most heartening tall stories came into being, circulated round Paris and reached the provinces with blitzkrieg speed.

This was the group's main activity. I recall the day when news reached France of the outcome, for a long time uncertain, and as it turned out disastrous for the Germans, of a tremendous battle between armoured units somewhere on the Russian front. The *Propaganda Staffel* had instructed the press to emphasize the scale of military resources brought to the engagement by both sides. The newspaper *Aujourd'hui* appeared with this banner headline across six columns:

LA BATAILLE FUT GIGANTESQUE.
[THE BATTLE WAS GIGANTIC.]

Which set everyone on the left bank humming the rest of that classic De Profundis:

> *Tous les morpions moururent presque*
> *A l'exception des plus trapus*
> *Qui s'accrochèrent aux poils du cul.*
> [The crab lice nearly all died
> The hardiest few alone pulled through –
> It was the pubic hairs that saved them.]

(Desnos was involved in the page layout.) Oh, Labadou's lot certainly had a good laugh that time. In short, while this team's activity was almost nil and never caused the least harm to Axis forces, at least our brave tipplers had excellent intentions. I'd never concealed from Labadou the possibilities available to me of communicating with London. He asked me to pass on the news of the existence of his group, '*Le Chat Qui*

Pêche'. Why not? I made a report to BCRA and the war went on.

During the street battles Labadou and his team were careful not to venture outside for any other reason but to stock up, on wine especially. 'We have other things to do,' they would say archly. Discipline being the chief force of the worst shambles, everyone regarded this as normal. So as soon as everything had more or less calmed down, and a few poor wretches had been bumped off for reasons that had nothing to do with national interests, and the splendid falangist police so hated only the day before had been feted, and the whores and the blacks from the Mid-West had through a process of mutual compromise invented their own curious Anglo-Saxon dialect, Franco-Allied pen-pushers took over from Wehrmacht-Gestapo pen-pushers.

Marius Labadou got himself and his group 'recognized'. A colonel who'd waged war from the safe distance of London offices, and a reenlisted NCO who selflessly kept up morale in the bars on Rue de la Huchette were destined to see eye to eye.

Marius Labadou was promoted to major without further ado, Fralicot and Domaom to captains, the rest to two-pip lieutenants. Who knows where they found the extremely smart, non-regulation uniforms with which they immediately rigged themselves out. Goering would have paled at the sight of what they displayed on their chests.

They didn't sober up for a whole week. Marius Labadou cut a fine figure in his uniform. And that's what brought about his downfall.

He was a widower. For some years he'd been living with a middle-aged woman, as husband and wife. She, Madame Félicienne, had a rather arrogant manner and was extremely houseproud. Her two-roomed apartment was crammed with knick-knacks, picked up here and there on Sunday strolls along the riverbanks or at fun fairs. And the china swans, Japanese tea cups, finicky brass ornaments, polished and buffed and patinated, gleamed with a heartwarming lustre. But Madame Félicienne seemed to reserve for these trinkets, embroidered tasselled cushions, and flower vases, an affection she withheld from human beings. With great thrift and capability she managed the household budget and took a dim view of 'her man' spending all his time in the company of his friends. For her, the Liberation should have marked the end of a dissipated existence she abhorred. Whereas Labadou, elated by his unexpected acclaim, saw things differently: in no hurry to take up his paintbrushes again, he preferred to saunter about in uniform, with one or two of his cronies at his side, and to keep the whole neighbourhood agog with his account of feats of arms no less astounding than imaginary.

So it was that he won the heart of Louisette, a former model turned barmaid. Quite pretty, though looking prematurely the worse for wear, Louisette managed to transform Marius's guardian angel into the demon of middle-aged lust.

The Major neglected his professional duties. Fed up with listening to Madame Félicienne's recriminations every day, he took advantage of a row between them to pack his lightweight suitcase and clean shirts at once and move in with the infinitely younger and more desirable Louisette. The newly-formed couple were now living together within a few hundred metres of the home he had forsaken. But such were the manners and morals of the neighbourhood, no one took any exception to this. Life resumed its humdrum routine. Madame Félicienne bided her time. She pretended to be on good terms with her rival, but those who knew her warned against putting too much trust in this. Especially as Marius was now getting a pension which meant that, come what may, there was always that little extra.

Meanwhile, Marius Labadou lost a bit of his swagger. He caught a chill that he didn't nurse properly. He was always doubled-up, coughing. His new mistress looked after him as best she could, but he drank far too much.

Until one dreadful morning during a spell of terribly cold weather that seemed to go on and on, when Marius, running a very high fever, had to be admitted to the Hôtel-Dieu where he was diagnosed with double broncho-pneumonia.

That same evening the sick man's friends met up at Le Chat Qui Pêche. They had fallen into two camps: the supporters of Madame Félicienne, with a respect for time-honoured conventions, in other words 'decent behaviour'; and those who saw in Louisette another chance for Marius to be young again.

Madame Félicienne and Louisette arrived separately. Louisette seemed terribly upset. Her rival by contrast looked calm and resolute. The situation was discussed.

Domaom suggested, 'Since there's nothing more we can do for Marius in terms of his medical treatment, the only chance we have of speeding his recovery is to go to see the Lancelin brothers and have him slept.'

Madame Félicienne expressed reservations. But she was easily persuaded there could be no serious objection to the Sleeper's letting his thoughts dwell for two hours a day on the man whose life they wanted to save.

'It's like praying for the dead,' said Fralicot. 'It may not do any good, but it certainly doesn't do any harm.'

This argument clinched it.

The evening wore on. Everyone related stories, embellished to the best of the narrator's ability, of miraculous cures brought about by the Sleeper and his brother. They all but resuscitated the dead. Madame Félicienne, however, had her own idea.

'And afterwards, when he comes out, he won't be fully recovered. What will he do, and whose place, eh, whose place, will he go back to?'

Louisette remained silent. Embarrassed, the others shook their heads. 'That's up to him,' said Old Collard. 'We're his friends, and we're friends of both of you. It's none of our business. You sort it out between yourselves.'

Domaom intervened.

'You both want to see him come out of there, don't you? Well, better do the same as in wartime: make an alliance to achieve your objective. For the time being, you should be working together. Come on now, Fralicot, as man to man . . .'

'You're something of an authority on the subject,' agreed Fralicot.

With their moist-eyed comrades looking on, the two men hugged each other.

'I'd love to know what dirty trick she's plotting,' said a voice.

Madame Félicienne's devotion exceeded all expectation. She'd rushed over to the Lancelin brothers' neighbourhood at the crack of dawn, and found out where they lived. She had to beg them: and so successful was she that when the wards opened to visitors the Lancelins were at Marius's bedside. He seemed very low. The Sleeper laid his hands on his torso for a long time, so long the patient complained, 'No more, it's tiring.'

As they were leaving Frédéric Lancelin, who was supporting his brother, said to Madame Félicienne, 'You know, we'll do our utmost, but it's going to be difficult.'

'You do everything you can, and I'll take care of you . . . For a start, come and have your meals at my house.'

And while Louisette did the washing-up, Madame Félicienne meanwhile busied herself preparing appetizing dishes. She fed the Sleeper most carefully.

'Truly, I wouldn't let anyone else but you do it,' said Frédéric, genuinely moved. 'Since he became paralysed, I've always been the one to look after him.'

The first day Marius was conscientiously slept for several hours.

Everyone at Le Chat Qui Pêche came by for news. Marius seemed better. His fever hadn't dropped but he was breathing more deeply and able to talk without too much effort. His eyes had brightened. And everyone was delighted. But whereas Madame Félicienne seemed mostly excited by the Sleeper's capabilities, Louisette couldn't conceal her joy: Marius was getting better. She was radiant.

This greatly vexed Madame Félicienne, who wasted no time in putting her rival in her place.

'You tried to steal my man. You see where that's led. Well, just you give him back to me. I've a rightful claim on him. For a start, he's still legally resident with me. He hasn't registered any change of address. You don't seriously believe, do you, that I'm just going to let you pocket his pension?'

'I don't give a damn about his money!' said Louisette.

Collard, you could tell, didn't much care for Félicienne.

'In any case,' he ventured, 'even if he does peg out, you can't count on getting the money. You'd only be his mistress, not his widow.'

'That's open to discussion. There have been similar cases brought to trial. The law isn't the same as before,' Félicienne declared authoritatively, a little put out nevertheless.

Fralicot, alias Les Eparges, who had reason to be well informed, said, 'Well, I wouldn't be so sure myself.'

Félicienne looked thoughtful. Her expression hardened. She directed a spiteful gaze at Louisette.

'One way or another, my girl, I'll get my own back on you,' she muttered to herself.

Félicienne only very rarely went to Pignol's. She happened to be there when Dr Troquemène was called out to see one of the lodgers.

'Will you have something, doctor?'

'No thanks. I never drink.'

'Listen, you couldn't tell me . . . I don't know what's wrong with me, I've not been able to stay awake for the past two days.'

'Do like me, drink less.'

'That's not the problem, I swear.'

Not bothering to answer, the doctor went off shrugging his shoulders. Suzanne, proprietress of the Sommerard hotel, was there.

'Oh, that guy's so disagreeable. I'll ask young Claude, one of my lodgers, this evening. He's a medical student.'

'Oh, that's really sweet of you. I'll drop by for a little chat later on.'

The next day the patient seemed to be out of danger. And the whole gang, confident of the virtues of the two treatments combined – that of the medical staff, and that of the Sleeper – drank to Marius's health and his speedy return. But all was not well. Along came the Lancelin brothers, one supporting the other. The Sleeper looked much weaker than usual. Obviously worried, Frédéric sat him down as if he were made of some extraordinarily delicate substance. The Sleeper was shivering slightly. He muttered in gasps, 'I don't know what's wrong with me. I've not been able to sleep. Not at all.'

'It's a disaster,' Frédéric lamented. 'For him and for our patients.'

'The best thing is for him to come and stay with me,' said Félicienne. 'I'll take good care of him. We'll sit up all night with him if necessary.'

Over the following days Marius's condition seriously worsened. But everyone's attention – except Louisette's – was somewhat distracted by the state of the paralytic. The Sleeper wasn't sleeping any more, was *unable* to sleep! By day or night. He complained of palpitations. He was no more than a shadow of his former self.

Félicienne made him swallow some gruel.

'He needs to keep his strength up.'

Louisette offered to help.

'No, no, I manage better by myself,' the older woman protested peevishly.

When she was told at the Hôtel-Dieu of Marius's death, Félicienne sobbed dry-eyed. Frédéric had stayed behind to look after his brother, who was practically unable to breathe. When the women returned he'd go and fetch a doctor – a good one. Maybe a shot of some kind of antispasmodic might bring some relief to the sleep-deprived Sleeper on the verge of exhaustion.

Frédéric went into the kitchen to fetch a glass of water, some sugar and a teaspoon. He opened a drawer.

When the two women got back, Félicienne said, 'It's all over.' She snivelled.

'It's all over,' echoed Louisette, pasty-faced and devastated.

Félicienne went to look for something in the room next door. Frédéric took the opportunity to signal to Louisette that he had something to tell her. He took four metal tubes out of his pocket – three empty and one half consumed. ORTEDRIN. Louisette didn't understand straightaway. Frédéric pointed to his brother.

'It was to stop him sleeping. She could have killed him *as well*.'

Louisette fainted.

The subsequent rumpus roused the neighbourhood. No one could make much sense of it. The temporary fit of madness that overcame Louisette and caused her to round on her rival with unbelievable violence was put down to despair. She tried to attack the older woman. Frédéric restrained her. Incoherent utterances were also heard, in which the words 'murder' and 'criminal' recurred amid sobs and rasps of rage.

Frédéric Lancelin demonstrated remarkable self-control and authority. Having calmed down Louisette, he asked her to help him take his brother home. Which she did, seemingly brought back to her senses. A car was found for them.

The next day Félicienne and Louisette ran into each other at Le Chat Qui Pêche. For a moment there were fears of another row.

To everyone's astonishment, it was Louisette who apologized.

'I don't know what came over me. I don't really remember. You know, I can't hold my drink very well.'

And for the second time Félicienne and Louisette made peace with each other. Or pretended to.

Friends in the neighbourhood turned out in full force to accompany Marius Labadou's hearse to Thiais.

People inquired after the Sleeper: he was able to sleep again and was back on the bridge, just as before. He had resumed his 'consultations'. But it was Félicienne who began to fall apart. She often wept without rhyme or reason, got drunk and fell into deep depressions.

'What have I done? What have I done?'

The neighbours would console her and take her home.

Louisette became her closest friend. One day she said to Félicienne, 'You're becoming a nervous wreck. I think you too should get yourself "slept".'

Félicienne refused with horror. But she'd lost her will-power. Louisette kept insisting, slowly and surely wearing her down. It was on the nape of Félicienne's neck, on her eyes and ears that the Sleeper laid his hands this time. Frédéric observed the procedure with a hardened expression no one recognized in him.

Félicienne has just been admitted to Ste-Anne. She'll be there till the end of her days – which are numbered. She vegetates, sunk in a mindless state of almost permanent lethargy. Which is just as well: whenever she comes to, nightmares and hallucinations cause her to utter dreadful cries.

I still go and see Pierre-Luc my friend on the embankment, but whenever we're obliged to walk past the Sleeper, I don't know what makes me take a huge detour.

Chapter XI

An historian is a kind detective in seach of the fact – remote or otherwise – that brings to a set of events apparently unconnected with each other, the link that unites them, their justification, their logic.

You cannot imagine what great delights this profession affords. It's as if, in every incunablum, consumed by worms and steeped in boredom, in every inarticulate scrawl, in every collection of forgotten chronicles, there presides a mischievous sprite, winking at you, who at the appropriate time confers on you your reward in the form of renewed wonder.

Marionettes and Magic Spells

Round Place Maubert and La Montagne, everyone was familiar with this slightly crazy Gypsy who a few years ago used to carve puppets, have clothes made for them, and sell them at Mayette and Vaubaillon.

Our man confined himself to making glove puppets, that's to say without legs, their costume serving to glove the hand of the puppeteer.

It was a labour of love, carving the figures, painting them, dressing their hair, 'finishing' them. In bars he made no secret of the pleasure he took in working his puppets. He improvised painfully funny playlets to suit his audiences' sense of humour. But it was all the same to him as long as peals of impersonal laughter – that 'frank laughter' Heine speaks of – rang in his ears.

I developed some interest in this woodcarving puppeteer, so much so that he inspired me to write some plays for puppets. (It's pleasant and relaxing, now and again, to 'concoct' folklore.) I penned five farces in the Lyons style. Vaubaillon and Billaudot published them. Through this entertaining friend of mine, I made the acquaintance of his main client: Monsieur Mayette.

About fifty years old. Long-time owner of a successful business, who'd started out as a conjurer and illusionist by profession. But above all a kindly and decent man, far from being uncultured, and most importantly instilled with that delicate sensitivity that does not deceive. What's all this leading up to? The fact that Monsieur Mayette should have established himself there and not elsewhere. It's always the same story.

With plenty of orders coming in, the Gypsy suddenly stopped making puppets. Yet, small-scale though this crafts-man's production was, his business was flourishing.

'I've had enough,' he said to me one day. 'I take too much trouble over my puppets. There's no profit in it.'

'Raise your prices!'

'If only it were that simple.'

I wasn't going to insist. On a previous occasion he told me he was 'too fond' of his creations – no two heads he carved were identical – and, although he'd produced hundreds of them, it was always a kind of wrench for him whenever he parted with one of his 'children'.

'I don't know whose hands they fall into . . . It's casting pearls before swine.'

Finally, he came out with the real crux of the matter, which at the time left me none the wiser.

'You know, a carving, especially if it's polychrome, is not meant to move. These faces, these half-bodies, when you animate them, they're more live than the living. They can be dangerous for those who don't really understand them. With contained energy, no one can predict what will happen when it's released.'

He began to paint frescoes in cafés and then I lost touch with him.

Some time later I was reading through a number of ancient documents relating to the history of the neighbourhood. Among a great many other things, I learned from them that in the immediate vicinity of the Mayette premises, near the Passage du Clos-Bruneau (in 1248 called the Rue Judas), a community of Orientals (Gypsies or Jews) had settled, who from before the Middle Ages had been engaged in making articulated dolls.

In my precious little *Privat d'Anglemont*, the following can be read on page 33:

> '*We had encountered wandering musicians, organ grinders, exhibitors of monkeys and other live animals: there are some houses here that are veritable menageries, and this is where the impresarios of marionette theatre have established their headquarters.*
>
> *These people have introduced an entire industry to Rue du Clos-Bruneau. They provide a living for the whole population, a quaint, gentle, kindly, almost artistic population vaguely reminiscent of certain characters in Hoffmann's fantastic tales. They are all employed in the production of puppets. There is first of all the woodcarver who makes the heads. He is both painter and hairdresser. He makes both simple and high-quality products. He sells his high-quality youths' heads for 2 to 4 francs; those of old men, with beards and white hair, for 10 to 12 francs; an ordinary wig, for 12 sous; curled and trimmed, for a woman or a Louis XIII courtier, 2 francs.*
>
> *Next door is the seamstress who makes the costumes; she is supplied with the fabrics. When she works for a well-established theatre, such as that of Monsieur Morin, Rue Jean-de-Beauvais, she earns 2 francs a day, without too much effort. Then come the shoemakers who make the satin slippers for the ballerina marionettes and the leather boots for the chevaliers. The shoes cost 4 sous a pair, the boots 15 sous. Finally, the real magician of this world, the one who wires up the puppet. Wiring up a puppet consists of attaching all the strings to make it move about on stage: that is what will complete the illusion. A certain expertise is required to do the job properly, because the person responsible for making the puppet dance must never be able to go wrong and mistake one string for another, make an arm move instead of a leg: the way in which the puppet is wired must be such that on seeing the detached strings anyone practised in these matters should be able to say: this one is for the arms, that one for the legs . . .*

So there you have it. And it was by chance that a trip to Switzerland, where he is still remembered, enabled me to reconstruct Brioché's adventure.

Jean Brioché, round about the year 1650, was a famous tooth-puller. In the winter he operated on the Pont-Neuf and travelled round the country during the summer.

The bridge was crowded with charlatans of every kind, artisans, streetvendors, beggars and mountebanks, while onlookers gathered to watch in front of the amazing trestle platforms of Mondor and Tabarin. On a kind of scaffold all festooned with multicoloured posters, Brioché attracted clients whom he relieved not very gently of their rotten tooth stumps. His victims, thus exposed to the gibes – or admiration – of an overexcited public, remained as stoical as the painful operation permitted. Brioché, whom the populace nick-named 'Remover of the Cobbles of Gob Street', deferred to contemporary custom by organizing a colourful and rowdy spectacle before each public extraction. Which was how he came by the idea of putting on a show of dancing puppets.

On the morning of December 24, 1649, a swarthy man stopped for a long time in front of the platform where Brioché was working his puppets. He patiently waited till the end of the performance. Then he approached Brioché, com-plimented him on his skill, and offered to make, exclusively for him, some much more beautiful marionettes, figuring the heroes of Italian farce: Pulchinello, Pantalon, Harlequin . . . as well as characters of religious inspiration that would allow him to stage the 'mysteries'.

Brioché followed the man to his workshop in Clos-Bruneau. The fellow showed him samples of his work. Brioché was charmed by them, and placed an order for a whole set of characters. A price was agreed, to be paid later, as the puppets were delivered. A final settlement date was decided on: a year to the day from when the deal was concluded.

It was stipulated that in the event the marionettes had not been paid for by that time, they would revert to being the property of their creator. Brioché paid a deposit, and the deal was done!

The puppets were duly delivered. The dolls were so beautiful, and so easy to work that Brioché, abandoning his instruments and chair of torture, became his own manager, trained some assistants and devoted himself exclusively to putting on marionette shows. He did well by it: within a very short time he'd made his fortune.

The swarthy man came to see him and demanded some of the money owing to him.

With bad grace the miserly Brioché paid him the stipulated first instalment of the total price.

The craftsman indicated that he was making his own puppets responsible for ensuring that Brioché met his commitments. Brioché shrugged his shoulders.

He went travelling round the country, where his takings exceeded his hopes.

There were reports of him all over Burgundy, then in Savoy. He forgot about his creditor.

The very day that had been fixed for making the last payment – Christmas Day 1650 – Brioché and his company crossed the border into Switzerland.

At Solothurn, he put on a show for a large invited audience. The Swiss were unfamiliar with marionettes: they marvelled at the complicated leaps and bounds performed by the characters in the first ballet. Three violinists played behind the scenes, while puppet musicians sawed away on stage on pretend instruments. But this was only a prelude of things to come.

The curtain rose amid general enthusiasm on the previously announced play: *The Damnation of Pulchinello* (which sounds like a curious transposition of Marlowe's *Faust*).

Then the most amazing thing happened: the puppets suddenly ignored their master! They knotted, tangled, broke the strings that were supposed to control their every movement: released, unfettered, they began to whirl, leap, quarrel, fight, and there was nothing anyone could do to arrest them.

The spectators declared that 'no one in living memory had

ever heard of such dainty and agile creatures, such chatter-boxes as these'. The audience was alarmed: there were fears of witchcraft. The dolls were said to be nothing other than a gaggle of goblins at the command of a devil.

The Swiss police tied up Brioché and escorted by a voci-ferous populace dragged him off before the judge. The judge wanted to see the evidence: the theatre was brought to him, with the wooden mischief-makers 'that he could not touch without shuddering', and Brioché was condemned to be burnt alive along with all his paraphernalia.

This sentence was about to be carried out when a certain Dumont, a captain of the Swiss Guards in the service of the King of France, happened to turn up. Curious to see the French magician, he recognized the wretched Brioché who had made him laugh so much in Paris. He hurried to the judge's house: having obtained a stay of execution for one day, he clarified the situation, explained how the puppets worked, and got the judge to order the release of Brioché.

This was no easy matter: for those witnesses at the trial who had been in the audience remained adamant and continued yelling accusations of witchcraft. The population of Solothurn were long divided on this issue.

Brioché returned with all possible speed to Paris. Nor did he rest until he had rushed over to Clos-Bruneau and settled his debt with the magician – I meant to write, with the craftsman – cash on the nail.

Thereafter, his fame only increased. He often performed before the Court.

Thus are legends born. I don't know what element of fiction there is in this story about Brioché: the fact is, there are contemporary documents preserved in Switzerland that record the circumstances of the trial, and everything reported above.

I'd very much like to meet again that Gypsy who told me: 'A polychrome carving's not meant to move. The reactions of contained energy are unpredictable.'

I found out that at the end of the last century Gabriele

D'Annunzio acquired some of Brioché's puppets. The most beautiful. They now belong to the poet and dramatist Guillot de Saix, the 'White-Bearded Child'.

The Old Man Who Appears After Midnight

Gérard is making progress. Séverin too. They've had a very good influence on Paquito, who's developing most satisfactorily. The three of them have organized an exhibition of their works in Rue de Seine. My fellow journalists have given them flattering reviews. Since then, their canvases have been selling as well as can be expected. Our 'general trading' friends, Géga first and foremost, are giving them a real helping hand. The group's relatively well off at the moment. But there's a shadow hanging over all this. And the name of that shadow is Elisabeth, whose eighteenth birthday we've just celebrated.

They're all more or less in love with her. My own feelings are more paternal. But I'm just as jealous of her as the others.

One fine evening last October a legionnaire out on the town fetched up at the Quatre-Fesses. I was there. I was in civvies. The soldier was absolutely determined to fraternize with everybody. He'd already come by during the day and buttonholed Olga. Not bad-looking in a rugged sort of way. A smooth talker – oh, yes indeed! – he'd made a good impression on her. In the evening he behaved in a likeable manner, and bought two drawings from Paquito. With no cause for mistrust, it seemed natural to invite him to join us at our table. He chose to sit in the corner, so he couldn't be seen from outside: friends of his might pass by and spot him and he wasn't interested in meeting up with them.

With a distant look in his eyes, he talked about Africa, Saigon, Shanghai, and Tonkin, where he'd fought.

He only gave the kid a polite distracted glance as he said goodbye. She didn't seem to care about him one way or the other. But she was petulant when Clément offered to walk her home, as usual. And we sensed that Clément was very unhappy.

The soldier came back every evening after that: and every time he brought a knuckle of ham 'to share among friends', he said. He spent a lot. 'Money! For all the use it is to me . . .' In a steady penetrating voice he recounted his adventures in Algeria, Tunisia, and Indochina where he'd been caught up in the Japanese invasion. But he'd 'taken to the *maquis*', he said – just like some ordinary guy in the Cevennes.

He described the endless voyages travelling in steerage. The torpor. The boredom. His mates, their lives, their stories. And then, at eleven thirty:

'Time to go. I've only got leave of absence till midnight.'

'Where are you going back to?'

'Vincennes. So long.'

And he would hurry off towards the metro. On one occasion, one of the regulars, Dédé, who owns a car, offered him a lift. He accepted. Twenty minutes later Dédé was back.

'So soon? All the way from the Fort de Vincennes?'

'You must be joking. I dropped him off at a hotel, in Rue de la Convention.'

Edmond was there. He muttered, 'I don't know what you lot think of him, but I don't much like the look of him.'

The next day the soldier said he could stay later. An itinerant accordeon-player kept the place crowded for part of the evening. It wasn't till about midnight that we were really on our own. Edmond, who spends more and more time with us, was sitting next to Elisabeth. He was awkwardly, touchingly attentive towards her.

The soldier had launched himself into a complicated account of an expedition in Tonkin, complete with parachute jumps, ambushes, belly-crawling through paddy fields. He was asked details about how he'd managed to get himself repatriated. At that point he hummed and hawed a bit, then recovered and began to impale and strangle the Japanese, or cut their throats. He was on to his twelfth when a chortle was heard, and that familiar little voice, 'Ha! Ha! Not true!'

The Old Man, tucked in his corner of the banquette, laughed, sarcastically this time, confidently, with the obvious intent of challenging the imposter. The latter rose to feet, white-faced. He was furious.

'What! How dare anyone . . .?'

'Well, yes, someone dares! Yes, I dare!' shouted the Old Man. 'Lying comes as naturally to you as breathing. You've never set foot in Indochina. Or Africa. You've just come out of prison! Clear out. Go on.'

It looked as though the legionnaire, beside himself with rage, was going to hurl himself at the Old Man. But then Edmond was on his feet.

'Now listen, pal. These other guys may have a subtle way with words, not me. We don't like your spiel. Now get out of here. Maybe you'd like a lift back. To the Fort de Vincennes?'

The fellow took himself off without another word. Elisabeth looked thunderstruck. Clément was jubilant.

I'd vowed to keep an eye on the Old Man when the party broke up. Why did Edmond have to take me aside at that very moment in order to tell me – I don't even remember what it was any more? Everyone was attending to something else: the minute our backs were turned, the Old Man was gone.

For a while Elisabeth received letters that her aunt's caretaker delivered to her 'personally'. She was completely changed, remote, distant, secretive, and often after modelling disappeared for several hours. Somebody told us that some guy met her at the Jussieu metro station. We checked it out: it was the legionnaire, but now in civvies. So as not to cause Clément unnecessary heartache, we agreed to keep him in the dark about these assignations. Once, Elisabeth didn't go home to sleep. Frantic, her aunt woke us at dawn: we swore that she'd been with us all night, at an artists' party that had carried on into the early hours.

A mouth, a face can lie. But not Elisabeth's body. That day, as soon as she appeared nude, we could tell that Elisabeth had lost her virginity.

A scarcely perceptible sagging of the breasts – her upper cleavage was gone; areas of her stomach that caught the light instead of dispersing it; heavier rings round her eyes; less looseness of the hips, which a kind of – yes, that's what it was – a kind of shame had infiltrated, infused, contaminated: none of this could escape us. We felt a stab of very bitter resentment. Our eyes must have been filled with reproach or pity: the poor girl couldn't withstand our gaze for more than five minutes. She suddenly covered herself with a curtain and started sobbing. We didn't press her.

Time passes. I've kept some sketches from 'before'. To tell the truth, since that day we take less pleasure in the work.

Elisabeth continues to meet 'her man'. We never mention him to her. And Clément, who's waiting his chance, continues to play the lovesick suitor.

Zoltan the Mastermind

At Military Intelligence HQ, my basic mission is to track down those comrades of ours who were arrested here and deported to the East.

I've been assigned an orderly. A young soldier with non-combatant status, who was determined to join Leclerc's army. Poor boy! It must have been out of pity that they drafted this wretched, woe-begone, bewildered creature, who, by some inexplicable miracle, escaped being rounded up by the Germans when they purged his street.

Father, mother, elder brother – Polish Jews – deported and exterminated, we now know. This feeble-minded boy – a bout of meningitis has left its mark – is afflicted with a curvature of the spine that precludes any physical effort. His face with very receding chin and bulging eyes is reminiscent of a bird at first, then a fish, and finally a rabbit. To cap it all, even his personal details are a joke. He has exactly the same name as what is generally referred to as 'a high-ranking political personality'. To avoid causing any offence, I shall call him Simon Baum.

The sole concern of the military authorities who drafted Baum was to ensure that he was materially reasonably well provided for during his few months' service. And maybe to save him from fits of depression that might prove fatal. I'm known to be susceptible to certain feelings of absurd pity. And I've been landed with this runt.

He drives me crazy. I've told him in the strongest terms that he's not to concern himself with my shoes or my clothes, or to go rummaging among my personal belongings. A secretary files my papers with which he has no reason to meddle. His uselessness oppresses him. As a soldier, he would like to have fought and conquered Alsace the way the kids of Montmartre fight over their potholes. I send him on impossible errands or give him magazines that he quietly pours over, huddled on a bench at the end of a corridor. I shall soon be more or less rid of him, at last.

Zoltan Hazaï has tracked me down again. He came into my office, with a suspicious policeman on his heels. I was pleased to see him.

'What's new?'

'No problems any more. I work for myself: resurfacing parquet flooring. At last I can work as hard as I like. I tell you, I really put my back into it.'

'And apart from that?'

'I'd like to get French citizenship as soon possible. I need a reference.'

'No problem.'

My Hungarian now speaks a heavily accented but very correct French. He tells me that he's living over in the Faubourg St-Antoine area, Simon Baum's home ground. This has suddenly flashed into my mind, and gives me an idea.

I hand Zoltan a document declaring that to my knowledge he hasn't commited any murder, sunk any allied submarine, handed over to the Gestapo any parachutist. And then: 'Tell me. You wouldn't be in need of some help? A young man who could carry your tools, run errands, a poor harmless lad . . .'

'I might consider it. Why not?'

I explained the case of Simon Baum.

'It's not just because I want to get him off my hands. He needs to be given the illusion of doing something useful.'

'OK.'

I called Simon. He gazed at me with those big honest eyes of his.

'This is a friend: he's from your neighbourhood. You need something to do, some exercise. I'm putting you in his charge. I'll renew your passes every two days. You'll come here to collect your linen, subsistence allowance and tobacco.'

Simon passively consented.

At last I've freed myself of the haunting prospect of hearing Simon furtively coming in to see me every hour, and asking in that scarcely post-pubertal voice, 'What should I do?' only to be rebuffed, often with an impatience for which I immediately reproach myself. If he were the poor innocent beast he resembles, I'd have showered him with kindnesses. But he's a human being, damn it! And as such, he exasperates me. He came to pick up his pass, allowance, and clean shirts. I gave him several K rations, and all the tobacco I could lay my hands on. He was fearful and subdued, as usual. (He has a marked Jewish accent.)

'So, how's the Hungarian?'

'Oh! he's kind, very kind to me. Teaches me lots of things . . .'

'Like what?'

'I collect the wood shavings and put them in a bag.'

'He's not encouraging you to drink, I hope.'

'Oh, no! Anyway, I never feel like drinking.'

I had difficulty reconstructing the scene.

Zoltan was bent over, breathing heavily, resurfacing the floor of an empty room. His moving torso sweated in the warm sunshine. Nearby, also on all fours and naked to the waist, was Simon. Zoltan stands up, dusts himself down, and goes off for a drink. Simon remains squatting: he gathers the wood shavings the way a child sweeps up dry sand to prevent his mud pies from sticking to the ground. In an ill-fated gesture, moving his left hand too quickly, a long splinter penetrates deeply between his thumb and palm. Intense pain. He faints.

Zoltan realizes something's amiss and approaches, slowly,

with a waddling gait, as is his wont when some unspecified danger lurks. He goes to fetch a chair, sits my comatose Simon on it. A panful of cold water and a repeated couple of slaps. Zoltan stares hard at the boy. 'Are you a man, or aren't you? Are you a man?' Simon's eyes open wide. He's still stupefied. Zoltan grabs the injured hand, sees the place where the splinter entered, rushes off to the caretaker, comes back with a pair of tweezers. Skilfully, but not gently, he extracts the thin sliver of wood. Now in good humour, he places his hands on Simon's shoulders, and gazes at him intently. 'Now, chin up, do you hear? Chin up, you little weakling!'

His eyelids half-closed. Simon remained silent, still, and apparently unconscious. Zoltan had hypnotized him without realizing it. At this point, the Hungarian committed a serious error. Instead of wakening his 'subject' with vertical hand movements, up and down – from the stomach to the forehead, and then aside, past the eyes – and failing that, instead of telephoning me, he grabbed a towel soaked in cold water and began belting the poor kid, who started screaming and struggling, stricken with a terrible attack of nerves.

It took him several days to recover, installed in the Hungarian's bed, while a mortified Zoltan looked after him like some inept clumsy nanny.

I went to see Simon every evening. It was easy to plunge him into an hypnotic trance, from which I immediately released him. But my attempts to waken him fully proved futile. He remained from that day on under the the Hungarian's influence, in complete thrall to him. Zoltan conceived a genuine remorse for this incident, and I confess to feeling tormented still by my own share of responsibility in the affair.

Once Simon had recovered, in appearance at least, he continued to trail after Zoltan, but no longer as his helper or assistant. The Hungarian was no longer 'the boss' but 'the master' of this too faithful, too submissive dog always at his heels. His hard day's work over, Zoltan felt the need to get away for a few hours, if only to court a certain little lady selling lemons (or aubergines, depending on the season). To do so, he found himself obliged to confine Simon to his room and put him to sleep – as simple as that – before he could bolt the door and slip out.

At first Zoltan found it a burden to have someone trotting along beside him all the time, reading his thoughts, anticipating his every move. And then he got used to it. And between these two individuals, so unalike, there came to be a flow of affection operating on a level that can only be described as psychic.

There was plenty of work. Zoltan was in demand for various reasons. Many families who'd gone into exile finally returned to Paris and wanted to refurbish their homes. They recommended him to each other. Zoltan's savings grew: he thought of setting himself up as a master craftsman. 'I'd certainly consider getting married,' he said to me one day, 'if it weren't for the kid.' The kid being Simon.

Just as many bilingual people are more likely to speak English to their animals, horses or dogs, Zoltan when he was busy spoke to Simon in Russian. Moreover, when the job to be done proved long and hard, that's to say a match for his abundance of physical energy, he would *think* in Russian. Recalling the tough years he'd spent in Odessa.

'There at least I had a good time,' he liked to say, flexing his biceps.

Simon had never learned a single word of Russian. Apart from his rudimentary French, he very vaguely knew just a few Yiddish phrases he'd heard his parents use in the past.

At first, as a joke, he taught himself to say to his master – badly pronounced – '*Zdravstute, gospodine*!' (Good morning, sir!) or '*Spasibo*!' (Thank you). That was all.

Last month, feeling drowsy on a stifling hot afternoon, Simon went to sleep on a sofa in a room adjoining the one where Zoltan was working. Zoltan suddenly pricked up his ears. Someone nearby was talking Russian. The person was saying, '*Ya umirayu ot zhazhde. Segodnja tak zharko. Davajte pit*!' (I'm dying of thirst. It's so hot. Let's have a drink.)

Utterly amazed, Zoltan got up and peered into the hall and the adjoining room. No doubt about it, he was alone, with

Simon asleep. Without waking him, he said, '*Ty govorish po-ruski?*' (You speak Russian?)

And in a more confident voice than when he was awake, without stammering in the least, Simon replied, '*Vot vopros! Nyuzheli vy nu znete? Ya vsegda govoril po-rousski.*' (What a question! Didn't you know? I've always spoken Russian!)

I was soon told of the phenomenon, which I've since verified several times. I questioned Zoltan. He confessed that he enjoyed putting Simon to sleep whenever he wanted a few moments alone. Then he would communicate his thoughts in Russian, he said, because he was more at ease in that language and he had the impression of being able to project his will more strongly.

He got hooked on it, and within a few weeks poor Simon, the idiot, the moron, began speaking Russian fluently, with no grammar, no textbook of any kind, no notebook.

That's the situation at the moment.

The Old Man Who Appears After Midnight

October

This morning Gérard came and woke me in a great panic. He was brandishing a newspaper.

'Elisabeth mustn't see this! Go and find her, keep her busy all day, whatever it takes.'

Filling two columns on the front page, with a sensational headline, was a report of the legionnaire's arrest. There was a photo of him, smiling and handcuffed, looking cocky. Thief, murderer, swindler and pimp. Everything you could wish for.

I rushed over to where the dear girl lived. I found her in the caretaker's lodge. She was reading a letter. As pale as could be. She was trembling. All she said was, 'You already know?'

'Yes, I know.'

It was a bundle of despair, a vulnerable and buffeted little bird that I dragged round the exhibits at the Salon d'Automne.

The girl eventually shared her secret with Séverin and me. Not knowing where else to turn, she asked us point blank to find her an angel-maker to perform an abortion. Round Place Maubert, they call this 'plunging the dipstick' in memory of an old woman who, in the 'conveniences' at Guignard's, would use a long needle to carry out this operation. We couldn't make Elisabeth listen to reason. We suggested taking a trip, going into hiding, staying in the country with one of our relatives until her confinement. Her aunt and Clément would know nothing about it. It was a waste of breath. She was obdurate. She gave us an ultimatum: it was either that or suicide. You can imagine our quandary.

It was very late. No one was talking. Elisabeth had in despondency hidden her face in her hands. Clément thought she was ill and didn't know what to do. Olga wanted us to eat. We weren't hungry.

In comes Marina, a little squiffy, accompanied by Batifol's wife, she too sozzled. They were bickering. They wanted cognacs.

'I'll tell you whether you're being cheated on, I'll tell you right now.'

They sat down. The Spanish woman took out her cards. She laid them out in a triangle, covered them, turned over spades, hearts and jacks. She gave a derisive laugh.

'What did I tell you? Cheated on, you are, right up to the hilt! He's only giving you as good as he got. Does he know? That Jeannot's not his. Eh?' (Jeannot is the Batifols' kid, just turned ten.)

In a fury Batifol's wife tried to slap the witch in the face. Olga intervened and separated them with a firm hand.

Then from his usual corner came the voice of the Old Man. 'Marina, go away! You're drunk.'

'Why should I go anywhere? I'll stay if I want to.'

'Marina, go away! You bring bad luck on children.'

'No children here.'

Then with his long index finger pointed at Elisabeth, who was sunk in despair, the Old Man said, 'Yes, there is, there's the child she's carrying.'

Elisabeth sat up, distraught, her fists to her temples. It was the cry of a she-wolf that she uttered. She made for the door and ran out into the night.

We would never have thought the Old Man capable of leaping up the way he did, on those short bandy legs of his. He threw aside his stick and went rushing after the girl: this time we saw him leave.

A blind dash through the clammy streets down to the Seine.

From the bottom of Rue du Petit-Pont, we heard two splashes in close succession. Clément had the presence of mind to bang on Felix's door to wake him up and telephone the fire brigade, and the police immediately afterwards. Ah! It didn't take long. In three minutes the River Police boat was there. Some big strapping lads, trained and ready for anything, fished out Elisabeth, who was floundering underwater. Meanwhile the fire brigade and the land-based police turned up. It was quite a party. A searchlight was turned on, but the Old Man couldn't be found.

About five o'clock we returned to the Quatre-Fesses to tell Olga what had happened and reassure her about the fate of the girl. Olga was fussing over her friend, who looked quite out of sorts and shot a terrified look at us (yes, us!).

'What's wrong? She's that upset by all this?'

'It's not so much the girl, it's the stick.'

The Old Man's stick had bounced on the tiles with a dull thud as he threw it aside to go running after Elisabeth. When she picked it up, Suzy remarked to herself how heavy it was. She laid it on the bench. Then, when the two women began to clear up, Suzy once again picked up the long stick, intending to carry it to the back of the room. As she was walking, she felt the object grow very, very light, so much so she turned round to share her surprise with Olga. At that moment the stick literally dissolved in her hands.

That was several days ago now. Suzy still hasn't recovered. You can't mention it in front of her: it makes her blanch and tremble like a leaf.

The day after her escape from drowning, we went to visit Elisabeth. She asked for news of the Old Man.

'He must have sunk like a stone.'

'I'm not really surprised,' she said.

She remained silent for a moment. And then she put her hands on her belly and decided to keep the child.

I said to Boucher, the inspector at the police station in Rue Dante, 'What about the Old Man? Any news?'

He shrugged his shoulders.

'We've enough work as it is, in your neighbourhood full of crazies. If we had to go looking for ghosts as well . . .'

The child will be named Patrice if it's a boy, otherwise Ghislaine. Clément's just waiting for it to be born so he can claim paternity and marry the baby's mother.

Chapter XII

On the Art of Accommodating the Dead

There's someone for whom those drowned in the Seine represent a real patrimony. This character is Poloche the shrimp-fisher.

Very small, his hands reaching almost down to his knees, like some chinless chimpanzee, Poloche lives on Quai de la Tournelle in a tiny room crammed with bizarre objects that derive exclusively from dredging and cleaning operations carried out on the riverbed. One day recently he caught sight of me on the embankment and accosted me with all the signs of violent indignation.

'You're someone that knows the big shots at Police Headquarters. You have to help me. I need you to do me a favour!'

'Sure. Although my influence isn't very great. What's the problem?'

'It's always the little guys that suffer in this bloody country. You want to know something? They're destroying us small traders, they want to kill us off. There'll only be room left for the big guys!'

'Quite so. But what do you want me to do about it?'

'Come with me.'

Poloche took me along the riverbank, having 'forced' me (a euphemistic term) to knock back a muscadet at the Bouteille d'Or. With a trembling finger, he pointed to the water, silt-laden at this point.

'Look!'

'Well? It's just water . . .'

'That's what you may think! It's a whirlpool, my whirlpool, where I've been laying my nets since before the last war. No one ever gave me a hard time about them till now. And every

200

season, the shrimps I collect I sell to the Bouteille, the Tour d'Argent. I've even sold some at the Eiffel Tower. And at the Vel' d'Hiv', every year during the cycling championships. After all, I wasn't doing anyone any harm.'

'And what's stopping you from carrying on.'

'Just listen. Apparently the whirlpool's disrupting traffic: it sends the barges off course, it's a threat to the bridge pier. Rubbish! Despite the fact the River Police are connected with Police Headquarters, they sent guys here from the Civil Engineering Department, the Forestry Commission, God knows what! And now they want to remove it. My whirlpool. My livelihood. You see, all the stiffs, as soon as they're light enough to be carried by the current – not bloated enough to float – whether they come down from Bercy, or Charenton, or much further upstream, this is where they "come to land".

'They're here for two or three days and then, phut, they're gone, they take themselves off. That's why this part of the river's always clean. But no more whirlpool, no more stiffs, and with no more stiffs, no more shrimps! Damn it! At my age, where are they going to send me to make my catch? Billancourt?

'Otherwise, they should pay me a pension. Can't you pull some strings to arrange that for me? We'd have a feast to celebrate. When we do, I promise you a basketful of shrimp. Still live and kicking. Word of honour!'

One-armed, one-eyed, lame and crippled, nearly all of them. They get through life on the crutches of their dreams.

In their world, according to their lore, a person passes away only to be immediately replaced: permanent reincarnation. They're more bound up with the dead than the living, and their behaviour makes them heirs to the mysteries of paganism dating back to the most distant times.

Respect for death in itself, and deference owing to the dead, is completely alien to them. But they steer clear of the dying, and carefully avoid contact with a corpse too recently deceased, that's to say one that's been dead less than twenty-four hours, or even going anywhere near one.

One of them, an Oriental, born in Mosul, in Persia, described to me the practices followed by one particular sect in his country, to ascertain the dead person's chances of attaining the sphere of the elect. The body is laid on the ground. A piece of bread is placed between its teeth. A dog that was unknown to the dead person is brought along. If the animal backs off, the dead person is damned. If it sniffs at the corpse, a period of time in purgatory has been allotted, which the dead person's relatives can reduce through prayer. If the dog actually climbs on to the corpse to take the piece of bread, then the soul of the deceased is in paradise, and this gives rise to great rejoicing.

It's true that dogs – not all of them, but many – are sensitive to certain emanations that are still a mystery.

Last winter carried off the Old Shepherd. He was eighty-four when I first met him. A big bearded fellow, standing tall and straight. He'd once been able to read, but no longer remembered how: to what purpose? On the other hand, he knew the names of hundreds of stars, which he'd point out without ever making a mistake. The various stages of his life were marked by the loss of a succession of dogs. Having become a rag-picker like everyone else, he carried within him the quiet contentment of the patriarchs. Once he said to me, 'On the plains of Beauce and the Perche, where for seventy-one years I led my flocks to pasture, there were nights when my dogs would howl to kingdom come. I knew then who in the nearby villages was sick or very aged, and it was no surprise to me that my dogs should demonstrate an unerring premonitory instinct. Now, on four occasions spaced out over the years, my dogs howled when as far as I knew there was no one for miles around in any immediate danger of death. On those occasions it was always young people that died, victims of unforeseen accidents: a horse that bolted, a blazing barn, an overturned truck.' And the Shepherd added, 'Death and nothingness are not the same thing. Death is a powerful force, less evil than is generally believed. To people who aren't afraid of it, it comes as a friend. When it strikes, it needs to finish the job without delay.

'Nothing can surprise me any more. You know, you learn a lot living under the stars.'

According to one enduring legend, when it's known that no one's going to come and claim the body of a person who's taking too long to die in a welfare-assisted bed, the last rites are administered. Destined for the dissection room and for pickling in formaldehyde, already carved up alive by professors and medical students, our dying patient receives the sweet restful dose that will despatch him *ad patres*. True or false? I've no idea. The fact is that our tramps, while fully appreciating a stay, even an extended one, especially in winter, in a warm room where getting enough to eat doesn't present a daily challenge, are reluctant to go into hospital when they feel their end is near. That 'nasty injection' inspires the vagrant with more horror, indignation and repugnance than the loathsome fate of those sentenced to death by the criminal courts. In their eyes the condemned man has committed the unpardonable sin of getting caught, and having thereby justified the existence of Their Honourable Cogs in the much abhorred machine: that of the police and a repressive system of justice.

However, the vagrants are well able to defend themselves against those among them who provoke and taunt the Grim Reaper by being too reckless or irresponsible. The story of Maurice is very telling in this regard.

Maurice is in fact none other than the son, illegitimate of course, of La Goulue, a famous dancer of the French cancan at the turn of the century. Remember the Moulin Rouge, Valentin the Contortionist. Maurice claims to be the fruit of his mother's liaison with Edward VII of England. In support of this assertion, he has been known to produce documents that make unsettling reading, to say the least. From scrutiny of these documents it emerges that the old man had a gilded youth, thanks to the munificence of His Britannic Majesty. The latter paid out a very comfortable monthly allowance from the royal coffers to his unacknowledgeable offspring. Of all this Maurice retains only two mementoes: a magnificent tattoo – a bust portrait of La Goulue, the work of Henri Toulouse-Lautrec – that adorns his chest; and a profile – his own – that bears a striking resemblance to the pennies stamped with the effigy of his putative father. It is in any case an undisputed fact that the sovereign, remembered for his dissolute life, kept up a long-lasting relationship with the famous dancer, both in London and in Paris (the couple would meet in Rue Montorgueil, on the first floor of the Rocher de Cancale, in an apartment designed by Gavarni). Maurice sank into beggardom in the interwar years. He's presently lodged at the Nanterre workhouse, where in all probability he will end his days. He's become a pitiful derelict.

He takes advantage of the days he's allowed out to return to La Maubert – I met him at Pignol's – and until recently would readily direct his footsteps to the area round Rue du Croissant, with which he had links.

There, he drank with the typographers, rotary printers and newspaper distributors.

He instigated some memorable scandals. But the story that will not soon be forgotten is that of the 'death' of Pussy.

The aforementioned, an unbelievably ugly and grubby streetwalker, had become Maurice's girlfriend right after the Liberation. This picaresque couple were wonderfully well matched. Maurice benefitted considerably from the generosity of his companion who occasionally, especially at night, managed to 'seduce' a drunk. One day, a black soldier with the American Army agreed to 'go upstairs' with Pussy. Instead of displaying any exotic ardour, the black guy began to lay into Pussy with the very clear intention of beating her senseless and robbing her. The girl screamed, the black guy took fright and fled. Maurice came running and found Pussy passed out. The 'king's son' wasted no time: he announced the sudden death of his partner throughout the neighbourhood, and appealed to everyone to make a contribution to the expenses of the decent funeral he wanted her to have. Everybody gave something. That evening, beaten black and blue, eyes half-closed, a puffy and tearful Pussy turned up while in a nearby bistrot there was Maurice in blithe spirits, tanked up with the numerous litres with which he'd washed down a substantial slap-up meal.

Maurice's regular drinking companions held council. They brought the culprit to book, made him admit his offence and took him to task for having fostered in people's minds, by falsely announcing Pussy's death, that letting-go, that extension of pity, that sentiment 'you only have once'. To 'stave off bad luck' three or four tramps went all round the area and asked the same people for a contribution equal to what they'd given for the 'burial'. This time the money was presented to Pussy who, with no hard feelings, paid for her man to get drunk.

Some time afterwards she died, worn-out, broken down and decrepit. And from that day onwards Maurice became a permanent outcast, banned for ever from Rue du Croissant, which he'd desecrated.

Keep-on-Dancin'

No, Fernand Fabre should never have done what he did to me. He began by convincing me he was no longer interested in the Keep-on-Dancin' affair. Besides, he'd just been transferred to National Security. He was only concerned now with suspect foreigners, when he was with me at least. What a relief.

I'd heard there were several occasions when Fernand had come looking round Rue de la Montagne without making any attempt to meet me. He'd appeared mostly in places I'd already taken him to. Friendly and good-humoured, never unwilling to buy a round, he'd quickly won over the locals. He readily engaged them in conversation and very cleverly made inquiries about Keep-on-Dancin' 's habits.

Once, a student told him how surprised he was by the fact this uneducated fellow should profess such a liking for François Villon, collecting different editions and books about him. They'd spent a whole evening discussing the subject. To Fernand Fabre, this was remarkable. So much so, he made some notes.

As soon as I was told about this, I declared covert war on my friend the policeman. I in turn began to pester everyone I knew, describing Fernand as a 'cop', a dirty rotten cop, a ruthless hypocrite. Nearly always, I'd get the reply, 'Bah! That's all a load of nonsense. He seems like a decent enough bloke. Even if he did book Jojo-the-Hustler. And besides, whether he's a cop or not, why should it bother us?' It was depressing. Eventually I ran into Fernand. Just ignoring him wasn't very subtle. Neither was questioning him. I preferred to let him do the talking.

We took a turn down Rue de l'Estrapade and quite naturally ended up at Place de la Contrescarpe. From there we descended Rue Mouffetard. As we were passing the Théâtre Mouffetard, just opposite the Vieux-Chêne, I noticed a poster:

Karel Kapek's
MARIONETTES

'Must be good, that show,' said Fernand. 'I read in the paper that at the end of every performance, the manager of this place – I think he's a painter – does recitations from Villon when he takes a shine to members of the audience.'

Villon. My heart leapt into my mouth. But I'd detected the trap and quickly changed the subject.

Change the subject. There was nothing that could be done to alter the course of events. Each person had their role to play, just like marionettes. The die was cast, the mechanism now set in motion such that to try and halt it was a presumption as absurd as expecting to turn back the clock.

A patient audience waited in silence for the three knocks to reverberate. Students and hard-up intellectuals – or those pretending to be – occupied half the rows. At last the lights dimmed and just two spotlights lit the opening item on the programme: a Slovak folk dance. Behind the scenes, someone played a piano. Against a rural backdrop, six dolls, facing each other in pairs, turned in time to the music, skipped, bowed and curtsied to each other with innocent charm. And suddenly there was total darkness: a power failure. Candles were produced. Everyone agreed to take a break until the lights came on again. There was a sort of family feeling among us. But the power cut went on and on. After a quarter of an hour, the manager of the theatre, Adrien, and a few of his assistants, began rounding up the spectators who had dispersed into the street.

Adrien had placed a petrol lamp on either side of the small stage. The somewhat greenish lighting cast splashes of pallor on people's faces ruthlessly outlined by the drastic darkness. That night's drama was the colour of herbal tea.

Fernand Fabre displayed an interest in the fresco covering the wall. I dragged him off to the other end of the room. Right next to him, I'd recognized Keep-on-Dancin'. But Fernand didn't notice.

'Under these conditions we're unable to stage the rest of the show,' announced Adrien. 'Your tickets will be valid for any other performance. But you won't have come here for nothing. This gloom gives us the opportunity to present a staging of Villon.'

The curtains parted to reveal the striking spectacle of four puppets swinging from a gallows. And Adrien, in his deep bass voice, began to recite:

> '*Frères humains qui après nous vivez*
> *N'ayez les cuers contre nous endurciz*
> *Car si pitié de nous pauvres avez*
> *Dieu en aura plus tost de vous mercy.*'
> [Fellow human beings living still
> Don't harden your hearts against us
> For if you take pity on us poor wretches
> The sooner will God show mercy to you.]

As the lines reverberated the puppet in the foreground, which was bigger than the others and had been very cleverly wired up, fell to pieces, losing one foot, then the other, then a hand, an arm, a thigh, until completely dismembered, it was no more than a skeletal torso with a hideous face whose eye-sockets a nightmarish bird came to peck at.

> *'Plus becquetz d'oilseaux que dès à couldre . . .*
> *De notre mal personne ne s'en rie:*
> *Mais priez Dieu que tous nous veuille absouldre!*
> [More pitted by beaks than a thimble . . .
> Let no one laugh at our misfortune
> But pray God He absolve us all!]

After this curtailed performance, entertainers and public met up outside on the pavement.

Across the street flickered the candles – there was still no electricity – hurriedly lit by the *patron* of the Vieux-Chêne.

Quite naturally it was there that most people ended up. I was with Fernand, whom I tried to lead towards the back. I was watching the door. Keep-on-Dancin' came in, the fool. And just behind him, two big lads I didn't recognize and who didn't much look like the type to be interested in Karel Kapek's marionettes. Keep-on-Dancin' – what an idiot! – spotted me in the smoky fug, came over and shook hands warmly. He saw Fernand, whom I'd introduced to him in the past, and stuck out his paw which the other didn't take straightaway, busy as he was – hmm! – rummaging in his pockets.

'No change? Don't worry, I'll pay for this round,' said Keep-on-Dancin' in his usual way.

He too searched his jacket, stuffed with small banknotes and coins. The first thing he laid on the counter was a dessicated human ear that looked as though it'd been tanned, a right ear.

Fernand smiled.

'What a coincidence!'

Alongside the right ear, he laid the one that matched it, the left ear, less well preserved than the other. It was slightly crumpled.

The two big lads had closed in on us.

'The game's up,' said Keep-on-Dancin', holding out his wrists.

'There's no hurry,' said Fernand. 'Take your time, finish your drink.'

We stuffed Keep-on-Dancin''s pockets with sandwiches. I borrowed two handkerchiefs and a blanket from the *patron*. No one noticed the handcuffs. As he went through the door, Keep-on-Dancin' uttered these three words: 'Free at last!'

Probably the last I'd ever hear from him. The police Citroen pulled away silently.

Zoltan the Mastermind

One day I took Zoltan and Simon to lunch at a Jewish restaurant in Rue des Ecouffes. I like this melancholy part of town, all squalor, and beards, steeped in legends and the Orient.

It was during those months when the survivors of the death camps were arriving in batches before travelling on to the countries of their choice.

Around us, incredibly thin people, their faces stamped for ever with definitive and seemingly age-old sadness, were slumped with dignity, if we can accept such a paradox. A woman who was once beautiful, with a five-figure registration number tattooed on her forearm, was serving mushy food that they swallowed slowly, with difficulty.

We were sat at a table. There was an uncomfortable oppressive silence. I was ashamed, and Zoltan too, of presenting these people with the spectacle of our good health, our freedom from care.

Simon, sitting next to me, seemed preoccupied, perhaps intimidated. His face gives little away about the feelings that stir him, or rather arrest him.

On Simon's left was a skinny young girl, in crumpled clothes, with a shawl over her head. Tentatively and with infinite difficulty she was trying to eat her way through a tiny portion of salmon roe.

Her hands were translucent. Cord-like veins throbbed in her neck. Zoltan had noticed this image of the most appalling distress. Simon seemed oblivious.

An ordinary Jewish meal: fish stuffed with bread, boiled beef with horseradish sauce. The pot of horseradish was close to the young girl. Zoltan asked Simon to pass it. Being clumsy, Simon knocked it over.

'Forgive me.'

'*Pozhalusta* (That's all right),' said his neighbour with a wan sad smile.

Simon gazed at us very proudly. He too was smiling. That was something we hadn't seen for a very long time.

Faltering at first, then more sustained, a conversation in Russian began between Simon and the young girl. Her name was Ida Bleivas, and she was from a remote village on the Russo-Lithuanian border. Liberated just in time from a camp devastated by typhus, she was part of a convoy of displaced persons on their way to the newborn state of Israel. She looked exhausted. We caught sight of her, in the back room, adjusting her shawl in front of a mirror. Her head was shaved. At last Simon had found a wretchedness to equal his own: he was happy.

Simon met up with his friend every evening. He became almost gallant. He offered her tea, held her hand, and took her wandering through the streets of the sorely depleted ghetto. They spoke little. These two afflicted souls didn't have much left to entrust to each other but their mutual presence.

Zoltan celebrated with me this unexpected turn of events. Finally, it was possible to envisage for our Simon the prospect of a more or less normal future.

Simon was disconsolate over the imminent departure of young Ida. But meanwhile difficulties arose in Israel where the arrival of thousands of helpless starving immigrants was viewed with some alarm. And Ida Bleivas's stay in Paris was extended.

One day she told Simon she'd like to have heard him speak Yiddish. That devil Zoltan more or less knew the language: and he starts repeating the same experiment as before on Simon. In less than two weeks he instilled in him not just enough to get by, but the ability to speak almost fluently.

Simon was transformed: quicker-witted and more lively,

with even occasional bursts of sheer joyfulness. When he spoke French his mispronounciations had almost disappeared.

One evening when we were taking the air together, Simon told us that he didn't after all much care about having French nationality, he wanted to share his life with the girl and follow her to Israel. I regarded this decision as his only hope of happiness and warmly approved it. But to my great surprise Zoltan became sullen.

From that moment I witnessed an extraordinary phenomenon: Zoltan was tormented with intense jealousy originating beyond any extremely improbable physical attraction. He'd developed such an attachment to the boy he called his 'burdensome beast' that the thought of their separation unhinged him. All my efforts to calm him, to make him see reason, proved futile.

One day he uttered these dreadful words in my presence: 'I shall wipe from his mind everything I put there.'

An expected assignment suddenly sent me off on a mission to Germany for six weeks. During my absence Simon's regular certificates of leave couldn't be renewed. But in the ordinary course of events he should have been free every evening.

I found out on my return that Simon had started stammering, then dribbling a bit.

He was admitted to Val-de-Grâce military hospital. He soon proved incapable of uttering anything intelligible whatsoever, even in French.

Then came the day when he was struck down with an epileptic fit. He was immediately invalided out of the army.

Ida Bleivas was woken at dawn one day by 'officials' of I don't know which organization, and given an hour to pack her meagre belongings and join a convoy on its way to Marseilles, as a first stop.

No sign of Zoltan. His landlord had to force the lock. His room was found neat and tidy, containing his clothes and work tools.

Where else would Zoltan be if not in La Mouffe?

Which is where I came across him several months later.

Terribly aged, emaciated, all he said was, 'It's worse than if I'd committed a crime. I don't know whether I can ever redeem myself. But I'm trying to.'

He wasn't resurfacing wooden floors any more. For a glass of wine, a bite to eat, often for nothing at all, he was teaching Russian to generous-spirited and 'committed' students. Let there be no misunderstanding: he enabled them to make such rapid progress that 'someone very respectable, wearing glasses and with a slight accent', became intrigued by his method of teaching and forcefully insisted on taking him on a journey. No one could tell me where.

There are in every ghetto in the world street-pedlars selling pumpkin or melon seeds – I'm not quite sure what they are. The Jews chew these the way others chew hazelnuts.

Over in Belleville, round République, there are cinemas where they often show pre-war yiddish films: *Yidl mitn Fidl, Der Yidisher Kenig Lir, Der Dibuk* . . .

At the entrance is a pathetic figure selling seeds, or trying to. He's constantly nibbling at them; he looks increasingly rodent-like.

He can't speak. From the sounds that issue from his constricted throat you can just about make out two syllables: I-da . . . I-da . . .

Chapter XIII

> *. . . the question is precisely*
> *to know whether the past has ceased to exist,*
> *or ceased to be useful . . .*

Bergson

1947

I'm trying to take stock of Paris, to rethink it. The convulsions that shook the world seem, in the eyes of those wilfully short-sighted people who reduce them to human proportions, to have subsided for a long period. I don't believe it. Nowhere in this City of mine, so thoroughly explored, so probingly questioned, so deeply penetrated, have I found the torpor, the weary calm that are symptoms of a lasting peace. People are tired, it's true. Tired and disillusioned. They're fed up with everything. But not the City. It's still edgy. Just as there remain, to the great disadvantage of arms manufacturers, enormous quantities of ordnance that have not yet been destroyed, are indeed being carefully preserved, there is pent-up rebellion beneath the paving stones. Anything could happen.

The events I've chosen to record are only the most spectacular manifestations of forces that – out of fear, ignorance, everyday stupidity – are deemed 'obscure'. But it's now an indisputable fact that the most innocent words, the most harmless gestures in certain places and at certain times acquire an unwonted importance and weight, and have repercussions that far exceed what was intended.

It's a joy, a pleasure to discover in Paris an oasis of calm – they're rare – and to visit it sometimes, returning from aggressive streets there to immerse yourself as if in a warm and placid lake.

The Place Dauphine is one such oasis. You feel somewhat captive in this shady, semi-provincial triangle, where the inhabitants are all known to one another by name and wouldn't know how to greet one another without a smile.

I'm particularly fond of Suzanne's grocery-cum-bar. She and her husband run a shop a few square metres in size that somehow manages to accommodate, in an amazingly restricted space, dried and cooked vegetables, tinned foods, litres of vintage wine, and the tiny bar counter behind which reigns Monsieur Suzanne, in other words Old François. At what is considered the time of day for an aperitif, the place is invaded by as mixed a crowd as you could hope to find. It ranges from drab young housemaids, who refer to themselves as 'governesses' here, to certain illustrious members of the bench who are not above standing a drink to persons of a disreputable and scruffy appearance (the jail is near by), or indeed clinking glasses with the gaolers and wardens of the Prison Service.

It was there, on a day 'unlike any other', that I met one of my old friends. A documentary work I was trying to put together was the reason I'd gone wandering round Rue des Blancs-Manteaux. At the corner of Rue Ste-Croix and Rue Aubriot there's a shabby little café with a Virgin watching over it, forbearing and indulgent, just like all the naive devotional images, Christs and saints installed by the populace of 'working men and women' for their 'own personal use'. I was proposing to chronicle the events that this congenial watering-hole might have witnessed, and depict the characters who'd surely drunk here over the course of bygone ages.

In the thirteenth century, a period when the present Rue Aubriot was known by the name of Rue à Singes [Monkey Street], one of the most interesting and colourful characters in the neighbourhood without a doubt was Sieur Michel de Socques. Before coming into possession of considerable wealth, this gentleman must have been some kind of strolling player or exhibitor of animals: for he devoted the rest of his life to assisting the former and offering a home to the latter. Whenever there was fear of certain types of epidemic, animals of exotic origin had to be placed in quarantine before their owners were allowed to exhibit them 'in the thoroughfares of the fair city'. So Sieur Michel would take in the animals whose exhibitors couldn't afford to keep them in isolation without their help to earn a living. His residence, 'Monkey House', gave its name to the street. A nearby passageway has retained this designation.

On bears and popinjays (parrots) there was an admittance toll levied, which was paid at the Passage du Petit-Châtelet, in front of the Petit-Pont. As for monkeys, 'The Rules Governing the Trades of Paris, by Etienne Boilève, Provost of this City', lays down the following:

'The Merchant who brings a Monkey to sell must pay four deniers: and if the Monkey belongs to someone who has bought it for his own amusement, it is exempt, and if the Monkey belongs to an exhibitor, the exhibitor must give a performance for the toll-collector, and in exchange for his performance be exempted on everything he buys for his needs: and minstrels too are exempted in exchange for singing one verse of a song.'

What this amounts to is that the animal exhibitor, instead of paying the four-denier toll the merchant has to pay, would pay his due in songs and capers. Hence the expression: *payer en monnaie de singe*, literally, to pay with monkey money, ie avoid paying a debt, with fine words and empty promises.

The Gypsies of Paris

So it was that after a pleasant stroll, my mind filled with gladdening thoughts, I quite naturally returned to the banks of the Seine and crossed the first bridge I came to.

It was evening. At Suzanne's, the regulars were as usual chatting quietly, sipping an inoffensive rosé. The man who came in was tall, bony and dark-haired, wearing a wide-brimmed hat and long khaki cloak, probably of military provenance.

Even then we were all intrigued by this new arrival: you never see a strange face at Suzanne's at this time of day.

The guy went up to the counter and ordered an anisette. To

pay and raise the glass to his lips he used only his right hand. Another glass. And another. Now where had I seen that face before? The collar of a large-checked shirt could be glimpsed under his cloak. That, the hat and the distant gaze more or less placed my man: he must work in a circus.

The guy noticed some little bags of macaroons hanging on the wall. He pointed to them, and said to Suzanne, 'How much?'

Still using only his right hand he tore open the packet, crushed one of the macaroons on the counter and, having tasted it, started to slip a tiny mouthful of cake inside his hermetically buttoned-up cloak. A hand emerged, a minute woollen-gloved hand, which grabbed the morsel. From under the cloak came a crunching sound.

Next to me at the back of the shop sitting on the only possible chair was Old Angélique, a somewhat simple-minded Breton woman. She does cleaning and shopping errands on the island, where any spurious ingenuousness is banished.

Angélique tugged at my sleeve, pointing to the hand that snatched the pieces of macaroon. 'What's that?'

There were a good ten or twelve of us asking ourselves the same unspoken question. The man then undid three buttons and perched on his shoulder a little old man, with beard and moustache – of cotton wool – black eyes that darted in every direction, a long turned-up nose, gloves, leather boots, black knitted trousers, a red jacket with a long hood.

The perfection of this impersonation amazed us. For the man must have had to tame his monkey with infinite patience to reach the point where the animal was prepared to tolerate this get-up – which didn't seem to bother it at all – and especially the papier-mâché nose and the mask of make-up.

The evening hour, fading light, peacefulness, and relaxed atmosphere reigning that day conspired to transport us within a few moments to a world of enchantment.

Angélique insisted. 'But what on earth is that, sir?'

'This? It's a dwarf, madame. As you can see, it's a dwarf, a very old dwarf.'

'A dwarf? But what . . . what kind of dwarf?'

'One of our forest dwarfs,' said the other, unruffled. 'Some still exist in my country.'

'That's just incredible! He's not mechanical?'

'Indeed not.' (He bent down a little.) 'Give him a piece of cake. You can shake his hand.'

'Oh! goodness me! It's for real!' Angélique was ecstatic. 'Let me tell you, sir, in my country too, in Brittany, we have forests like yours. And I was told that dwarves lived there, *farfardets* we call them. As well as goblins riding white mares, and then women who are taller, but mean no harm, the *milloraines*. Well, I believed in all that, as if it were the Gospel, until the age of fourteen. Yes, sir, fourteen. And then I went to work in Rennes, and they told me it was all humbug. Then, since I'd never seen any, in the forests or on the heath, I didn't believe in those dwarves of yours any more. But here I am at the end of my life – you see, I'm getting on for sixty-eight and not in very good health, monsieur – and I can believe in them again, really and truly, for good and all? Ah, monsieur! If you only knew how happy you've made me!'

Everyone was choked. No one dreamed of making fun of the good-hearted woman. The man with the monkey was having a private conversation with Suzanne.

Angélique rummaged in her skirts, drew out a large battered-looking purse. In it were a few small notes, carefully folded. 'Monsieur, this is worth celebrating. François, give everyone here a drink. It's not that I'm very rich, but that's done me good, ah la la, that's made me happy.'

'That's all right, dear, you keep your money, we wouldn't dream of taking it,' said François, filling the glasses.

The man put his monkey away, buttoned up his cloak, and said goodbye with a smile addressed to all. He cast a glance in my direction. A knowing glance. Now fancy that. He was at the door when Angélique called out to him, 'Hey, monsieur! Where was it that you found your dwarf?'

With a very broad sweep of his hat, 'In a legend, madame.'

The man with the monkey had on the quiet given Suzanne a thousand francs, to pay for Angélique's bag to be filled with provisions after he left.

217

Now I've placed him. It was the Gypsy from Rue de Bièvre, Gabriel, who was my godson for seven years. He's simply shaved his beard off. He must have been living abroad for quite a while: you can tell from his accent.

When I leapt out of bed on Sunday I didn't need to waste much time wondering how to spend the morning. Even if I'd decided otherwise, my shoes would have walked me to the St Médard market. I had fun poking about among those humble old bits and pieces, shook hands with the Captain, ran into La Puce, La Lune, Trouillebave. But that wasn't the only reason for coming. The Gypsy had agreed to meet me. By himself this time: he only takes his monkey out for two hours in the evening.

His name's not Gabriel any more, but Mikhail. His new 'godfather', my successor, is Rumanian. We shall soon make each other's acquaintaince: Mikhail — since that's what we must call him — has invited both of us to a feast that his clan is hosting to celebrate his forthcoming marriage. There, eating straight out of the family cooking-pot, we shall savour together the *niglo* (hedgehog) of true friendship. Mikhail is for the time being manager of the travelling circus-cum-theatre that his future in-laws own. He let me see a photograph showing the eyes of his betrothed. Only her eyes. The rest of her face was concealed by a piece of white masking paper folded over, stuck down on the back. Apparently, 'among their own' — I don't know whether this term includes the entire race or only one clan — this is the custom for a very specific period during the betrothal.

We went to Olivier's, where naturally I spoke to him about Keep-on-Dancin', goatee-bearded Klager and the 'ill-intentioned prayers' that people offer up in front of the sign of the Quatre-Sergents.

'And you thought you were an expert on Paris, that you knew it all. I could teach you a lot more things I'm sure you don't know,' he said to me.

'Gladly. You're making my mouth water. But how long are you going to keep me dangling?'

'How should I know?'

Olivier called me over into a quiet corner.

'Have you heard the rumours going round?'

Apparently, they want to abolish the market, 'our' market.

'Who's "they"?'

'The police authorities, of course.'

'But that would be heinous, and idiotic. Why? For what reason? And under what powers?'

'The normal powers of the local administration. They're perfectly entitled to revoke a concession that may have existed for centuries but isn't registered in any written text. It would help us out if you could write a few articles on the subject.'

'That's certainly within the realms of possibility.'

'And if you could try and trace the origins of that concession in the City archives. Apparently it goes back a very long way.'

'Sure. I'll get on to it right away.'

'Let me know what you find out,' said the Gypsy. 'If your research confirms what they say in my family, you're in for a few surprises.'

'How on earth . . . in what way can a Gypsy community's folklore have anything to do with the St Médard market? In fact, do you mean the market, or the church?'

'Both. The church is a place of pilgrimage assigned to us, some of us at least, from way back: every seventh generation. No more questions for now. You've work to do.'

The St-Médard Concessions

What a City of marvels! I turned myself into a detective, and followed the trail through indecipherable manuscripts and old books. It was in the City that the story began. Here it is.

The present Rue Chanoinesse, which winds its way in the shadow of Notre-Dame, was not in the Middle Ages disturbed by the noisy presence of our motorcyclist guardians of the peace. It was called Rue des Marmousets: on the site of the motorcycle garage was the corner of Rue des Deux-Ermites.

And there, until 1884, it was possible to gaze on the remains of a generally neglected monument, so-called Dagobert's Tower, which included a ninth-century staircase set into the masonry, of which the thirty-foot handrail was fashioned out of the trunk of a gigantic oak tree. Here, according to tradition, lived a barber and a pastry-cook, who in the year 1335 plied their trade next door to each other. The reputation of the pastry-cook, whose products were among the most delicious that could be found, grew day by day. Members of the high-ranking clergy in particular were very fond of the extraordinary meat pies that, on the grounds of keeping to himself the secret of how the meats were seasoned, our man made all on his own, with the sole assistance of an apprentice who was responsible for the pastry.

His neighbour the barber had won favour with the public through his honesty, his skilled hairdressing and shaving, and the steam baths he offered. Now, thanks to a dog that insistently scratched at the ground in a certain place, the ghastly origins of the meat used by the pastry-cook became known, for the animal unearthed some human bones! It was established that every Saturday before shutting up shop the barber would offer to shave a foreign student for free. He would put the unsuspecting young man in a tip-back seat and then cut his throat. The victim was immediately rushed down to the cellar, where the pastry-cook took delivery of him, cut him up, and added the requisite seasoning. For which the pies were famed, 'especially as human flesh is more delicate because of the diet,' old Dubreuil comments facetiously.

The two wretched fellows were burned with their pies, the house was ordered to be demolished, and in its place was built a kind of expiatory pyramid, with the figure of the dog on one of its faces. The pyramid was there until 1861.

But this is where the story takes another turn and joins the very best of black comedy. For the considerable number of ecclesiastics who had unwittingly consumed human flesh were not only guilty before God of the very venial sin of greed; they were automatically excommunicated! A grand council was held under the aegis of several bishops and it was decided to send to Avignon, where Pope Clement VI resided, a delegation of prelates with a view to securing the rescindment if not of the Christian interdiction against cannibalism then at least of the torments of hell that faced the inadvertent cannibals. The delegation set off, with a tidy sum of money, bare-footed, bearing candles and singing psalms. But the roads of that time were not very safe and doubtless strewn with temptation. Anyway, the fact is that Clement VI never saw any sign of the penitents, and with good reason.

Notre-Dame had not yet disappeared from the bright horizon when these prelates of ours, their feet already sore, anticipating the hardships of their journey decided to stop in some suitable place and discuss what decisions should be taken. They circled round Paris, skirted the estates of the Comte de Boulogne bordering the Bièvre, and found at a place called Pont aux Tripes (Tripe Bridge) – more or less the site of the Gobelins intersection – a welcoming inn where the owner didn't mind being overrun by the Grand Provost's footsoldiers. Having eaten their fill, and appreciative of the generous fare provided by their host, our clerics postponed their journey till a later date and settled round the small market town of St-Médard. They very soon found themselves in need of replenishing their funds. They turned themselves into mendicant friars, some calling themselves *Hubains*, that's to say, 'those cured of rabies by St Hubert'; the rest, *Coquillards*, who'd made the pilgrimage, so they claimed, to Santiago di Compostella or Mont-St-Michel. Thus divided into two allied bands, our 'penitents', who were somewhat forceful in getting the tardy traveller to donate alms, were not however looked on with a favourable eye by their rivals: the *Rifodés, Malingreux, Francs-Mitous* and *Piètres* – highway robbers all of them – were only too anxious for a chance to pit themselves against these intruders. It duly arose. One autumn night in 1352 Monsignor Jean de Meulan, formerly Bishop of Noyon and recently appointed Bishop of Paris, was returning to his estate that lay just beyond the church of St Médard, along the Rue de 'Mont-Fêtard'. Armed horsemen were escorting his carriage. But his guard would have had to yield to the attack

221

launched by a gang of brigands determined to rob the bishop and his entourage if the former 'Penitents', alerted to what was happening, had not come running and fought a pitched battle. Jean de Meulan was able to regain his property, safe and sound.

In gratitude for their intervention, perhaps due to some lingering scruple in which a kind of vocational biais may be detected, he absolved the *Coquillards* and *Hubains*, granting them permission to sell, on his land and adjoining meadows, all kinds of goods and objects whose provenance would not be questioned.

And as Pope Clement VI was unable to intercede on their behalf and solicit any indulgence from Heaven, that's why the souls of those ill-fated prelates, priests and monks too fond of good eating have been stewing for centuries in the cooking-pots of hell.

The authorities who exercised control over the land round St Médard, and were responsible for policing it, changed many times. But throughout the ages, despite the unheavals and disturbances of History, the concession under which the St Médard market operated remained in force. Until now.

The Gypsies of Paris

The Gypsy was reading the *Aboi de Paris*, rubbing his chin. He was smiling.

'So, what do you think of it?'

'That's it. That's exactly right. Let's go for a walk.'

He put the periodical in his pocket, and at the first newspaper stand bought another five copies of the same issue.

'I'd love to know what your people have to say about St Médard.'

'Try to free yourself for a couple of hours, and come with me. I'd like to introduce you to my family. We're camped over by Montreuil.'

There were doe-eyed children swarming under the caravans. One of them, a tiny thing with his bottom in the air, had nose-dived into the dog's bowl. And the mutt was so tickled by this that it frisked about and every so often, with its muzzle, nudged the toddler into its bowl again. Two adolescent girls were carefully combing and smoothing the fur of a good-natured brown bear eating a beetroot.

A man holding a long piece of rope was making a young horse with no harness circle round an imaginary ring. The half-wild animal would rear up, its mane flying out, rising on its hind legs and flailing the air with its hoofs – then set off again, subdued, seething with resentment.

A little monkey I thought I recognized was searching the hair of an old woman busy feeding fresh twigs into a crackling fire. A hearty soup bubbled and simmered in the copper pot with a handle and feet made of sturdily wrought iron.

There were some women scrubbing dishes and linen all mixed up together in a tub. Mikhail seemed to be regarded as the boss. Everyone cast meek and vaguely fearful glances in his direction. Mikhail grabbed a stick lying to hand, went up to one of the caravans and knocked twice on the shutter, and then once again. The door opened. A slender girl of regal bearing, with her hair loose, descended the four steps.

'My wife,' said Mikhail.

She smiled graciously, extending her hand.

I was in the middle of nowhere. The gaudy clothes, the horse's white coat made the surrounding landscape, which was flat and rather squalid, take on a different hue. This Gypsy encampment could have been located in any corner of Europe, America, or Asia Minor.

'All we need's a bit of music,' I said.

'Stay with us,' said Mikhail. 'You shall have some this evening.'

There are things he'd like to tell me, loads of things, revelations I await with impatience. But these fail to come. What the nature of his latest qualms is, I do not know. So I can't attempt to allay them. He finally makes up his mind, without conviction, and opts to question me.

'Have you ever needed to be forgiven for something serious?'

'That depends. If you mean, have I ever committed a serious sin, probably yes. But have I thought of "seeking forgiveness"? To start with, from whom?'

'Not from your fellow men.'

'Then no. Definitely not. You can't redeem a wicked deed: you can, if possible, make amends. I'm willing to be punished for all the ill I might do. I want to pay my dues. But I don't believe that past deeds can be cancelled out. Nor the intentions a person might have had. The intention: that's the important thing in my view.'

'You don't recognize any other judge?'

'No. Besides, I'm more severe than anyone else. For me, any notion of humility, of submission, is unthinkable.'

'So you reject the very principle of confession.'

'Absolutely. It offends me. Infuriates me. It's a humiliation, a degradation I can't accept.'

'Of course, that's a valid point of view.'

We were walking through the grassy rises and depressions of that outlying area. We circumvented an animal carcase. A tyre ring, worn down to the canvas, lay abandoned among the nettles. Mikhail picked it up and put it on his shoulder. I wonder what use he can possibly make of it.

After a pause: 'But if you felt there existed inside you, in your physical body, something bad, impure, taboo . . .'

'There's always penicillin.'

'Don't joke about it.'

He expended his anger by giving a hefty kick to all the tins that lay in his path.

'How am I going to get you to understand?'

'I don't know. I've never had that experience.'

He decided to change tack.

'Have you never had the impression, whether it took the form of a memory, intuition, or whatever, of having lived in some previous age?'

'Oh, yes indeed. Actually, in two different ages, a little over two centuries apart, which I could pin down to within a few years.'

'And where was that?'

'Here. In Paris.'

'And it was really you, you're not just identifying with some other character?'

'No. Exactly the same person, with same face, the same body, in every detail.'

He looked relieved.

'Some common ground, at last. Now, I hope you'll be able to understand.'

Mikhail's family-in-law belong to the same clan. They're all more or less cousins. I'd noticed they had more sophisticated, more highly developed features than most of their like: no thick lips, clearly separated eyebrows, broad foreheads, ears that originate at the level of their eyes and not above. They live in a patriarchal community under the rule not of a 'leader' but as is customary among the Gypsy people of a king, not elected by his subjects: it's an hereditary position. Now, according to family tradition – which corresponds to a very deep-rooted belief – every seven generations, it's the very same king who reappears to regenerate his dynasty. The authority of his forefathers and descendants, 'kings' too but mere links in the chain, is infinitely less great than his. Which is absolute and extends to every domain. The crown princes – the eldest sons – are expected to procreate as soon as they become physically capable of doing so: that's to say, between thirteen and sixteen years of age. Which leads to a 'reincarnated' sovereign every century, more or less. The law of the clan lays down that on his death the king should not be buried but cremated and his ashes scattered to the wind.

A detail arises at this point that caused Mikhail to hesitate a long while before revealing to me the secret of a tradition that, appalling as it was, no one will ever dare to violate. A funeral banquet, organized according to an immutable rite, will bring together the dead king's sons, and more generally speaking all his male descendants. Among other classic delicacies, they'll have to partake of the deceased's brain, heart and testicles, prepared however it suits them.

And then, even if they're on the other side of the world,

they'll have to hurry to reach Paris and come to do penance at St Médard, praying in earnest for nine consecutive days. At St Médard, and nowhere else; for only there is the sin of cannibalism absolved.

'Now, you're free to regard me as a savage.'

'Not at all. I wasn't expecting to hear what you've just told me. It's still too fresh in my mind. And anyway, far be it from me to pass judgement. But have you already attended such a meal, experienced a ceremony of this kind?'

'No. The last "Great King" was cremated on the island of Oléron, in 1880. It's a problem in France, for we don't have the right to dispose of our dead, or even to transport them.'

'So what will you do next time?'

My question seemed to provoke in him a certain unease.

'Everything's arranged. He'll be shut up in a box filled with salt and the caravan will travel until it finds some uninhabited or remote spot, far from any village, in the Landes, for example.'

'And where have you got to in your dynasty?'

'My father's the present king, he's number six, and the oldest son is me.'

It was my turn to feel somewhat uncomfortable. Gabriel himself, Mikhail here, destined for the cooking pot!

'So you're the reincarnated king. But how old are you?'

'Thirty-eight.'

'No children yet?'

'Sixteen, including four daughters.'

'And it's only now you're getting married?'

'For the fourth time.'

'I didn't know your people practised polygamy.'

'They don't. I'm allowed to. No one else is. I'm allowed to do anything.'

'But how come you were a rag-picker when I met you?'

'All of us, the kings just like everyone else, are obliged to spend some time alone and in extreme poverty. It's the oldest member of the clan, not necessarily the king, who decides when it's time to go and how long the ordeal's to last.'

'What determines that decision? His mood? His judgement? Some sixth sense?'

'Certainly not. With us, it's much more complicated. Accounts have to be settled.'

On this point, he refused to be drawn any further.

'I can't understand why your people pretend to profess the Catholic faith while on the other hand their customs seem contaminated with pagan practices from the most distant past. Not to mention this ritual cannibalism, which is a little too reminiscent of the nineteenth-century travel journal. Admittedly, in that case, it was happening in a place like Caffre or Papua New Guinea.'

'I want to show you something.'

The back of a caravan is set up as a shrine. A flame flickers on a glass of oil. A faint smell of incense hangs in the air. Vases attractively filled with fresh flowers stand on the shelf that serves as an altar. An extraordinary virgin of blackened silver is in the centre of an icon.

Dominating all this is a polychrome wooden crucifix. It's very old. Of Hungarian or Rumanian craftsmanship. It's no ordinary Christ figure: the head is raised, the eyes look skywards. The left hand, detached from the cross, is raised in a gesture of farewell – or appeal. The effect is ungainly.

'Listen carefully.'

He makes two rapid movements to indicate the two structural elements of the cross. From top to bottom, from left to right.

'That's time. That's space. They're mutually restrictive, they imprison each other. A man cannot conceive of one except in terms of the other. True or not?'

'That's quite true. It's indisputable. We weren't made to transcend those givens.'

'Indeed. Man stuck in the middle. Right? At zero point. We can't escape that. We've no right to. That's Christian humility for you. That's obedience. That's discipline.'

He gives a contained sarcastic laugh. His eyes are shining. An insane pride is stamped on his brow. He points to the free hand.

'There, that's our secret, our ... my heritage. We've managed to escape. To transcend everything. We're no longer subject to any constraint. Think about that. Often.'

Time, the x-axis. Space, the y-axis. The rest of us stuck in the middle. I promise you, Mikhail, to think about it much more often than I'd like to.

Chapter XIV

Berlin, February 1948

I took the tram from Tegel, the U-bahn from Wedding. Brandenburg Gate: ten kilometres of houses blown up on Unter-den-Linden. It's freezing cold. There are children tobogganing amid the devastation.

I walk up towards Stettiner Bahnhof (their Gare du Nord). Near the urinals, a young nancy-boy on crutches – about seventeen, with the face of an angel, he has only half a leg – asks me for a light. Apparently, with him, for three marks, it's 'a deal'.

Inside the station: police raid. German cops and Russian NCOs search the rucksacks of gaunt individuals hurrying to board gloomy carriages fitted with plywood panels instead of glass windows.

Round the station, black market trading in potatoes, matches and horrible Rusky fags ('*Papyruski*', they say). And who do you think it is, wearing a Jerry cap and grey-green combat jacket, that sells me a packet?

Tricksy-Pierrot! Pierrot from Keep-on-Dancin' 's gang!

He hasn't heard. He's stunned by the news.

Keep-on-Dancin's first trial was annulled. The second dragged on for ages. He was condemned to death by two different courts on loads of charges. He was guillotined ten days ago.

'Topped! They did that to him! And you think that's going to be the end of it? To hell with it all! I'm going back to Paris!'

'Please, Pierrot, don't be a fool.'

Keep-on-Dancin'

Keep-on-Dancin' had been executed, and no one was protesting about that. 'Those were the rules of the game,' in his own words. He shouldn't have let himself get caught in such an idiotic way like that. But around Mont-St-Geneviève we'd all known him, and everybody began to consider and comment on the actual process of execution. And outraged by it, everybody declared it was degrading to all of us, appalling, disgusting. It's the beheading that sickens them. An Arab told us that the beheading of a single Muslim, however abominable a criminal he might be, causes millions of fists to be raised against the sacrilegious Christians. A Muslim does not present himself before Mahomet purged of all his earthly sins with his head under his arm. Dolly-the-Slow-Burner was terribly upset. It became quite another matter when Tricksy-Pierrot showed up, bearded, bespectacled, unrecognizable.

In the back room at Quarteron's they rallied a few supporters and held a kind of war council. Everyone agreed 'it shouldn't end there'. Dolly's unbridled anger verged on hysteria. It was she who had the nerve to reach the conclusion, 'Either we've got guts, or we haven't. I say, we ought to do in a cop.'

Feelings were running high among the others. Pierrot backed Dolly.

'Absolutely, they need to be taught a lesson. If the law's left to the fuzz, it means the death of the petty crook . . .'

A little later Alexandre Villemain turned up. Drunk, like he was every evening. And like every other evening when he was drunk, he came out with the same old story.

'I'm like you . . . I'm with the police . . .'

Everyone stared at him with interest.

It's curious how the waters of the Seine act differently on the drowned, depending on whether they've eaten or drunk, or the proportion of unabsorbed alcohol circulating in the system. When two days after the memorable meeting between the friends of Keep-on-Dancin', Villemain was fished out on Quai du Marché-Neuf, his hands and feet had become chalk-white and enormous. His dosser friends organized a collection.

So he didn't have to be buried in an unmarked grave.

Solange is inconsolable. She's made up a little bag that she wears next to her skin like a scapular. She's tucked inside it the last memento she has of her friend. An exhibit that was produced as evidence in court, stolen during the trial. A human ear, a right ear, tanned like leather, long and a little pointed.

I've treated her and her girlfriends to a bottle of champagne. They're wondering if I've come into an inheritance, or something. It's made them feel slightly uncomfortable. This is no way to 'bury' a friend.

Today I've lost all sense of modesty. For the first time I'm celebrating an award. I've been decorated. I show Solange the citation from which I've cut out the verbiage:

'Resolution no. 1347 dated 18th November 1945 . . . on the 4th June 1944 uncovered a Gestapo agent who came to him to join the network. Killed him and disposed of the body . . . thereby saving the organization', etc.

Solange made an effort to smile. She said, 'All that's down to Keep-on-Dancin'. I realize more and more he's not as dead as all that, which bucks me up. Besides, it's being taken care of . . .'

'Oh? By whom?'

'You're not one of the family yet. It takes a long time, you know. You'll work it out for yourself later, much later.'

And off she went, saying, '*Bye-bye.*'

A client was waiting for her out in the street.

Chapter XV

The Shipwreckage Doll

October 1951

Doctor Garret and his wife, Priscilla, are in Paris. He, a northern god, of powerful build beneath luxuriant white hair. She, small, dark and plump, and always laughing.

For the past week I've been acting as their guide. We've thoroughly explored the districts of the old City. As well as the catacombs, the quarries, the underground tunnels of Belleville, the course of the Bièvre. I'm determined that Garret and his wife shouldn't miss out on anything I can provide them with, in terms of stories, specific information and, to the extent that Paris colludes with me, enchantment.

Garret was keen to walk down Rue Zacharie – Witchcraft Steet – at sunset, like the blind man in the legend. We rowed on the Seine (in this season!), ate sausages at Bicêtre, bought a fake mumified 'mermaid' at St-Médard (they're made in Japan, apparently), and La Lune gave us a harmonica recital at the Vieux-Chêne. They're in seventh heaven.

I've never met a Parisian who's shown more interest in things relating to his City, or been more fascinated by them than Garrett. He turns out to be absolutely incapable of articulating a single word of French. Yet he's at home here: every evening we dine with the Bretons in Rue Grégoire-de-Tours where Garret expresses himself fluently in 'maho' with the *patronne*. It's always a pleasure to tell him a story because every time he draws an unexpected conclusion from it, a surprising 'essence'.

From London, Garret had sent off the complete collection of his works, which are of immense interest to me. I don't know how to repay him. We try to outdo each other in kindness.

'That's better, isn't it?' says Old Georgette, the doyenne of La Maube, whom we treat every morning at the Trois-Mailletz to a glass of the liquid stuff.

Garret has permanently established his laboratory, library and collections in B, the pretty Welsh town where his wife continues to run the gynaeological department of the local hospital.

I showed them my votive doll, the statuette I'd found down in the cellars of Rue de Bièvre. Garret studied, examined, stroked, fingered it, weighed it in his hand, admired it for a very long time, as though entranced. He said to me, 'This piece is extremely rare if not unique.'

He wanted to explore the underground passageway where I'd found it. I mobilized the old gang. We had to repeat the expedition of ten years earlier, and it wasn't so easy this time round.

Garret is categorical. 'The evidence this object represents is of the utmost importance to me. It allows me to draw up for the entire hemisphere the "magic" ground plan that your friend Keep-on-Dancin', to his considerable credit, had worked out for Paris alone.'

They've left. On the station platform – they don't like flying – I gave them my statuette, all carefully wrapped up, for them to take care of. They were as happy as sandboys. What nice people!

September 1952

One morning at about ten o'clock, at the beginning of last month, Garret turned up at my place. This time he'd come via Air France. Haggard, red-eyed, his face drawn. Looking crushed.

A little marmelade fortified him. I urged him to speak.

'It's the doll, the wretched doll. Oh, how dreadful! I'm no sorcerer myself, damn it! What can I do?' He found it difficult to express himself less incoherently. At last he succeeded, and told me the following.

'Having returned to B, I hastened to prepare a glass case in

233

which to install "your doll". And I conceived a strange desire to restore it to its original appearance, that's to say, with brown hair, probably quite long, implanted with wax.

'I asked the only hairdresser in our little town, if she got the chance, to put aside a few locks of dark hair of the requisite length. This, I told her, was for the purpose of an experiment of no great consequence. I was in no hurry. One day the hairdresser gave my wife a package: it was two long thick tresses of very beautiful chestnut hair. Everybody in B knows each other. We realized this was the hair of little Eve J, an eleven-year-old whose mother had decided to have her braids cut off.

'From time to time, in the evenings, I applied myself to the task of replacing the hair that had been missing from the statuette for centuries. Very patiently, very carefully, in my usual way, I implanted the hair in little tufts into the twenty-four holes in the skull. For these locks of hair, I used not wax but the paraffin for preparing my microscope specimens. The doll looks quite different now. It makes quite an impression. See for yourself.'

And he showed me a photo. There was no denying it.

'Some time later I tried to determine within the bounds of possibility the antiquity and origin of this extraordinary object. I made several tests on splinters of wood of different types, from different periods. And then I decided to remove a few fibres from the magic doll. I made the tiniest nick where it couldn't affect the outward appearance: between the legs. Oh, dear me, what have I done?'

'So? How old is it?'

'Its age can't be determined. The piece of oak your statuette was cut out of had been in sea water for so long before it was carved, it was treated like stone, not wood. Then there were the tannic properties of the waters of the Bièvre. The doll is now a kind of artificial fossil. It's almost impossible to date it beyond two hundred years. The nails were introduced into already existing holes. But from all this, I deduce the doll was carved out of shipwreckage. It doesn't come from the East, as you seemed to believe, but from the Far North. And that would be all well and good, if . . .'

'Quick, go on.'

'The very day after I'd removed that splinter – in other words, the day before yesterday – little Eve J was brought into hospital, where by good luck my wife was on duty.'

'The little girl with the braids?'

'Precisely. The child had a fever, was somewhat delirious, and complained of terrible pains exactly where I'd cut a nick out of the doll . . .'

'And?'

'Right now the child has a terrible inflammation – solely exterior, fortunately – of her private parts. Blood tests have revealed nothing. She's like a starfish consumed with pain, and my wife's trying to treat her without success. We alone know the true cause of her illness: my imprudence. Because of the hair, the child became identified with the statuette. We must find a remedy. Fast. The resources of medicine are all powerless. It's a genuine sorcerer or an extremely effective exorcist we need to consult. The Anglican priest of our town advised me to come straight to you. What can we do now?'

I must declare at this point that I've never in my life had recourse to the services of a priest, Catholic or otherwise. Don't pass judgement or stick any kind of label on me: whatever it is, it will be wrong.

I shared Dr Garret's distress so much, and tried dispassionately to consider the matter from every possible angle. I don't know any 'practising sorcerers', and in any case I'd be wary of them. We needed to find a recognized exorcist and follow his instructions. There was no getting away from that.

Extremely perplexed, I headed over to the St Séverin neighbourhood, with Garret in tow. A friend of mine has a bookshop there that specializes in the history of religions, and of course the occult sciences. I explained the problem. He strenuously advised me to consult one of his clients, a clergyman, curate of a Parisian parish with a most eventful history.

I was dreading this meeting. I was afraid the priest I was going to see would display a certain sectarianism, take umbrage and turn down our request with horror. This was not so.

I greatly regret being unable to give more details of the place where we went and the person who received us. But I was sworn to secrecy. The priest greeted us very courteously. There was a young cleric doing accounts in the sacristy. He was dismissed with a glance. We felt at ease.

I described the 'case', leaving out nothing. The priest listened attentively, without interrupting. When I'd finished, his first question astounded me.

'When you came into this church, did you put any money in one of the collection boxes?'

Taken aback rather than embarrassed, I replied, 'Goodness, no. It didn't even occur to us.'

Garret was trying desperately to follow what we were saying.

'Good! Very good!' said the priest. 'Now, listen to me: even if you come back here in ten or twenty years' time, you must never leave so much as a sou. Nor the doctor.'

'Ah! but I saw that you had some pamphlets on sale relating the history of the parish. I was intending to buy a copy.'

'I'll let you have one strictly for cost price. It's imperative that I do not make the least financial gain from you, or allow you to do me any kind of service, even indirectly.'

This was becoming offensive.

'In your mind, we're such evil people, are we? My word, you're placing us under taboo!'

A smile. 'Not at all. Even devils with horns wouldn't scare me very much, if I happened to come across them. It's got nothing to do with yourselves, but with what I may be able to do for you. It has to be – how can I put it? – unilateral.'

I translated for Garret what had just been said. He screwed up his eyes, wiped his brow, and breathed deeply.

'*Fine. I think we're on the right track.*'

The priest added, 'And remember this: the instructions I shall give according to my conscience might not please the authorities to whom I'm answerable. Promise me never to reveal . . .'

We promised.

And the curate went on. 'What you need is an exorcism,

pure and simple. And it's necessary to use very powerful means straightaway. For your doll seems to me to be exceptionally "highly charged". To tell the truth, I don't know whether I'm capable of performing the operation. And we have no time to lose. Ordinarily I'd be obliged to consult the bishop, who after endless discussions and symposiums would make unforeseeable decisions. . . I'm convinced there's only one solution, and it's one that will surprise you. Here's an address. That of a priest who's not of the Catholic faith – in these circumstances that's actually of no importance – and who has proved to be a first-rate exorcist. Go to him straightaway. And try not to mention my name unless you can't avoid it. Now, remember what you've promised, and keep me informed as much as possible of how things are going.'

Father Mathias, of the Arian denomination, at the chapel in Rue du Château-des-Rentiers. Honestly! There we were, Garret and I, wandering round Porte d'Ivry, looking for the chapel that was hard to find.

This neighbourhood looks a bit provincial. There are small gardens in front of the houses. An old buffer, sitting astride a chair, smokes his pipe outside his front door. Reluctantly, I ask for directions.

'The chapel? Ah! yes, the place belonging to the. . .' (He doesn't complete the name – it must be that Garret intimidates him – he merely taps his forehead. He assumes a mischievous look.) 'Next door, at the back of the yard, in the direction my pipe stem's pointing.'

Laughing openly now, he watches us go off. What on earth are we letting ourselves in for? A kind of converted greenhouse: it has new tiles and it's been whitewashed. The only window has been raised to make a gothic-style arch. On the firmly-shut heavy door a discreet plaque: Sunday Service 10.00 am–11.30 am. That's all. No bell. We knock. No answer.

'Excuse me, ma'am, Father Mathias?'

'Mathias? You mean, Monsieur Roger. He must be in the café at this time of day. Go and have a look, it's down there on the right.'

The woman waves at her neighbour with an air of complicity. They both appear to be ready for a laugh.

'I'm looking for Monsieur Roger ... Well, Father Mathias ...'

'Wait here, he won't be long.'

I dissuade Garret from ordering lemon tea.

'In place like this, that'll draw even more attention to us. We've attracted quite enough already. Two cognacs, please!'

Enter three sporty-looking lads in pullovers, laughing and joking, and landing each other hearty slaps on the back.

'Roger, these gentlemen have been waiting for you.'

The tallest of the three comes over. No more than thirty, well-built, down-to-earth sort of chap.

'What can I do for you?'

I say, 'It's a professional matter.'

'Sure, sure, I'll be with you right away. Take a seat over there, we'll be more comfortable.'

He directs us to the back room.

Monsieur Roger joins us: a glass of beer is brought to him. I try to pay for the three drinks. He won't hear of it.

'No, no, I don't yet know what it is you want. I'll pay for myself. Don't insist.'

Garret winks at me. He's reassured.

The priest had listened to me without uttering a word. Monsieur Roger – Father Mathias – constantly breaks in with exclamations of gleeful surprise. Finally he erupts.

'Well, I never! That's amazing! This is the real thing! My goodness!'

And he punctuates these excited remarks with a gesture – a raised thumb – that doesn't seem very priest-like at all.

Then he questions me, asking for countless details. Garret thinks back, replies, and I translate. This goes on for a good hour.

'There's no time to lose,' concludes Monsieur Roger. I haven't had the chance to ask him anything about himself yet. 'Go for a walk. Meet back here in two hours.'

He dashed out and hailed a taxi.

That evening Monsieur Roger was dressed up as Father Mathias: black jacket, very high-buttoned waistcoat, clerical collar. He was almost unrecognizable. Moreover, he seemed very preoccupied, almost anxious.

'This is a fascinating case. I don't know what I would have given to deal with it myself. But I've just been to see the master who's dissuaded me from doing so. Many factors are involved: power, forms that have to be observed, a training I don't yet have. And then there's a question of proximity that comes into play. This is what you must do. Call England and get news of the sick child. And hurry to Cherbourg: you have a train at eleven. Tomorrow morning, go to X, a little village near the port of Carteret. Ask for Monsieur Bruhat. He's a defrocked priest. To my knowledge, he alone can save you from this predicament. No need to say I sent you: you'll be well received in any case. As you might expect, in such circumstances!'

We offered, not to pay Father Mathias for his services, but at least to reimburse him for the taxi.

'No, no, absolutely not!'

We insisted on paying for his drink.

'Don't start by ruining everything.'

Somewhat reassured, Garret was thinking ahead. He granted his large frame ten minutes to relax, to unwind, in anticipation of future expenditure of energy. Father Mathias didn't seem to be in too great a hurry, and I'm eternally grateful for that moment's respite which I used to conduct a kind of interview.

'Have you already carried out many exorcisms?'

'Actually, no. Maybe two in the three years I've been specializing in this sort of thing. But I've treated hundreds of people.'

'Meaning?'

'Well may you ask. What I do consists mostly of comforting my clients – female clients mostly, in nine out of ten cases – listening to their complaints. They describe themselves as possessed, persecuted, or jinxed, under an evil spell cast over them by someone they know. Of course, that's nonsense, but it's pointless trying to get them to admit it. So I put on an act, perform an ineffectual pantomime. In fact not so ineffectual: they're taken in by it. I send them away if not cured, feeling better at least. We can't keep everyone locked up.'

'In short, you're dealing with the semi-deranged.'

'Alas, you wouldn't believe the number of neurotics, obsessionists, fantasists and hysterics there are.'

'And the two operations that you performed – what were they?'

'Listen, the word "exorcism" is actually a misnomer, used for want of a better term. For in the symptoms those two sick people presented – yes, two sick people, that's all – I may have found something out of the ordinary, rare, peculiar, but it wasn't as if they bore the same signature stamp, as it were.'

'Do you have any points of comparison?'

'Yes. Otherwise I'd be doing something else. My first subject was a twenty-year-old student. Sickly as a child. Well-off family. Very spoilt. He fails one exam, then another. It's arranged he should have private lessons with the choice of teacher left to him. He commits a terrible crime, one that is still attributed to a gang of ruffians "that got away". Obviously they're fictitious. He has no misgivings. He starts studying furiously. In no time, he's retaken the exams and passed. He was about to sit his final exam in order to qualify for his degree when we met by chance in Rue de Buci. Within the space of one evening he'd confided in me, unburdened himself of his dreadful secret. It was high time! The poor boy was possessed of a murderous instinct so domineering he was about to strangle a child.'

'Good heavens!'

'I'm not exaggerating. He'd already assassinated a member of his family in the past. You're the first person I've ever told.'

'Why take me into your confidence?'

'I have my reasons. As I was saying, the poor sick fellow had been lurking round Square de l'Archevêché every evening for several days. He'd picked out a little boy to whom he'd been offering lollipops: he was just waiting for an opportunity to lure him to a building site. And despite the disconcerting lucidity he displayed as he made his confession, he couldn't help himself. This compulsion, this obligation to do evil, absurd evil, came from somewhere. I'd no trouble discovering the source of it. My "subject" was under the influence of a foreigner, supposedly a doctor, who was giving him lessons in German and, so he claimed, "psychology". This "professor" gave me the impression of being very suspect. Under the pretext of "practising" pychoanalytic experiments, he'd taken such control over his student's mind, so dominated him, that committing a crime through an intermediary was just a game to him. I succeeded in subduing my potential executioner, not as you might think with reasonable words but using methods the practice of which constitutes what I call my "profession". Then I tried to meet the professor. I was not mistaken. That diabolical creature – and I know what I'm talking about – exuded a will to evil, a delight in evil, that was evident a mile off. If I could have rendered him incapable of causing harm, I assure you, I'd have had no scruples.'

'Even in eliminating him?'

'Perhaps not, for he's the kind of person who's even more dangerous dead than alive.'

'Please explain yourself.'

'Allow me to do no such thing. In short, I had great difficulty in gaining the necessary ascendancy over my sick young man. In the end I went to his parents and impressed on them the need to get him away from Paris. Which is what happened. He's much better now. But I keep an eye on him from a distance.'

'And the second case?'

'That's less dramatic. An ordinary decent woman, wife and mother, had for several years been acting as a medium for a group of old bats who used to meet not far from here in a caretaker's lodge, for table-turning sessions from five to seven. You know the type.

'Her name was Madame Hache, and she was a seamstress. Of feeble constitution, extremely impressionable. One day outside in the street she witnesses a serious accident: a crash between a car and a lorry. The sight of two bloodied corpses is too much for Madame Hache. She faints and doesn't regain consciousness. She's taken to hospital. There, in a semi-comatose state, in the presence of a flabbergasted intern, she starts delivering a seemingly coherent speech but in some foreign language. Yet certain sounds were familiar to the intern. Not surprisingly: it was ancient Greek! What happened next we don't know. Because from that day on, Madame Hache would fall into a trance more or less at the drop of a hat, and start raving: once in Latin, getting all her declensions right; mostly in Greek; occasionally in dialects about which learned professors from the School of Oriental Languages are not in agreement. For this case has become known, and medical experts have taken an interest in it. Especially psychiatrists. They call this phenomenon "xenoglossia". On several occasions Madame Hache's utterances have been tape-recorded. After regaining consciousness, she's never been prepared to accept it was her own voice that was played back to her. But these experiences were debilitating, and it was her parish priest who asked me to take her in hand. I restored her to a state of health and equilibrium that were as good as lost to her. Don't ask me what I think – or don't think – about all this, and let's get back to your doll: tell Doctor Garret that if he telephones home he should give strict instructions that no one, absolutely no one, is to touch that object.'

I did as he asked.

Garret said, 'What if I told them to burn that piece of wood?'

Father Mathias gave a start.

'That would inevitably spell the child's doom. Take my word for it, and don't do anything untoward. Now, good luck, and do come back to see me.'

'Thank you!'

'Just what you shouldn't say!'

We telephoned from La Bourse. The child's condition had deteriorated. Very high fever with nightmares the previous night. The inflammation was worse. Mrs Garret begged us to 'do something'.

It was a dull dawn in Cherbourg. A fine, freezing-cold, biting rain greeted us. We weren't prepared for such miserable weather. At once shivering with cold and boiling with impatience, we dived into a bar where we waited for the tourist office to open. There was no bus to Carteret until the afternoon, and then it was a six-mile walk inland to where Father Bruhat lived. We hired a taxi.

'You're looking for Monsieur Bruhat? Look, that's him over there.'

The road climbed a little. Next to a hedge, a man was securing two empty barrels onto a cart. His horse looked thin and weary. As soon as he saw us, the man remained motionless until we came up to him. He was chewing his cherry-wood pipe. Very clear, penetrating eyes. Weathered complexion.

'Monsieur Bruhat?'

'That's me. What can I do for you?'

'We've come from Paris to see you.'

He looked wary and vexed. 'Ah! you've come from Paris at this time of day? What's it about then?'

'A matter of. . . of witchcraft, of black magic.'

'Oh, but you mustn't talk about that here, lads. There's a place for everything. Indeed!'

We walked down the hill without speaking.

A west country man for sure, but not from here: he doesn't have the Cotentin accent.

He stopped in front of a modest-looking house. He patted the old horse and carefully covered its steaming back with two sacks.

'Come in, this way.'

An unmade bed. Above it a plaster crucifix with a faded twig of blessed palm. A few very old books. In the back room an indescribable clutter of all kinds of junk piled up in a corner or hanging from the walls. Bits of wooden beams from burned-out houses. Fragments of fuselage from crashed aeroplanes. A very old ship's figurehead: a mermaid, spit in two. And two miniature ships in bottles.

'You'll have a glass of cider, won't you?'

He invited us to sit down and placed an enormous jug of sweet cider on the table and a litre of brandy.

'So, what's the story?'

Well, he didn't miss a word of it. His clear gaze, direct and unwavering, guided my thoughts. When I'd finished, he said, 'Good, very good. But have you brought some of the hairs with you?'

I couldn't help looking to left and right to see if someone else was present: his voice had completely changed, the peasant accent was gone. It was the priest speaking. I repeated his question to Garret.

He was dismayed. 'No, I haven't, as you well know. I should have thought of it.'

'It's not the end of the world,' said the priest. 'I'm going to harness Basil's horse and take you to Carteret. There are some Canadian tourists sailing for Jersey this evening in their motor launch. From St Helier the doctor will surely find some fast way of reaching the English coast. He must bring me back very quickly a lock of hair belonging to the sick little girl, which should be cut off at the very last moment, and about half of the doll's hair. Above all, don't pull out any of the implanted hair. Cut it mid-length. And handle the object with the utmost care. I'll also need a map of the area round B. You,' he said to me, 'go back to Cherbourg, from where you can call B to get news of the child and let them know the doctor's arriving. I'll try and call you at your hotel this evening.'

Damn the Normandy railways! Wretched stopping trains! It was much more complicated calling from a phone box in Cherbourg than from Paris: I had to call London, then Liverpool, before finally getting put through to the hospital in B. Fortunately Mrs Garret happened to be there. The little girl's condition was unchanged. Still running a high temperature, the inflammation just as bad. Very weak and debilitated, the child was drowsy. Bruhat, as promised, rang me that evening. I learned that the Canadians had raised no objection to taking Garret in their boat.

Garret was back by midday two days later. That was a considerable achievement: in Jersey, he'd gone to the airport where the pilot of a private plane was only too happy to fly him straight to Liverpool. Even the weather, which contrary to all forecasts had cleared, was in their favour.

Return trip by train Liverpool-London and Paris-Cherbourg. From London to Paris, a British Airways flight.

Garret was bearing two precious envelopes: the locks of hair – those of the child, those of the doll. Furthermore, he had obtained a map of England, a 1:10000 scale military map of the part of Wales where B is located, and a survey map of the town on which the hospital and his own house were clearly marked.

Father Bruhat examined the documents carefully, felt the hair.

I noticed that after having touched the doll's hair, he moistened his fingers with some liquid – water, probably – poured from a little bottle, before touching the lock of hair taken from the child.

He poured three enormous brandies, filling the glasses to the brim.

'Now go away and leave me,' he said to us. 'I'll be busy for two days solid. I'm battening down the hatches. Tomorrow and the day after, find out how the child's doing, put it in writing for me and drop it through the letter-box in an envelope. Don't knock. I have my part to play now. Good-bye. Till Thursday evening if all goes well. If not, Friday.'

Twenty-four hours later the child was no longer in pain, her temperature was back to normal, the inflammation decreasing with astonishing speed.

After two days all signs of illness were gone: the child was cured, quite amazed to find herself in hospital, unaware of the seriousness of the harm she'd escaped.

It was evening. We'd just brought the good news. We were pacing backwards and forwards, indifferent to the gaze of mystified neighbours.

At last, a clunking sound of the door being unlocked, and then it was flung open.

Father Bruhat came towards us. Hunched, drawn, exhausted, in a pitiful state. But his eyes gleamed with contentment.

'Well, now! You've certainly put me through the mill,' he said in a voice striving to sound cheerful. 'This problem of yours has aged me a good ten years, but I'm indebted to you for the greatest satisfaction of my life.'

Like the Parisian parish priest and Father Mathias, he declined with indignation and nervous apprehension our offers of 'compensation'.

'What should I do with the doll now?' asked Garret.

'Whatever you like. It's permanently neutralized, you can take my word for it. As for the little girl, she won't have any recollection of this distressing experience. She's also safe from quite a number of illnesses.

'By the way, when you get back home, send me a photo of her. I'll think of her from time to time, it will be good for her well-being, and give me great pleasure.'

Chapter XVI

'Why do you not seize the Absolute?'
'Why does it not come to me?'

The Gnostics

March 1954

While adhering to the truth as closely as possible, all I have done in the course of the preceding chapters is to record a series of events of various kinds, which are more or less perplexing and classified by myself as belonging to the category of phenomena that should occasion much more serious reflection and verification than idle fancy and acceptance.

No one will ever know what manifold difficulties I've had to overcome in order to bring to a conclusion this first part of my chronicle. In certain dreams you feel leaden, numb, paralysed, incapable of moving even though frightful and ferocious enemies are closing in on you. A constraint, curb, impediment of this order were a constant obstacle to the, oh, so very long and arduous composition of this work. And yet with every one of these stories the fact of having committed it to writing relieved me of a genuine millstone. My only regret is not to have completely unburdened myself. I'm still sadly short of reaching that target.

The tumult has never subsided. Actually, it never will. But I don't yet know the day when I'll be free not to be so closely involved in it. I can't allow myself to set out here equations whose constituent parts already exist, which will be resolved at some time in the future, and whose results I need to validate. For a length of time that remains uncertain, I'm in the same predicament as the maniac incapable of finding a piece of string in his path without picking it up and tying a knot in it. But whatever the space given to the narrator throughout this chronicle, I'm well aware this isn't about my own life but the thrilling, rich and generous life of my City.

These scruples compel me to remain silent about some astounding things that I wasn't in fact the only one to witness, and whose protagonists I don't wish to identify. In the circumstances, it would be sheer dishonesty to change or modify names, dates and places.

I should like one day, as some anonymous pedestrian revisiting the scenes of these memories, to follow on the heels of an attentive reader – there are some – and to relish his delight when, with this book in his pocket, he finds himself in the presence of one of the characters described, mentioned or referred to earlier on, who do exist, large as life, and wittingly or not perpetuate their legend. I'd like people to investigate, to verify. You need to be an extremely well-informed reader to identify all the 'keys' scattered throughout these pages. Many readers may find among them the key to their own front door.

In any case, what you need to know is this: in certain areas of Paris, the supernatural is part of everyday life. Local people accept this and have some involvement with it. I rely on two easily verifiable examples that hundreds of people will confirm.

Henri the Breton, a decent and good-hearted old soak, was a porter at the Wholesale Fish Market. Those who knew him – they are many – still meet up at his headquarters: Pagès, the coal-merchant-cum-bistrot on Rue du Haut-Pavé. One evening in July 1950, Henri borrows a hundred francs from Pagès, supposedly to bet on the horses. By ten o'clock he's at the Vieux-Chêne, already fairly tipsy. When he was drunk, easygoing Henri developed fixed ideas and tended to raise his voice.

'No rowdiness from you,' the Captain told him.

'No danger of that, Captain, I'm a Breton, an' I'm a Christian, an' I'm a gen'leman,' says Henri, with an unfortunate gesture sending an empty glass flying. He insisted on paying for damage on the spot.

Along comes Honoré Thibaudaut, as though by chance of course, the man with a blasted reputation, the burns man, the blabber. Thinner and more pasty-faced than ever, constricted rather than dressed in black, with eyes that couldn't be more sunken.

Henri says something to him. The other refuses to reply. Henri loses his temper. 'Anyway, I don't like you, you carry a whiff of damnation about you. Where I come from, the parish priest wouldn't have looked very kindly on you.'

Once uttered, those words 'parish priest' release a flood of distant memories in Henri the one-time choirboy. He pictures himself serving at mass in Kirity-Penmarc'h. He makes huge signs of the cross in the pipe smoke. In a rush of emotion, he berates the other with these terrible words:

'Damnation! There's a whiff of damnation about you, with that whey-faced expression of yours, like a cat shitting on hot bricks! You sold out, you sold out to the devil! You're dead, dead, deader than all the dead put together! And you don't even deserve to be pitied! Bugger off! You stink! The cemetery's the place for stiffs!'

This was verging on insanity. Henri started declaiming melodramatically, '*De profundis clamavi, Domine, Domine . . .*'

Thibaudaut's sallow complexion had turned ashen. 'Stop it! Stop it! What are you doing?' He was jigging about in terror.

His persecutor went on, '*Fiant aures tuae intendentes in vocem . . .*'

Thibaudaut fled. The Captain threatened to get angry if the Breton didn't leave straightway. Henri complied.

'I can't help it,' he said, hiccuping, 'I can't stand people who stink. Of anything but fish.'

Henri must have had something to eat and sobered up a bit.

At four o'clock in the morning there was a sudden storm. A single flash of lightning lit up the tower of St Jacques (in the middle of a garden square planted with big trees).

Henri was found close by, beside the railings round the square, struck down by the lightning, with his hands clenched on his trolley, his face blue.

André Gantot was a butcher in the south-east suburbs of

Paris. Three times a week, he would drive in on his scooter to Les Halles, where he would buy his meat supplies. He was in the habit of eating at Raymond's restaurant, on the corner of Rue de Pontoise and Quai de la Tournelle, in a house that only two hundred years ago was still part of the Meat Market (the cattle port was right opposite).

Gantot was a pretty unpleasant character. Thick-set and dull-witted, a big-mouth and a braggart, he annoyed everyone with his infelicitous remarks. On the morning of April 1st, 1947, news phoned through to Les Halles took two hours to cross the Seine: André Gantot, who'd left Raymond's very late the night before, had had a fatal accident driving home that night. His scooter had skidded. Hit a tree. He was killed instantly.

His fellow traders at Les Halles immediately organized a collection and bought a huge wreath there and then that was placed in front of the stall where he usually made his purchases.

On the stroke of midday, stupefaction: looking fresh as a daisy and very pleased with himself, André Gantot turned up to enjoy the effects of what he considered a good joke. All he encountered were stony faces. No one failed to convey to him the general disapproval. Sheepishly, he thought he'd get away with just buying everyone a drink.

On April 1st, 1948, exactly the same news spread through Les Halles and made the usual round.

'He's really going too far,' said his colleagues. And no one thought any more about it. At La Tournelle, everyone agreed this inveterate stupidity could rebound on him badly.

Little did they know how right they were. The next day it turned out that the butcher, having set off late the day before, had stopped off at several bars along the way. He'd even offered a young man a lift. Five hundred metres from his house, sure enough, André Gantot had factured his skull against a tree. The young man was unhurt. We later saw him. 'André bled like an ox,' he told us. 'He didn't skid, he drove straight into the tree at top speed. As if he were attracted by the obstacle, drawn towards it. I'll never be able to make any sense of it.'

Of course he won't. But the lads who all knew Gantot, and didn't much care for him, don't see this as anything but perfectly normal. The incident is still well remembered in the neighbourhood.

Rue des Maléfices

I didn't have the nerve to tell Dr Garret during his last visit to Paris what happened in Rue Zacharie – Rue des Maléfices – during the summer of 1950. This incident so deeply affected me, I avoid mentioning it. And until the very last moment I felt prevented from describing it here. It makes you think that if there is a pervasive spirit, it's wariness that hangs in the air. *Who* is apprehensive, *who* has reason to fear such evidence should be brought to the attention of mankind, *what* is feared, and *why*?

I'd like this final anecdote to have the austerity of a report.

My work on the Vieux-Pont had prompted a film producer to conceive of a short documentary devoted to 'legendary neighbourhoods'. Among these legends, that of the blind man – the Man-Who-Sings – which Garret related to me in his London retreat, seemed to us the most poetic. I was commissioned to write a synopsis of the script. By common consent, we decided to call the film *Rue des Maléfices*. A female street-singer was to play the leading role. I'd written the lyrics for two theme songs that my brother, a professional musician, was to arrange.

So it was that one warm night conducive to fruitful ruminations, three companions, pondering on their projects and puffing on their pipes, walked down that street in the footsteps of the medieval couple. They were the journalist Raphael Cuttoli, my brother and I. Luckily – it was two o'clock in the morning – there was one small restaurant still open: the Athènes, run by Denis the Evzone. There was only one customer there, eating rice: Serge B, a big Gypsy fellow, whom I vaguely knew from having met him at the Friday poetry meetings of the Islanders on the Ile St-Louis.

'I didn't know you lived round here.'

'Yes, nearby, at number 16. A garret. But it's a hassle. I have to keep the light on all night. So I'm running a night-light off the downstairs neighbour's meter, without him knowing.'

'Why do you need the light on?'

'You mean you don't know? It's the Blind Man's room.'

I was stunned. Cuttoli and my brother, to whom I'd related the story maybe a quarter of an hour earlier, were thunderstruck.

'What blind man? Tell me, quickly, tell me.'

'Some cock-and-bull story. An old, very old tradition is attached to this garret – this attic rather. No subsequent tenant has managed to stay more than a few weeks. It seems that the ghost of an unkempt blind man who walks with a limp appears to them in their sleep. And without waking them, the blind man passes over their eyes a long broad hand that's luminous, translucid and icy-cold.

'These people wake up full of anguish. They have some recollection of a horrible nightmare, and they have the sensation that the blind man has drawn the light out of them: they see less clearly, their eyes blink and can't take the sun. In the end it gets too much for them. They leave. The owner, an elderly woman, fed up with all of this, didn't want to let the room any more, at any price. I had to beg her. But although I've never encountered any ghost, these things unnerve me. So I leave the light on all night, as an additional precaution. And so far I've slept soundly.'

I subsequently had the opportunity to check out what this fellow had said: it was true. My old acquaintances from the Maube – Georgette, Old Marteau, Jean the mattress-maker, and many others – have all, everyone one of them in turn, been through that experience with the old man. You really have to worm it out of them. They talk of it solely with dread. All of them complain of defective eyesight which they attribute to their stay in 'the Attic'. Most of them wear dark glasses.

'I must visit your room.'

'All right. Come tomorrow during the day.'

'No. Right now. It's urgent. It's important. It's essential.'

I buy a litre of Samos wine. And now all four of us are climbing the stairs. Halfway up, Serge says to me, 'I share the room with a friend. An actor. He may be in. Otherwise, he'll be back any minute.'

To enter 'the Attic', you have to duck, follow a long corridor – like a kind of trench – and climb another few dangerously worn steps. Here we are at last: a rather squalid mess, not at all amusing despite the inscription painted on the peeling plaster: *You're not at home here, keep these premises in a shambolic state*. We made ourselves comfortable as best we could on some rickety chairs, and filled some sticky glasses.

'And now,' says Serge, 'tell me a little bit about why you have such a keen interest in this pad?'

I was already steeped in 'my' film, and without immediately tackling the legend of the man who was going to die, I paint a picture of St Séverin in the thirteenth century, with its hordes of beggars: *Malingreux*, *Sabouleux*, and *Rifodés*. The door creaks. In comes number two. A young guy. Tall, untidy, check shirt, with a thick head of hair. A fine handsome head, but a little drunk. Introductions are quickly made.

'My mate Thierry,' says Serge. Right.

Thierry sits down beside me. I tell the story of the man overcome with weakness, the woman who becomes identified with the night, the tree on the riverbank, the rising darkness.

Serge was standing behind his friend. But Cuttoli, my brother and I observed with anxiety Thierry's eyes, his trembling hands, his pale face: he was going out of his mind.

All stories come to an end. I couldn't drag it out for ever. When I concluded with the word 'blind', it was met with a howl.

Thierry went beserk. No longer able to control himself, and his strength increased tenfold by a desperate surge of long-contained fury, he leapt on us. Despite our efforts, he managed to smack Cuttoli's face, and in the scuffle Cuttoli lost a shoe. It was only after having torn out the electric wires that we succeeded in reaching the staircase, then the street, leaving behind our briefcases crammed with documents, scores and manuscripts – the fruit of weeks of work.

We needed to get it back, which meant a lot of hassle, involving the police . . . So the three of us, my brother, myself and a bloodied Cuttoli, end up at the Panthéon police station, where no one could make any sense of the fact that a guy could suddenly go crazy at the relating of a legend.

For a long time afterwards Thierry was not at all well. He too complained of problems with his eyesight. And his mental health.

I'd recounted this distressing incident to my friend D, an official in the city administration. The next day he came to see me, thoroughly rattled, and asked me point-blank, 'Who was Provost of Paris in 1268, which is when that legend dates from?'

'Easy.' I consult my Lazare. 'Augier, Jehan Augier.'

'Right. And what was he doing in 1268?'

'Well, we just settled that: he was Provost of Paris.'

'Maybe so. But he was still in the East, returning from a crusade carried out by order of the king St Louis, at the request of the Infidels themselves. Who for once wanted to join forces with the Christians, as far back as 1240, in order to drive out of their lands the hordes of Genghis Khan. Augier had set sail, and was heading towards the coast of Africa.'

'So?'

'Back in Paris, he'd delegated his authority to various individuals: in particular to one of the churchwardens of St Séverin, whose name was Thierry de Sauldre. A Flemish nobleman. Thierry de Sauldre fell under a spell – at least it was the activities of a sorcerer that were blamed for the ailment he was stricken with, which gradually deprived him of his eyesight. In 1269 he issued a decree prohibiting access to Rue des Maléfices to "all who are blind, whatever the origin of their blindness." We can trace the fortunes of his family since then. In the eighteenth century the De Sauldres emigrated and became colonists of Guadeloupe. The last descendants returned from there just recently. And Guadeloupe, by the

way, is where *he* was born, your aggressor the other night, the
raving lunatic.'

'Is that so? As a matter of fact, he's also called Thierry.'

'And do you know his full name?'

'No.'

'Thierry de Sauldre!'

Thierry de Sauldre exists. I've slightly altered his name. He's
a talented young man from a very respectable family, and
I certainly wouldn't wish to cause him any harm.

So I can't disclose here the unbelievable ransom that in
order to preserve his light Thierry has to pay to Darkness. Yes,
Darkness. Or let's say, to the colour black.

Having observed or instigated these incidents, in any case
having been personally involved in them, constitutes the
most dreadful ordeal, and affords the most marvellous, most
unhoped-for satisfaction.

My happiness has not followed the same paths as the
Gypsy's.

But like his, it knows no bounds.

Translator's Notes

Chapter I

p.14 *the site of the old morgue*

From 1804 located on Quai du Marché-Neuf, it moved in 1864 to a new building on Quai de l'Archevêché, behind Notre-Dame. The Morgue became a veritable tourist attraction in the 19th century, even included in the Thomas Cook tour of the city, offering the spectacle of cadavers of unknown persons laid out on slabs that they might be identified and claimed for burial. It figures large in Emile Zola's *Thérèse Raquin*, in which the murderer is daily drawn to the place to see if his victim has been discovered. It was eventually closed to the public in 1907.

p.14 *La Tournelle*

The Quai de la Tournelle runs between the Pont de l'Archevêché and the Pont de la Tournelle that connect the Left Bank to the Ile de la Cité and the Ile St-Louis. It takes its name from a tower in the City walls built by Philip Augustus at the beginning of the 13th century, from which a chain running across to the Tour Loriot on the right bank could block the river passage for the protection of the City. The Tournelle tower was demolished in 1787.

p.14 *Boult-sur-Suippe*

Village in the Marne, occupied by the Germans on 10 June 1940.

p.15 *the Ghetto, behind the Hotel de Ville*

More a Jewish neighbourhood than a ghetto, this is the area round Rue des Rosiers, Rue des Ecouffes and Rue Ferdinand-Duval, formerly Rue des Juifs, where the Jewish community settled in the early 13th century. There had been an earlier Jewish neighbourhood round Rue de la Juiverie, now part of Rue de la Cité on the Ile de la Cité, with a Jewish synagogue that was torn down in the 12th century and replaced with a church.

p.15 *Rue des Grands-Degrés*

Between Place Maubert and the Seine, near the Pont de l'Archevêché.

p.15 *La Maube*

Place Maubert, one of the places of public execution in Paris's turbulent past, famous for its barricades during the Fronde, the anti-royalist insurrection of the mid-17th century, and the Revolutionary period.

p.15 *Château-Rouge*

(Also known as La Guillotine, on rue de Galande) and *Père Lunette*, so called because of the glasses worn by its proprietor that were replicated as this establishment's shop-sign, were notoriously squalid entertainment-halls-cum-doss-houses. Both places are graphically described by J.K. Huysmans in his description of the St Séverin neighbourhood, in *La Bièvre et St Séverin*, 1898.

p.15 *Rue Lagrange*

Opened in 1887, running north off Place Maubert towards the Pont-au-Double.

p.15 *Austerlitz*

Napoleon's great victory against the Russian and Austrian armies on 2 December 1805, the first anniversary of his coronation as Emperor, in which the French suffered losses of 1305 dead and 6940 wounded against 11000 Russian and 4000 Austrian casualties.

p.17 *Robert Desnos*

Leading Surrealist poet (1900–45), active in the Resistance, arrested by the Gestapo in February 1944, he died of typhus at Terezin concentration camp on 8 June 1945.

p.18 *Privat d'Anglemont*

Born in Guadaloupe 1815, died in Paris 1859. *Paris Anecdote*, his recorded observations of Paris life, culled from night-time wanderings round the City, caused a sensation on its first publication, generally given as 1854. Extract quoted p.184.

p.18 *Arrests Memorables du Parlement de Paris*

Case law studies that started to be published from the mid-16th century, establishing legal precedents and reflecting social mores.

p.18 *Nationale, Arsenal, Ste-Geneviève, Archives*

Bibliothèque Nationale: could be said to date back to the 14th century and the first royal library of Charles V, whose inventoried collection of 917 manuscripts was housed in what came to be called the Library Tower of the Louvre, which could be consulted by scholars, but as this collection was dispersed on his death the real founder of what came to be the National Library was Louis XI who ruled 1461–83. Legislation requiring a copy of all books published for sale in France to be deposited in the Royal Library was passed in 1537. The royal collections were transferred in the early 18th century to Rue de Richelieu and renamed the National Library after the Revolution. Constant acquisitions and the need for more space led to the decision taken in 1988 by President François Mitterand to build new library premises. Designed by Dominique Perrault, this controversial edifice, comprising four towers, is located on the Left Bank between Pont de Bercy and Pont de Tolbiac.

Bibliothèque de l'Arsenal: rebuilt several times over the centuries, destined for demolition by Louis XVI, a part of the old Arsenal, on Rue Sully between the river and Place de la Bastille, now houses a library of books and manuscripts relating to the history of Paris.

Bibliotheque Ste-Geneviève: 8 Place du Panthéon.

Archives Nationales: Hôtel Soubise, 60 Rue des Francs-Bourgeois.

p.18 *Charles the Bold*

Charles the Bold, who succeeded to the Duchy of Burgundy in 1467, led an alliance of nobles, known as the League of the Public Good, including the Duke of Britanny and the King's brother Charles, Duke of Berry, in a feudal revolt against royal authority. The humiliation of Louis XI was achieved by the Peace of Peronne in 1468, but the king survived long enough to see the ambitions of the Duke of Burgundy, who died on the battlefield in 1477, completely thwarted. The Duchy of Maine was united with the Crown in 1328 when Philippe of Valois became Philippe VI of France, the title having been assumed by then by the Counts of Valois.

Chapter II

p.22 *La Montagne*

Mont Ste-Geneviève. The hill on the Left Bank, rising from Place Maubert to Rue Mouffetard, that under the Romans was called the Hill of Lutetius.

p.23 *Vieux-Chêne*

69 Rue Mouffetard.

p.27 *Africa Disciplinary Battalions*

The so-called *Bat' d'Af'* were special units for recruits with a previous criminal record.

p.27 *La Mouffe*

Rue Mouffetard, which runs through the middle of the 5th arrondissement, lying between Place Maubert and Les Gobelins.

Chapter III

p.32 *'quickening peg'*

Quotation from Rabelais' *Gargantua and Pantagruel*, Author's Prologue to Book Three: '*on nom . . . des quatre fesses qui vous engendrerent, et de la vivificque cheville qui pour lors les coupploit*' [in the name of . . . the four buttocks that engendered you and the quickening peg that served to join them].

p.33 *Xavier Privas*

Born Antoine Paul Taravel in Lyon 1863. Poet and celebrated singer who made his debut in Paris cabarets around 1890. Rue Zacharie is now known by the name of Rue Xavier-Privas.

p.34 *Petit-Châtelet*

Originally a defensive structure dating back to Roman times that stood at the end of the Petit-Pont on the site of today's Place du Petit-Pont, it was rebuilt several times, later serving as a tollgate, and then from the 14th century as a prison until it was demolished in 1782.

p.34 *St Louis*

Ruled France as Louis IX 1226–1270. He led the Seventh Crusade to recover Jerusalem in 1248, and died in Tunis at the start of the Eighth Crusade. After his death and canonization in 1297, a record of his saintly life was written by his devoted subject and crusading companion Jean de Joinville.

p.34 *Sorbonne* and *Irish College*

In the mid-13th century Louis IX's chaplain Robert de Sorbon (the name of his native village in Picardy) founded a small theological college for poor students, at the time just one of the many colleges, most of them attached to the great abbeys and churches of the City, that came into being from the 9th century on and attracted students from all over France and Europe, so great was the renown of their teachers. (The most celebrated of whom was Peter Abelard (1079–1142), who taught first at the Cathedral school and then at the school of St Geneviève). It eventually established itself as the great court of appeal on matters theological, and became synonomous with the university of Paris. By the 17th century there were 65 colleges in Paris. The various schools were incorporated into a single body designated the *université* in 1212, with statutes regulating who was entitled to teach. Students enjoyed considerable privileges and freedoms that led to violent clashes with the ecclesiastical authorities and with the townspeople.

The Irish college was founded by two Irish priests, Patrick Maginn and Michael Kelly, who in 1671 and 1681 received letters patent from the King authorizing them to take over the Lombard college on Rue des Carmes, founded in 1334 for students from Italy, which by the 17th century was falling into ruin.

p.39 *Tour Pointue*

A popular name for the Prefecture of Police, dating from the 19th century, and deriving from the shape of the tower on the corner of Rue de Jerusalem, on which the Prefecture was originally located, a street on Ile de la Cité that no longer exists, and so called because pilgrims to the Holy Land used to stay there. After these original premises were set on fire by the Communards in 1871, the Prefecture moved into a new building, the Caserne de la Cité, constructed as part of Baron Haussmann's scheme for the remodelling of Paris.

p.39 *Henri Vergnolle*

Author's note: Henri Vergnolle was to become Chairman of the City Council after the Liberation.

p.40 *La Source* and *D'Harcourt*

Two cafés in the Latin quarter, the Source at 35 Boulevard St Michel, D'Harcourt at Place de la Sorbonne. D'Harcourt was the name of a canon from an old Normandy family who in 1280 founded a college in Rue de la Harpe for poor students from the dioceses of Coutances (where his brother was bishop), Bayeux, Evreux and Rouen. In 1820 the Lycée St-Louis was erected on the site of D'Harcourt's college.

p.42 *Fréhel*

Marguerite Boulc'h (1891–1951), music-hall star, born in Paris of Breton origin, who began her career under the patronage of La Belle Otero, singing first under the name of Pervenche and later Fréhel (after Cap Fréhel in Britanny). Her most famous song is '*La Java Bleue*', recorded in 1939. She also appeared in a number of films including Julien Duvivier's *Pépé le Moko*, starring Jean Gabin as a French gangster. Personal tragedy and unhappiness led to attempted suicide, drug addiction and alcoholism, and she ended her days in misery.

p.43 *Georges Darien*

Anarchist writer (1862–1921), whose scathing exposé of military justice and the army's *Bat' d'Af'* disciplinary units in North Africa (referred to in popular parlance as Biribi) was published in 1890.

p.43 *Montehus*

Born Gaston Mordachée Brunswick (1872–1952), popular song-writer, whose anti-militarism and socialist sentiments won him the admiration of Lenin during the latter's four-year exile in Paris 1909–12. Awarded the Légion d'Honneur in 1947.

p.46 *beauceron*

A type of sheep-dog of ancient origins, used on the agricultural plains round Paris, with the same sort of colouring as a rottweiler. Also called a *bas-rouge* (literally, 'red sock') or a *Berger de Beauce* (literally, 'Beauce sheepdog').

p.49 *Hôtel-Dieu*

Literally, Hostel of God. Hospital dating back to the 7th century, when St Landry, Bishop of Paris, began treating the sick in the monastery of St Christopher, on the site of which the Hotel-Dieu was built during the 8th century. Under Louis IX the hospital was restored, enlarged and richly endowed. Rebuilt in 1878, it now stands on the north side of the Ile de la Cité between the Pont Notre-Dame and the Pont d'Arcole.

p.49 *St-Louis*

Hospital specializing in dermatology, in the 10th arrondissement on Place Dr-Alfred-Fournier.

Chapter IV

p.51 *Laughter is proper to the man*

Reference to Rabelais' *Gargantua and Pantagruel*, dedication To the Readers: '*Rire est le propre de l'homme.*'

p.52 *Glacière*

A district to the west of Les Gobelins, in the 13th arrondissement.

p.53 *François Villon*

Author of one of the most celebrated lines of poetry – '*Où sont les neiges d'antan*' [Where are the snows of yesteryear?]. (Another of his lines '*autant en emporte le vent*' was adopted as the French title of Margaret Mitchell's novel *Gone with the Wind*). Born in Paris in 1431, date of death unknown. Villon's small body of surviving work reflects his disreputable life and criminal associations that earned him arrest, imprisonment, and eventually a death sentence commuted to ten years' exile from Paris.

p.54 *'the days of wanton youth'*

Villon's '*Testament*' verse XXVI: *Hé! Dieu, se j'eusse étudié/Ou temps de ma jeunesse folle,/Et à bonnes moeurs dédié,/J'eusse maison et couche molle.* Oh God! If only I'd studied/In the days of my wanton youth/And cultivated good behaviour,/I'd have a house and a soft bed.

p.54 *Auteuil*

The southern part of the wealthy 16th arrondissement in south-west Paris.

p.56 *prohibited zone*

Under German occupation, France was divided into Vichy France in the south and Occupied France in the north. Furthermore,

Alsace-Lorraine was incorporated into the Reich, while the very north and the Pas de Calais were put under the administration of Occupied Belgium. In the north-east, from Picardie to Lorraine, there was a so-called prohibited zone, where the population that had fled during the exodus was not allowed to return, and land belonging to these exiles was appropriated for cultivation by German farmers.

p.63 *Argonne trenches*
To the west of Verdun, where some of the fiercest fighting of WWI took place.

p.63 *Fort St-Jean*
At the mouth of the harbour in Marseilles.

p.64 *Sidi-bel-Abbès*
From 1832–1962 headquarters of the French Foreign Legion, founded in 1831 by King Louis-Philippe for the conquest of Algeria.

p.64 *Monastir*
The name by which present-day Bitola, in southern Macedonia, was known under Turkish rule.

p.67 *Hendaye*
On the border between France and Spain, at the mouth of the Bidassoa estuary on the Atlantic coast.

p.68 *Kharkov*
Also in the Ukraine, west of Kiev.

p.71 *Marquis de Ste-Croix* and *Brinvilliers*
Notorious murderers of the 17th century, Marie-Madeleine d'Aubray, wife of the Marquis de Brinvilliers, and her lover Gaudin de Ste-Croix, conspired to murder her father and her two brothers, who were scandalized by their liaison and tried to oppose it. Ste-Croix died in his laboratory, overcome by the fumes of a poison he was developing, which prompted an investigation that led to Brinvilliers being brought to trial and sentenced to death. Mme de Sevigné (1626–96), whose famous *Letters* were published in the 18th century, saw her taken to be executed, in 1676, and Alexandre

Dumas (1802–1870), author of *The Three Musketeers* and *The Count of Monte Cristo*, recorded the affair in his *Celebrated Crimes*, published in four volumes, 1839–41.

p.73 *St-Denis plain*

To the north of Paris, beyond Porte de la Chapelle, where the basilica of St Denis is located.

p.73 *Lariboisière*

Hospital on Rue Ambroise-Paré near the Gare du Nord in the 10th arrondissement, completed in 1854 to a pavilion plan that won the approval of Florence Nightingale, who came to see it when it was newly opened.

Chapter V

p.74 *Tell me who you haunt . . .*

Nadja, an 'anti-literary' prose work published in 1928 by poet and author of the *Surrealist Manifesto* André Breton (1896–1966), opens with following words: *Qui suis-je? Si par exception je m'en rapportais à un adage: pourquoi tout ne reviendrait-il pas à savoir qui je 'hante'?* [Who am I? Suppose I were to make an exception and fall back on an old adage: why shouldn't all be explained by knowing whom I 'haunt'?]

p.75 *Jehan de Chelles*

One of the masons of Notre-Dame, who has left his name on the south portal of the cathedral, together with the date, 12 February 1257, on which building work began.

p.76 *Gentilly*

On the southern outskirts of Paris.

p.80 *Salle Adyar*

Assembly room at 4 Square Rapp in the 7th arrondissement.

p.82 *Les Halles*

The central market in Paris originated in the early 12th century when Louis VI established a market on land belonging to the priory of St Denis-le-Chartre (on a site where even in Roman times there had been a market). It expanded under subsequent monarchs, with new halls added for the various goods sold. When the market was moved out of cenral Paris in the 1970s, the twelve enormous glass-and-iron pavilions of which it consisted by then, ten of which erected under Napoleon III, the others dating from 1937, were demolished and replaced by the shopping centre known as the Forum des Halles. A classic 19th-century description of Les Halles is to be found in Zola's *Le Ventre de Paris*, 1873.

Chapter VI

p.84 *Brétigny*

The aerodrome at Brétigny-sur-Orge, some thirty kilometres to the south of Paris. (Also the site of the Treaty of Brétigny signed in 1360, during the Hundred Years War, under the terms of which King Jean II of France was exchanged for an enormous ransom.)

p.84 *Marolles-en-Hurepoix*

A village a few kilometres south of the aerodrome.

p.87 *Quatre-Sergents*

In September 1822, during a period of great political instability in France and Europe, four young army officers, Goubin, Pommier, Raoulx and Bories, who were members of a Republican secret society, were executed on the Place de Grève for conspiring to subvert their regiment, which deployed from Paris to La Rochelle, and for taking part in an abortive insurrection led by General Berton at Saumur. Because of their youth, courage and defiance, they came to be regarded as martyrs for the liberal cause.

p.89 *Belle-Ile*

Island off the south coast of Britanny with two notoriously grim detention centres for young offenders, one housed in what was originally a military prison, which were closed in 1979. Offenders would sometimes graduate directly from Belle-Ile to the *Bat' d'Af'*.

p.90 *Casque d'Or*

The nickame of a golden-haired beauty for whose favours two rival gang leaders confronted each other on the streets of Paris in 1902, a story that inspired Jacques Becker's film of 1952, in which Simone Signoret starred as Casque d'Or ('Goldilocks', or 'Golden Marie' as the film was titled in English), Serge Reggiani her lover *Manda* and Claude Dauphin as the apache gangster *Leca*.

p.90 *Val d'Amour*

The name by which Rue Glatigny (which no longer exists) on Ile de la Cité was also known. (At the beginning of the 19th century there were over 50 streets and some 20 churches or chapels on the Ile de la Cité; by the 1870s urban replanning had opened up this insalubrious warren and reduced the number of streets to no more than a dozen.)

Until the mid-12th century attempts were made to banish prostitutes from the city altogether, but it became clear this was never going to be achieved. In legislation attempting to control prostitution, Rue Glatigny and several other streets – including Tiron, Chapon, Brisemiche – were designated areas where prostitutes were allowed to ply their trade in houses dedicated to that purpose – and which were taxed – although regulations were hard to enforce and much flouted.

p.91 *Aliscans of Paris*

The Aliscans, or Alyscamps (Elysian Fields) in Arles, in the South of France, is a large necropolis founded by the Gallo-Romans, renowned as a site of great spirituality. It was also the site of a crushing defeat of the Christians by the Saracens, recounted in a 12th-century *chanson de geste*. There are paintings of the Alyscamps by Gaugin and Van Gogh.

p.92 *Uncle Guillaume*

Villon, *Le Testament*, LXXXVII: '*mon plus que père,/Maître Guillaume de Villon,/Qui m'a été plus doux que mère/A enfant levé de maillon*' . . . [more than a father to me,/Maitre Guillaume de Villon,/ who's been kinder to me than any mother/towards a child raised from infancy].

p.92 *Pomme-de-Pin*

A tavern mentioned in Villon's *Lais*, XIX, and *Testament*, CI. Also mentioned by Rabelais. According to one 19th-century historian, located in Rue de la Juiverie (now part of Rue de la Cité) on the Ile de la Cité.

p.92 *The Ballad of the Gallows-Birds*

Sometimes called Villon's 'Epitaph'. See ch.12, pp.207 and 208.

p.94 *Melun*

The prison in the prefectural town of the departement of Seine-et-Marne, located some forty-five kilometres to the south-east of Paris, occupies the entire tip of the ancient island centre of the City. There is a pun here, linking the prison, called the Maison Centrale, with the École Centrale, the State School of Engineering.

p.94 *Arbre-à-Liège*

10 Rue Tiquetonne, running between Rue Montmartre et Boulevard St Denis.

p.96 *Alexandre Arnoux*

Poet, novelist, playwright (1884–1973).

p.96 *St-Germain-l'Auxerrois*

Formerly the royal chapel, opposite the Louvre.

p.99 *exodus*

The German invasion of the Low Countries in May 1940, followed by the collapse of the Somme-Aisne front, and the withdrawal of the French government from Paris on June 10, led to a mass exodus of some three-quarters of the population of the City, around two million people, over a period of three days. A census carried out three weeks later indicated that around 300,000 had returned.

p.106 *Gobelins Factory*

The famous Gobelins tapestry factory established in Paris at the beginning of the 17th century by a family of that name, which for a brief period under Louis XIV produced other types of furnishings for royal residences. The factory premises at one time included houses and gardens for the weavers and their families.

p.108 *Bagneux*

Cemetery at Chatillon-Montrouge, to the south-east of Paris.

Chapter VII

p.112 *Ferdinand Lop*

French humorist and writer (1891–1974), a prototype Screaming Lord Sutch who repeatedly stood for President with the slogan '*Tout pour le front Lopulaire*' (a personalized Front Populaire). The author of, among other works, *Petain and History: What I would have said in my induction speech at the Académie Française had I been elected to it* (1957), from 1946 to 1958 he stood on an electoral platform promising the abolition of poverty after ten o'clock at night, the extension of the Boulevard St Michel to the sea, the nationalisation of brothels, the award of a pension to the wife of the unknown soldier, and the removal of Paris to the countryside so that its citizens could enjoy some fresh air.

p.112 *Au Pilori*

Anti-Semitic weekly published under German Occupation with an allocation of paper that allowed a printrun of 90,000 copies.

p.112 *Raymond Duncan*

Artist, printer, and designer (1874–1966). Eccentric brother of the dancer Isadora Duncan, whom he encouraged in 1900 to join him in Paris, where he had already taken up residence. He accompanied her to Greece in 1903. Finding shoes obnoxious, he was making his own sandals and now took to wearing ancient Greek-style robes. An article written by Grace Tibbits in 1917 (which appears on the Virtual Museum of San Francisco website) refers to the stir caused when he and his wife (Penelope, sister of the Greek poet Sikelianos) and their young son arrived in winter on a visit to the US, dressed in this fashion. 'The authorities in New York said that Mr and Mrs Duncan might dress as they pleased, but the small Duncan would fall into the hands of the Society for the Prevention of Cruelty to Children if he weren't more warmly garbed.'

p.123 *as Attila was wont to say*

Attila the Hun is supposed to have said, 'Where my horse passes, grass no longer grows.'

p.126 *Roi des Aulnes*

Der Erl-König (The Erl-King, or King of the Alders) is the title of a narrative poem written by Goethe in 1782, based on a folk legend about Death snatching a child. Schubert wrote a song based on this poem, which was orchestrated by Berlioz in 1860. There is a translation of Goethe's poem by Sir Walter Scott.

p.126 *Kostis Palamas*

Greek poet (1859–1943), author of *The Twelve Lays of the Gypsy*, a long lyrical philosophical poem from which these quotations are taken, figuring the Gypsy-musician who is celebrated as the symbol of freedom, art, patriotism and civilisation.

p.130 *Admiral Horthy*

Hungarian dictator (1868–1957), who served as Admiral of the Austro-Hungarian fleet during WWI and as regent from 1920 to 1944. Allied with Germany and Italy at the beginning of the war, Hungary began negotiating a separate peace with the Allies in 1942, but was occupied by the Germans in 1944 and then invaded by the Russians.

p.130 *our own concentration camps*

St Cyrien, Argelès-sur-Mer, Bacarès, Noe, Gurs, Vernet, Les Milles, Pithiviers, Rivesaltes ... When the Spanish Republicans were defeated in 1939, thousands of refugees fled to France, including many who had fought with the International Brigades. They were herded into camps where conditions were appalling and kept under armed guard. After the fall of France, anti-Fascists of various other nationalities were interned. Many internees died in the camps, others in transit. Others were handed over to the Germans and deported to Germany. Jews who were rounded up in raids that began in France in 1941 were transferred to transit camps, such as the one at Drancy (a police barracks before the war), before being deported to the death camps in Germany.

p.131 *Clamart*

A village some five kilometres to the south-west of Paris.

p.131 *Panaït Istrati*

Romanian writer (1884–1935), who wrote in French as well as Romanian, and led an adventurous and peripatetic life. *Kyra Kyralina* was published in 1923, with a preface by Romain Rolland and became the first of the Adrien Zograffi cycle. A radical who became disillusioned with Soviet communism after visiting the USSR and witnessing the Stalinist regime at first hand, he is celebrated for remarking, 'All right, I can see the broken eggs. Now where's this omelette of yours?'

p.137 *Grande-Chaumière*

Famous art school in Rue de la Grande-Chaumière, off Boulevard Montparnasse, that still offers the opportunity for life drawing of nude models.

Chapter VIII

p.139 *Patriotic School*

During WWII the Royal Victoria Patriotic Building, originally an orphanage for daughters of servicemen killed in the Crimean war, located in Wandsworth, south London, became the so-called London Reception Centre, and often referred to as the Patriotic School, where foreign refugees were screened by British security officials from MI6 under the direction of Colonel Pinto. The reference to Duke Street, however, suggests that Yonnet is alluding to the Free French Intelligence headquarters (see note p.275 on *BCRA*, ch.X p.174).

p.139 *Berlemont*

Victor Berlemont, who in 1916 took over the York Minster at 49 Dean Street in Soho, which he ran as a pub and restaurant and which became known as the French Pub. In 1947 his son Gaston took over the management of it, eventually retiring on Bastille Day, 1989.

p.139–40 *West Norwood, Harold Road and Convent Hill*

In Croydon, South London.

p.141 *Huysmans*

French writer of Dutch descent (1848–1907), author of *A Rebours*, whose central character Des Esseintes embodies the *fin-de-siècle* spirit of decadence with its horror of banality and glorification of life as art, and *Là-Bas*, an investigation into the 15th-century sadist and child murderer Gilles de Rais, which leads the narrator into satanic circles in contemporary Paris. Huysmans, who became a devout Roman Catholic, was particularly fond of the church of St Séverin, of which he gives a fascinating historical account in *La Bièvre et St-Séverin*, 1898.

p.143 *Henry V*

Following a period of bitter civil strife between the factions of Burgundy and Orleans, by the Treaty of Troyes signed in 1420 Henry V of England took Catherine, daughter of Charles VI of France, for his wife, and was himself named heir to the French throne in preference to the King's son Charles, the young Dauphin. Charles VI and Henry V entered Paris together to celebrate this agreement. However, Henry died in August1422, leaving a nine-month-old child as his heir, and Charles VI followed him two months later. Inspired by Joan of Arc, the Dauphin pressed his claim, and the English were eventually driven out of France.

Chapter IX

p.146 *I. G. Farben*

German company that originally specialized in producing paints and dyes and expanded into a huge chemicals conglomerate that closely collaborated with the Nazi regime, for which its directors stood trial at Nuremburg. The company had to pay compensation for its use of forced labour and was eventually liquidated.

p.147 *Sainte-Chapelle*

Built on the Ile St-Louis in 1246–8 by St Louis in order to house the Crown of Thorns, which he acquired from Venetian merchants who had received it in exchange for a loan to the Emperor Baldwin of Constantinople, the Sainte-Chapelle was described by Ruskin as 'the most precious piece of Gothic in Northern Europe'.

p.147 *Pont-au-Double*

Built in 1634. So called because the toll was a double denier. All tolls on bridges were abolished in 1848.

p.148 *Rifodés* and *Malingreux*

Cant names – along with *Hubains, Coquillards, Francs-Mitous, Piètres* – dating from the Middle Ages, for various types of vagabonds and scoudrels who made their living by deception and importunity, some of whom might be found cured of their piteous physical ailments within the precincts of the courts of miracles, so-called precisely because of these 'miraculous cures'.

Rifodés: accompanied by their womanfolk and children, they bore a certificate attesting that their homes had been destroyed by the hand of God.

Malingreux: malingers who faked either dropsy or skin ulcers.

Hubains: bearers of a certificate testifying to them having been cured of rabies by the intercession of St Hubert, the patron saint of hunters and trappers in the Ardenne.

Coquillards: identified by the shells they wore (the shell being the symbol of St James of Compostella), brigands posing as pilgrims who infested the highways after the Hundred Years War. Villon was associated with them and his *Ballads en Jargon* are written in the still impentrable cant of the Coquillards.

Francs-mitous: fraudsters so good at faking being taken ill in the street, even doctors were fooled by them.

Piètres: imposters who pretended to be cripples, and went about on crutches.

p.149 *Hector Malot's 'San Famille'*

A classic children's story, first published in 1878, about a little boy called Rémi, who discovers at the age of eight that he is a foundling. His impecunious and embittered foster father sells him to a kindly old man named Vitalis, who with his troupe of performing animals makes a living as a street entertainer. This picaresque novel recounts Rémi's long and eventful life on the road until he finally discovers his real identity and finds his true home. Hector Malot (1830–1907), is the author of some seventy novels, of which *Sans Famille* is by far the most enduring.

p.158 *April 1814*

Napoleon's catastrophic campaign in Russia during the winter of 1812 marked the beginning of the end of his rule, with declarations of war by Prussia and Austria in 1813 leading to defeat at the Battle of Leipzig in October, the capitulation of Paris on 30 March 1814 to the invading armies of the Czar and the Prussians, who were actually welcomed as liberators by the anti-Napoleonists (see following note), the abdication of Napoleon on 6 April, and the restoration of the Bourbon dynasty.

p.158 *'a certain lack of dignity'*

Author's Notes:

De Bordier: '. . . the conquerors blushed at such contemptible behaviour . . . countesses threw laurels on the Kalmuks and rode pillion behind the Cossaks . . .'

De Vaulabelle: 'The saturnalia in the streets and public squares belonged that day to rich and titled ladies.'

p.163 *Truie Qui File*

Literally, 'the Running Sow', a café near Montmartre.

p.163 *Rue aux Oües*

The original medieval name of a street now called Rue aux Ours

(Bear Street), which runs between Rue St-Martin and Boulevard de Sebastopol, *Oües* being the old French version of *Oies*, meaning 'geese': the name changed as the number of roast-houses gave way in the 12th century to an influx of furriers. In 1789 a decree was passed putting an end to a centuries' old tradition of burning a wicker man here on 3 July every year, supposedly the effigy of a Swiss soldier said to have desecrated a statue of the Virgin on the corner of the street.

p.163 *Panier Fleuri*

There was a brothel by this name on Boulevard de la Chapelle, near the Gare du Nord. Legislation closing brothels was passed on 13 April 1946 which came into effect six months later.

Chapter X

p.169 *Luc Berimont*

Pen name of André Leclercq (1915–83), poet, novelist, writer and broadcaster. Active in the Resistance, he was awarded the Croix de Guerre, and made a Chevalier de l'Ordre du Mérite and Chevalier de l'Ordre des Arts et Lettres. *Domaine de la Nuit* was published in 1940, in roneotype format, with a preface by Sergeant Maurice Fombeure.

p.171 *Liberation of Paris*

After the D-Day landings on 6 June 1944 and the successful advance of the Allies through Normandy, the liberation of Paris was anticipated by an insurrection of the local population in which the police played a prominent role. Fearful of German retaliation against an ill-equipped popular uprising, and also of losing the initiative to the Communists, the Allies authorized General Leclerc, commanding the 2nd French Armoured Division to march on Paris. The German military governor of Paris, General von Choltitz, surrendered to General Leclerc on 25 August. General De Gaulle reached Paris the following day and with his provisional government was able to claim uncontested control of the country.

p.172 *Les Eparges*

Ridge some 30km from Verdun which was the scene of very heavy fighting and great loss of life during WWI.

p.173 *Propaganda-Staffel*

The occupying forces' Propaganda Department under the control of the German military commander of Paris (and therefore not directly under the control of the German propaganda minister, Dr Goebbels). Also called the Propaganda Abteilung.

p.173 *Aujourd'hui*

Parisian daily newspaper published during the Occupation.

p.173 *The battle was gigantic*

A scurrilous popular song describing an internecine conflict between crab lice.

p.174 *BCRA*

Bureau Central de Renseignements et Actions, the Free French intelligence agency, under the direction of André Dewavrin (1911–1998), codenamed Colonel Passy, based at 10 Duke Street in Central London.

p.180 *Thiais*

Cemetery south of Paris.

p.181 *Ste-Anne*

Psychiatric hospital on Rue Cabanis in the 14th arrondissement.

Chapter XI

p.182 *Heine*

German poet and man of letters (1797–1856), who moved to Paris in 1831, and died there, at his home in Rue d'Amsterdam. He wrote a great deal about France and French culture and his own ironic style of lyric verse had some influence on French writers. He used to say that a traveller could tell how close he was to Paris by noting the increasing intelligence of the people, and that even the bayonets of the soldiers there were more intelligent than those elsewhere.

p.185 *Mondor and Tabarin*

In the 17th century Mondor, a vendor of quack medicines, teamed up with a street entertainer by the name of Tabarin, whose quick wit and comic satire drew appreciative crowds and buyers and won the admiration of Molière and La Fontaine.

p.187–8 *Gabriele D'Annunzio*

Italian poet, novelist, dramatist, journalist, patriot and war hero

(1863–1937). His home for the last seventeen years of his life, Villa Cargnacco at Gardone on Lake Garda, together with the monumental complex that he built up around it, he conceived of as a celebration of his 'glorious failures' and his legacy to the people of Italy: called the Vittoriale degli Italiani, it is a remarkable phenomenon.

p.188 *Guillot de Saix*

Poet and playwright (1885–1964), one of whose poems was set to music by Reynaldo Hahn. Among the items he left to the Bibliothèque Nationale's Performing Arts' Department is a collection of twenty-two 18th-century Venetian puppets.

p.189 *Cevennes*

The *maquis*, which became synonymous with the French Resistance, is Mediterranean scrubland, and the expression 'take to the maquis' originated in Corsica, where bandits would go into the wild to escape the police. French resistance fighters in the south of France sought similar refuge in the mountainous landscape of the Cevennes region.

p.189 *Vincennes*

Vincennes lies to the east of the 12th and 20th arrondissements, the Château and the Fort standing some 3km's distance from Nation outside the Porte de Vincennes on the edge of the Bois de Vincennes, one of the two great wooded parks of Paris.

p.196 *Salon d'Automne*

Founded in October 1903 by Franz Jourdain and Yvanhoë Rambosson, an annual art exhibition held (after the initial success of the first show) at the Grand Palais, which established itself as a showcase for all kinds of new artists. Charles De Gaulle met Yvonne Vendroux, who was to become his wife, at the 1920 Salon D'Automne. The 1945 show featured a celebration of Matisse, and introduced work by Nicolas de Stael and Bernard Buffet.

Chapter XII

p.200 *Bouteille d'Or*

Restaurant on the Left Bank at 9 Quai de Montebello.

p.201 *Tour d'Argent*

Dating back to 1582, the Tour d'Argent, on the Left Bank at 15 Quai de la Tournelle, has a distinguished history. In 1947 Claude Terrail took over the management of this establishment from his father, André, who bought it in 1911. When Claude died in 2006, his own son, André, succeeded him. During WWII Claude Terrail walled up the cellar to keep the wine reserves from falling into the hands of the Germans. The Tour is famous for its *'canard au sang'*, a dish first served in 1890, every duck being numbered, and a register kept of diners to whom it was served. The Prince of Wales (later Edward VII, see note for p.203) in 1890 consumed duck number 328, the Duke of Windsor, in 1938, number 147,844.

p.201 *Vel' d'Hiv*

The Velodrome d'Hiver, an enclosed stadium on Rue Nélaton near the Quai de Grenelle in the 15th arrondissement, built in 1910 for track cycle racing. An annual six-day non-stop cycling event, in which pairs of riders competed (one cycling while the other rested), attracted huge numbers of spectators. The Vel' d'Hiv has become notorious for the round-up, carried out by French police on the 16th and 17th of July 1942, of thousands of Jews who were held in the stadium before being deported. Most died at Auschwitz. The stadium was demolished in 1959. In July 1994, a national commemoration day was instituted, and in 1995 President Jacques Chirac spoke officially of the nation's collective responsibility for the deportation of French Jews.

p.202 *Mosul*

City in Iraq that at one time fell within the ancient Persian empire, but has never been part of Persia, or Iran, proper.

p.203 *La Goulue*

The French cancan dancer Louise Weber (1870–1929), who performed at the Moulin Rouge 1890–95, until she became too overweight, owes her nickname (meaning 'the Glutton') to her enormous appetite. The subject of a number of works by Toulouse-Lautrec, she ended up alone and destitute, and died at Lariboisière Hospital.

p.203 *Moulin Rouge*

Charles Zidler opened this celebrated nightclub at 90 Boulevard de Clichy in 1889.

p.203 *Valentin the Contortionist*

The stage name of Etienne Renaudin (1843–1907), who was La Goulue's dance partner at the Moulin Rouge, and featured in works by Toulouse-Lautrec.

p.203 *Edward VII*

Eldest son (1841–1910) of Queen Victoria, he succeeded to the throne in 1901. As Prince of Wales, he was known for his racy lifestyle and numerous mistresses. In *God's Fifth Column: a biography of the age: 1890–1940*, William Gerhardie writes of 'the frigid silence which greeted [Edward VII] as he drove through Paris on his arrival. "They don't seem to like us," said his companion. "Why should they?" said the King. But he liked French ways and French cooking. And when on the fifth day of his stay he drove to the station through Paris, the crowds, this time, cheered him.' As Gerhardie puts it, Edward VII 'liked to swing a loose leg in Paris'.

p.204 *Henri Toulouse-Lautrec*

Severely crippled by a congenital bone disease, Toulouse-Lautrec (1864–1901) found models for his paintings among the dancers, actresses, and artistes in the world of Parisian entertainment to which he was drawn. He had his own table at the Moulin Rouge and at various times lived in a brothel. When La Goulue left the Moulin Rouge, he decorated the fairground stall she had at the Trône Fair on what is now Place de la Nation. He was a friend and advocate of Van Gogh, an admirer of Oscar Wilde and James Whistler, whom he met in London, and was greatly influenced by Japanese prints.

p.204 *Rocher de Cancale*

A restaurant at 78 Rue Montorgueil, the successor to an earlier and very successful restaurant by the same name at no.59 that features in several of Balzac's novels. (The actual Rocher de Cancale is a rock formation that stands in the sea off the Britanny port of Cancale, famous for its oysters, for which the original restaurant too was celebrated.)

p.204 *Gavarni*

Lithographer and painter (1804–1866), who specialized in genre scenes.

p.206 *Karel Kapek*

Czech writer (1890–1938), anti-Nazi and anti-communist, credited with inventing the word 'robot' and author of the anti-technology play *RUR*, he explored many themes taken up by later science-fiction writers and wrote pieces for Czech puppeteers, who were persecuted by the Nazis for their underground opposition.

p.206 *three knocks*

A theatrical tradition dating back to Roman times, whereby it is signalled to the audience with three knocks on the boards that the performance is about to begin.

p.207 *Frères humains qui après nous vivez*

This is the first line of Villon's 'Epitaph', or 'Ballad of the Gallows-Birds'.

p.211 *Val-de-Grâce*

A military hospital, formerly a Benedictine convent founded in the 17th century by Anne of Austria, at 1 Place Alphonse-Laveran on Rue St-Jacques in the 5th arrondissement.

p.212 *Pre-war Jewish films*

Yiddle with his Fiddle, Poland, 1936, a musical written and directed by Joseph Green, starring Molly Picon; *The Yiddish King Lear*, USA, 1935, adapted from a play by Jacob Gordin, directed by Harry Thomashefsky; *The Dybbuk*, Poland, 1937, based on the play by Sholem Ansky, directed by Michael Waszynski.

Chapter XIII

p.215 *Etienne Boilève*

Etienne Boilève (also Boislève, or Boileau) was appointed Provost of Paris by Louis IX in 1254. He won a reputation for zeal and integrity, as Joinville recorded in his *Life of St Louis*. Boilève was responsible for *Le Livre des Métiers* (Book of Trades), a compilation of the rules and regulations governing all the merchant guilds authorized to trade in the city of Paris.

p.220 *Dagobert's Tower*

At 18 Rue Chanoinesse, a fifteenth-century structure that served the old port of St Landry, named after Dagobert I, a Merovingian king who ruled 623–639.

p.221 *Pope Clement VI in Avignon*

After the election of a Frenchman as Pope Clement V in 1305, the papacy settled at Avignon. This was the beginning of what is referred to as the Babylonian Exile. Clement VI was Pope 1342–52.

In 1376, Gregory XI returned to Rome, where he died. The election of an Italian successor, Urban VI, led to a schism in the church, with Robert of Geneva elected contemporaneously as Pope Clement VII residing in Avignon, which had been made over to Clement VI by the Angevin Queen Giovanna I of Naples in 1348.

p.221 *Hubains, Coquillards, Francs-Mitous, Piètres*

See note p.272 on *Rifodés* and *Malingreux*, ch.ix, p.148.

p.221 *Mont-Fêtard*

Supposedly one of the interim deformations of Mons Cetardus, the origin of Mouffetard.

p.226 *Oléron*

Island to the south of La Rochelle, off the west coast of France.

Chapter XVI

p.249 *Kirity-Penmarc'h*

Important fishing port on the Penmarc'h peninsula to the south-west of Quimper in Brittany.

p.249 *De profundis clamavi, Domine, Domine. . . Fiant aures tuae intendentes in vocem . . .*

Out of the deep have I called unto thee, O Lord: Lord hear my voice./ O let thine ears consider well: the voice of my complaint . . . Psalm CXXX.

p.254 Lazare

Dictionnaire administratif et historique des rues de Paris et de ses monuments, Felix and Louis Lazare, Paris, 1844, 2nd ed. 1855.

p.254 *Jehan Augier*

From 1268 to1276, Jehan Augier was head of the ancient guild of merchant shippers an extremely powerful body in the early history of Paris, whose Provost was known until the late fourteenth century as the Prévôt des Marchands d'Eau and effectively acted as head of the City Council, based from the mid–14th century in what was to become known as the Hôtel de Ville.